MW00803272

The Act and the Place
of Poetry

YVES BONNEFOY
The Act and the Place of Poetry
of Poetry SELECTED ESSAYS

Edited and with an Introduction by

JOHN T. NAUGHTON

Foreword by JOSEPH FRANK

THE UNIVERSITY OF CHICAGO PRESS
Chicago & London

YVES BONNEFOY's critical works include *Peintures murales de la France gothique, Arthur Rimbaud,* and *Rome, 1630, l'horizon du premier baroque.* Of his many books of poems, five are available in English translation. JOHN T. NAUGHTON is associate professor of Romance languages and literatures at Colgate University. His *The Poetics of Yves Bonnefoy* is published by the University of Chicago Press.

The University of Chicago Press, Chicago 60637
The University of Chicago Press, Ltd., London
© 1989 by The University of Chicago
All rights reserved. Published 1989
Printed in the United States of America
98 97 96 95 94 93 92 91 90 89   5 4 3 2 1

∞ The paper used in this publication meets the minimum requirements of the American National Standard for Information Sciences—Permanence of Paper for Printed Library Materials, ANSI Z39.48-1984.

Library of Congress Cataloging-in-Publication Data

Bonnefoy, Yves.
    [Essays. Selections]
    The act and the place of poetry : selected essays/Yves Bonnefoy; edited and with an introduction by John T. Naughton; foreword by Joseph Frank.
        p.   cm.
    A collection of essays translated from French.
    ISBN 0-226-06449-2 : $23.95
    1. French poetry—History and criticism. 2. Shakespeare, William, 1564–1616—Criticism and interpretation. 3. Poetry. I. Naughton. John T. II. Title.
PQ412.B66 1989
841'.009—dc19
                                                            88-21547
                                                            CIP

Contents

Foreword
Joseph Frank

I HAVE BEEN ACCORDED the privilege of saying a few words to introduce this first publication in English of some of the major essays of Yves Bonnefoy, and I should like to use the occasion to express a very personal sense of why both his poetry and prose seem to me so uniquely precious and valuable. They have always possessed for me, ever since I first became acquainted with them and their author more than thirty years ago, a very rare quality—a quality that can only be characterized in words that run the risk, especially in English, of sounding ponderous and grandiloquent. But there is no help for it, and there are some subjects (this is, I believe, one of them) for which a certain elevation of tone is amply justified and even obligatory.

What first struck me about the man, aside from a complete absence of any pose or pretension, was a quiet and tranquil spiritual integrity, a determination—never asserted but simply felt directly as part of the personality—to go his own way and to follow his own path. The nature of this path gradually became clearer to me as I immersed myself in his work and began to acquire a sense of the deep wellsprings of inspiration from which it sprang. For I realized that Bonnefoy was writing poetry originating in a metaphysical impulse of the highest order—a poetry that, for someone like myself whose native language is English, inevitably recalled some of the most soaring flights of the Wordsworthian muse. I do not know if the comparison has been made by others in the now quite voluminous Bonnefoy literature, but his French has always seemed to me to have the same stripped simplicity and bareness as Wordsworth's English, creating an effect of sublimity by its very bleakness; his predominantly rural imagery has the same mysterious and infinitely expansive resonance; and he too conceives of poetry as communicating to the reader a sense of a higher order of being—those revelatory moments, those "spots of time," when

> . . . with an eye made quiet by the power
> Of harmony, and the deep power of joy,
> We see into the life of things.

Bonnefoy, however, is a man of his time; and in comparing him with Wordsworth, or in stressing the predominantly metaphysical or even quasi-mystical aspect of his poetry, I do not wish to imply that he has sought for ways to escape the burdens and responsibilities of living in the turmoil of the present. Quite the contrary, he exposes himself to the withering breath of modern negativity with a full awareness of its overwhelming strength, a full realization of the collapse in modern times of any coherent system of values giving sense and meaning to human life. My own first encounter with Bonnefoy took place in the early 1950s, in a Paris that, along with the rest of Europe and the entire world, was just beginning to emerge from the catastrophes and horrors of the second World War. Existentialism, what-ever else one may say about it, attempted to find ways of responding to these horrors in its literary creations and Bonnefoy's preoccupation with the themes of death and destruction, though rooted in more independent per-sonal sources than mere adherence to a philosophical movement, fit in very well with this mood of the moment. He was in any case quite familiar with the work of such thinkers as Kierkegaard, Heidegger, and Léon Chestov (I use the French spelling), the last a Russian emigré essayist whose impact on Bonnefoy can hardly be overestimated (he has referred to it himself quite frequently), and whose ideas take their origin in an impassioned meditation on the great Russian novelists, particularly Dostoevsky.

The poetry of Yves Bonnefoy may thus be described as an anguished dialogue with death, a dialogue that throws into the balance against extinc-tion and negation all the forces of the earth, and the occasional gleams of transcendence—what he calls "presence"—which occur in those blessed moments when he perceives "all things in the continuity and the sufficiency of a *place,* and in the transparency of *unity.*" These primordial opposites are constantly played off against each other; and the poetry explores, with an indefatigable and inexhaustible tenderness, all the harrowing uncertainties of the human condition in its oscillation between hope and despair. A passage that particularly moved me, and where much of what is central to Bonnefoy is admirably expressed, is the tribute he offered to the memory of his old friend Boris de Schloezer, another Russian emigré of great impor-tance for him, and a man, as he has told me, of a pure and abiding religious faith. Schloezer was of course well known as the influential music critic of the *Nouvelle Revue française* in its great period between the two wars, and also as a man of letters—a novelist, literary critic, and translator from the Russian. In Bonnefoy's lines, the faith of Schloezer is rewarded by an unearthly music played for him alone:

> Et Boris de Schloezer, quand il est mort
> Entendant sur l'appontement une musique
> Dont ses proches ne savaient rien (était-elle, déjà,

La flûte de la délivrance révélée
Ou un ultime bien de la terre perdue,
"Oeuvre" transfigurée)—derrière soi
N'a laisse que ces eaux brûlées d'enigme.

And Boris de Schloezer, when he died
Hearing on the landing a music
His loved ones knew nothing about (was it, already,
The flute of the promised deliverance,
Or some last gift of the disappearing earth,
"A life's work" transfigured?)— left behind
Only these waters charred by enigma.

For Bonnefoy, whose work shows no traces of any belief in the "deliverance of revelation," such music could only be "a last gift of the disappearing earth"; it is the music arising from a harmony suddenly felt *within* life and human experience, a "life's work transfigured" whose earthly provenance does not prevent it from communicating the same sense of deliverance. In his enchanting spiritual autobiography, part memoir and part reverie, *L'Arrière-pays,* Yves Bonnefoy has described his obsession with the idea that somewhere in the world—somewhere in the *arrière-pays,* the back country, away from the beaten paths and off the well-trodden roads—there exists a Great Good Place that is the physical and terrestrial embodiment of such an epiphanic plentitude of being. But this obsession is also a temptation—a Gnostic temptation, as Bonnefoy calls it in his own appropriation of the term. Just as the Gnostics believed that their doctrines marked out the way to salvation and enabled the soul to escape from death and hence from time, so the same ambition, he suggests, inspires this quest for a perfection that could be *entirely* realized within the boundaries of human life. To long for such perfection means to long to escape, like the Gnostics, from the hazards and uncertainties of human finitude.

In *L'Arrière-pays* (which cries out for translation), Bonnefoy depicts, with a bemused and half-melancholy humor, some of the moments when he felt he had reached his goal—whether in art, literature, travel, or simply through the verbal magic exercised by exotic place-names. Surely *there* it would be found! Somehow he could never surrender this belief, not so much in the Incarnation as in the final fulfillment of the messianic promise concentrated, by some miraculous dispensation, in one small plot of earth. But Bonnefoy also evokes, in words of haunting beauty, how each time he approaches what seems to be the accomplishment of the claim to such fulfillment, he is seized by an emotion of both exaltation and disquiet. "Everywhere where people have wanted to add to a wall, or decorate a facade, build terraces, and have appear there, to be heard by the rising or setting sun, a music that sings of the dissolution of the illusory self, but on a foundation of rock and in the midst of architecture that is a lived form of permanence; in all these places one can affirm, yes, I feel at home—at the very moment that I aspire to the unlocatable place that repudiates them." For he is always uneasily aware, once having reached a spot at which mankind has wished to affirm its triumph, that there is in reality no such privileged place; there is no art or architecture, however imperious its claim to "a lived form of permanence," that can guarantee eternity to such an aspiration. The search for transcendence must continue forever, guided only by one unassailable certainty—that its elusive "presence" can flash forth at any moment from the simplest and humblest object or artifact as well as from the greatest creations of the human imagination. Or to put the same idea in the words of another great philosophical poet, Wallace Stevens, who also writes out of the metaphysical solitude of modern man, and whose work, despite a sharp dissonance of stylistic register, contains unexpected thematic affinities with Bonnefoy:

> If ever the search for a tranquil belief should end,
> The future might stop emerging out of the past,
> Out of what is full of us; yet the search
> And the future emerging out of us seem to be one.

These, then, are some of the dominating themes and preoccupations of Bonnefoy's poetry, and they infuse his critical essays as well. His criticism is that of a poet, not in the sense of being eccentric or idiosyncratic, or concerned with the quarrels of literary coteries and the jockeying for position amid the rapid changes of literary fashion, but in the sense of which the same could be said of Baudelaire, Mallarmé, and Valéry. Their criticism also came out of the same vision of life and was infused with the same values as those expressed in their poetry; and Bonnefoy's criticism should be seen as a worthy successor of the line begun by Baudelaire's *Curiosités Esthétiques* and continued in Mallarmé's *Divagations* and Valéry's *Variétés*. Such criticism is not primarily that of scholars and teachers (though Bonnefoy's scholarship has never been faulted, and he has taught for many years, most recently to packed amphitheaters in the Collège de France) but of creators actively engaged in the literary process and who, if they concern themsleves with the past at all, do so in their own terms and in the light of their own problems. Such criticism instinctively accomplishes that "fusion of horizons" that has recently become a rallying cry for a whole group of literary theoreticians; like Monsieur Jourdain, knowing nothing about rhetoric but speaking in "prose" all the same, poet-critics have always been exemplary hermeneuticians unbeknownst to themselves. I cannot help wondering, however, whether the sovereign self-certitude of such great creators should really be recommended to every fledgling student of literature as an example to follow.

The virtues to this type of criticism derive from its vital relation to the experience of creation, and from the richness of mind, the profundity of insight, the wisdom and sensitivity that its authors bring to bear on the subjects that come under their scrutiny. It is not my purpose to illustrate in any detail how brilliantly Bonnefoy lights up the literature of both past and present, and how the illumination afforded by his perceptions and categories, the suppleness and imaginative ingenuity with which he employs them, lead to surprising and unexpected but totally persuasive interpretations of long-familiar figures and their historical epochs. I leave to the readers the pleasure of discovering these treasures, and they can turn for reliable guidance as well to the introduction by John T. Naughton. There is, however, one essay—Bonnefoy's inaugural address on assuming his chair at the Collège de France—which is of such outstanding importance in the present state of literary criticism that I should like to dwell on it a little futher.

Bonnefoy is not given to literary-critical polemics; for the most part he contents himself with setting down his own ideas and letting them speak for themselves, without feeling any need to quarrel with others about *theirs*. But, naturally, he is fully cognizant of the contemporary critical scene, and well aware of the extent to which the status and stature of literature has been undermined by recent theories. If we accept such theories, the work of literature itself, as well as the consciousness of the creator in whom it originated, both crumble into nothingness "in the ruins of the cogito"; what is left are only "thousands of levels of the fleeting clouds of this language of which, for our passing moment, we are only a slight ruffling of the structures." And he knows perfectly well that his own insistence on asserting the reality, even if elusive and transitory, of those blessed moments of "presence" runs smack against the fierce campaign waged by Jacques Derrida, with all the untiring remorselessness of Captain Ahab hunting down the Great White Whale, to uncover and expunge all the lingering traces of the "metaphysics of presence" anywhere and everywhere it can be detected, whether in philosophy or literature.

Yves Bonnefoy thus felt called upon, in the solemn and celebratory moment at which he officially acceded to the chair of Roland Barthes, to enunciate and defend his own position; but it is typical of the man that he does not do so simply by rejecting what he opposes. For who, after all, if not the poets, were aware of "what criticism has stressed recently concerning the role of the signifier in writing and concerning the part played by the unconscious in their decisions?"

> . . . and, on the threshold of our modernity, which began as a breakdown of the Romantics' absolute idea of the self, they had already made this role their primary preoccupation. Rimbaud was not unaware of the autonomy of the signifier when he was

writing his sonnet "Voyelles," nor was Mallarmé when he put
together his "Sonnet en yx."

Indeed, so far as the most powerful thrust of the deconstructive attack on
literature is the denunciation of its claims to any sort of truth-value, Bon-
nefoy even radicalizes its underlying animus. For he argues that recent
criticism, remaining on the level of language and the signifier, has not gone
far enough and really fails to expose the *true* source of illusion in literary
creation.

As a poet, he knows that this unquenchable source, "a desire as old as
earliest infancy," is the Gnostic tempation to create a world alternative to
our own and to revel in it according to our heart's desire. Literature destroys
the world through language in order to fashion a self-enclosed universe that
claims its own autonomous reality; its personal idiolect, which simply ex-
cludes what it finds incongruous, is "a semblance of the golden age." He
vigorously denounces what he calls the false cult of the Image, which he
defines as "this impression of a reality at last fully incarnate," though "it
comes to us, paradoxically, through words which have turned away from
incarnation." "The Image," he declares, "is certainly a lie, however sincere
the maker of the image"; and he agrees that "it really was time for textual
criticism to come along and analyze and even to undermine the ever-trun-
cated perspectives which pile up in the literary use of speech." More deeply,
he is hostile on principle to all attempts, whether through the arts or in
philosophy, to construct an order presumably immune to the existential
fragilities of the human condition.

So far as recent thought has worked to destroy all such attempts, Yves
Bonnefoy welcomes its salutary labors, which coincide so closely with so
many of his own idea-feelings (to use a Dostoevskian coinage). But, in the
midst of the ruins of all past certainties, life must still continue; and it is out
of this realization that he begins to assert his own values, tentatively but
firmly, against the consequences of such limitless sapping of the founda-
tions. Do we not, after all, "when we speak . . . say 'I,' and do we not say it
in the urgency of our days and in the midst of a condition and a place which
remain, whatever may be their false pretenses and their groundlessness,
both a reality and an absolute?" Moreover, "if the deconstruction of the old
ontological ambitions seems, on a certain level, an imperative of conscious-
ness, their weakening, in any case in concrete situations, is accompanied by
a risk of decomposition and death." Yves Bonnefoy thus reaffirms the moral
and social needs of human existence and human community against the
epistemological iconoclasms of the reigning doctrines, and he sees the task
of poetry precisely as the continual rememoration of such needs, the refusal
to allow them to be forgotten.

"If being is nothing other than the will that there be being, poetry is nothing itself, in the estrangement of language, but this will understanding its own nature—or at the very least, in dark times, keeping the memory of itself." The term "being" here has primarily a social meaning; it designates the values that knit a community together just as "presence" suddenly unites the accidental dispersal of nature; and Bonnefoy illustrates its significance in a poignant passage where he imagines a handful of people, the survivors of some disaster, painfully struggling to reestablish their lives. In so doing they make the decision, without even thinking about it, "that *there is being*: these people having no doubt, beneath the collapsing rock, that one's relation to oneself, even if nothing founds it, is origin and suffices to itself." They learn (or relearn) "that *what is* is what responds to [their] project, what allows for exchange, and must first of all have done this to find a place in language: for instance, the main features of the place, the tools of labor, later perhaps the materials of a first moment of rejoicing—one will say then the bread and the wine. . . . Words which name a sacred order, words which welcome us on earth!"

It is such words, Yves Bonnefoy believes, that it is the task of poetry to pronounce and continually to revivify. "Whatever may be the driftings of the sign, the obviousness of nothingness, to say 'I' remains for them [the poets] the best of reality and a precise task, the task of reorienting words, once beyond the confines of dream, on our relation to others, which is the origin of being." So while the poet will go hand in hand with the semiologists and the deconstructive philosophers for a good stretch of the road, he parts company with them when it comes to an ultimate vision of what is basic and fundamental to human existence. It is not, as we see, on the level of the concept as such that Yves Bonnefoy defends his point of view, and I believe he is profoundly right in having refused to do so; finally, it is out of one's deepest sense of the foundations of human life that one chooses for or against *any* metaphysics.

This inaugural lecture, so finely comprehensive and so gravely discriminating, will, I am certain, eventually come to be seen as one of the major documents of twentieth-century criticism, and may well already be on the way to attaining this position. The growing international reputation both of Bonnefoy's poetry and of his criticism, obtained entirely on the basis of a firsthand acquaintance with his work (he has never made a public statement about anything but his poetry and has shirked any kind of personal self-display), may well be seen as a sign of the times, and an indication that the values he has always expressed with such moving and tragic serenity (if I am allowed this expression) have now come to respond to a long-felt need of the contemporary sensibility. This is how I would see it, at any rate, and I can only hope that my conjecture will turn out to be accurate. Even if it should prove fanciful, I can only rejoice at the existence of such a voice sounding amidst the modern cacophony, when so much of what is considered culturally exemplary is all too often inspired by a hysterical rage for violation and desecretaion.

Yves Bonnefoy is a devoted admirer of the late great Greek poet George Seferis, and I should like, in conclusion, to quote some lines from his reverent portrait of the man even though it is not included in the present selection. Seferis served as Greek ambassador to Great Britain, and Bonnefoy recalls a visit to him in London when he was greatly worried by his official duties. Nonetheless, Bonnefoy found Seferis "so gravely absorbed, so firmly attached to a single thought, despite the cares of the moment which were still visible on his face, that it was truly for me—and I say this with no desire to magnify things, but simply to define a quality of soul through the play of those analogies that unite us with things—an exigency so pure, a sound so just amid the discord of the day, that I felt that the star of being, however deeply sunk beneath our horizons, must not have ceased to exist. A great poet is a man who suffices." I cite these words because they seem to me to apply so perfectly to Yves Bonnefoy himself, and I am sure that the readers of this volume, as they peruse its pages, will find them being confirmed in their own responses again and again.

Introduction
John T. Naughton

HERE IS THE HEART of Yves Bonnefoy's poetics: a number of his most important essays on the French poetic tradition from the *Song of Roland* to the Surrealist movement, together with a sampling of his highly personal readings of Shakespeare whose work he has been translating since the fifties. By now, most English-speaking readers of poetry know who Yves Bonnefoy is. His presence over the years at poetry festivals such as the ones held at Cambridge, his lectures and visiting professorships at Princeton and Yale, at Williams College, Brandeis, Weslyan, and the University of California have established his reputation as a leading spokesman for poetry in France. Two of his books of poetry were recently published in translation by Random House, and selections from his work have appeared in *Poetry, Ploughshares*, the *Hudson Review*, the *New Yorker*, and other important journals. In Anglophile circles, he remains, however, more admired than really studied, and many readers, feeling somewhat disoriented by his work, have felt the need to know more about his poetic orientation and philosophy.

Born in Tours in 1923, Bonnefoy was, like Rimbaud, whom he reveres, a brilliant young student, graduating with honors from the *Lycée Descartes*. Like Rimbaud, too, Bonnefoy lost his father—a worker whose job involved assembling locomotives—at an early age. After his father's death, his mother took a job as a teacher at a grade school outside Tours and looked after the education of her son. Bonnefoy eventually received an advanced degree in mathematics and philosophy before coming to occupied Paris in 1944. There, he became involved in the Surrealist circles, met André Breton, and edited his own small review called, with appropriate iconoclasm, *La Révolution la nuit*. He also married and taught mathematics and science for a time. The publication in 1953 of his first major book of poetry, *Du Mouvement et de l'immobilité de Douve (On the Motion and Immobility of Douve)*, immediately put him at the forefront of the new generation of French poets. Four other books of poetry have since appeared—*Hier régnant désert (Yesterday's Desert Dominion)* (1958), *Pierre écrite (Words in Stone)* (1965), *Dans le leurre du seuil (In the Lure of the Threshold)* (1975), *Ce qui fut sans lumière*

(What Was without Light) (1987)—as well as translations of most of Shakespeare's major plays and a selection of the poems of W. B. Yeats. His election to the Collège de France in 1981—to fill the seat vacated by the death of Roland Barthes—gave official recognition to a supremely, if quietly, distinguished career. In addition to his poetry and translations, Bonnefoy has also steadily produced a body of remarkable criticism: reflections on the act and place of poetry, on the visual arts and their relation to poetry, on Shakespeare and the English poetic tradition. It is the experience of these important works that the present volume seeks to provide.

❦

As is usually the case when choosing among the works of a writer of considerable range, the decisions about what to include were not always easy. Bonnefoy's admirers will surely regret the absence of his essays on Saint-John Perse, on Pierre-Jean Jouve, on Paul Celan, or wonder why we have not translated any of his essays on the visual arts for this volume. What the present collection offers is a coherent statement of poetic philosophy and intent—a clear expression of the values and convictions of the French poet whom many critics today regard as the most important and influential of his time. What guided us in our choices was this sense of continuity and coherence. The essays, published over a nearly thirty-year span beginning in the fifties, do in fact respond to one another, the more recent pieces taking up for renewed consideration ideas developed in earlier meditations. And so, though essays of incontestable merit may not have been included, the present volume will at least possess a certain element of integrity and completeness. It was with this aim in mind that we also decided to group together in a single volume Bonnefoy's essays on the visual arts. This collection, edited by Richard Stamelman of Wesleyan University, is now in preparation.

Though we sought to establish a certain coherence, we did want to include essays from various periods, and thus the essays from the fifties, say, will obviously be animated by different critical categories and awarenesses than those published quite recently. We decided, however, to arrange the essays not in order of their dates of publication but rather according to the material discussed, thus establishing, though somewhat artificially, a chronological order to the discussion of what amounts to almost the whole sweep of French poetic tradition. And so, the essay on *The Song of Roland,* for instance, though written much later, precedes the piece on Baudelaire, just as the recent analysis of Rimbaud's relation to his mother is placed before the essay on Valéry from the sixties. Each of the essays, regardless of its vintage, while grounded in a thorough learning, is above all else animated by a depth of feeling and conviction that perhaps only the practicing poet can summon to a similar degree. For Yves Bonnefoy, the experience of poetry is always inseparable from the experience of living, and his entire poetics is built around the insistence that the world of words must never be permitted to replace the real world, that it is only to the extent that words allow themselves to be absorbed into the real that they become true and living speech.

Despite their diversity, furthermore, and the years separating many of them, the essays do tend to elaborate upon a common core of values, and rather astonishingly consistent attitudes may be traced from the earliest to the most recent pronouncements concerning poetry. This is not the place for anything like a detailed discussion of Bonnefoy's poetics, especially since nothing can speak as eloquently as the essays themselves about these matters. The critical literature on Bonnefoy, moreover, grows steadily with each passing year, and the reader interested in his work will now find quite a large number of books and articles devoted to his poetry and poet- ics. Nevertheless, a few of the dominant preoccupations should, perhaps, be noted here. Bonnefoy's essays on Shakespeare focus on the fascination in Shakespeare's work with the "weakening of that faith in the meaning of the world that ensured the survival of society" and stress the fact that this is the obsessional center around which his entire opus turns. Something of the same sort could be said of Bonnefoy himself, since the search for mean- ing in a world where it seems to have vanished completely is surely at the heart of his enterprise. Thus, despite the repeated assertions that he is of a generation that "comes after the gods," that his starting point is the defini- tive collapse of traditional systems of value and sacred order, Bonnefoy's idea of poetry is inseparable from a certain form of affirmation and hope- fulness. "I should like to bring together, almost to identify poetry and hope," he wrote in 1959. This hopefulness is situated in the midst of human limitation, however, and Bonnefoy, expanding upon Baudelaire's contention that sorrow and suffering are necessary to poetic con- sciousness, insists that death itself is indispensable. Recognition of finitude—of the restrictions that bear upon us from all sides, that check our inevitable tendency toward self-aggrandizement and escape through dreaming, and of which our mortality is the supreme form and proof— this recognition is our existential starting point, since it unites us with others who share the same fate, and since in moments of extreme illumina- tion this awareness allows us to perceive the greater unity in which all finite things participate.

The affirmative dimension of Bonnefoy's poetics is closely associated with an insistence on *presence*. Though the idea of presence is clearly the touchstone of his poetics—since it is the presence of things that gives meaning to the world—and though the term is repeated in a great variety of contexts, Bonnefoy never defines it simply or once and for all, and each of his essays tends to invest the notion with new meaning or special emphasis. In his earliest formulations, Bonnefoy seeks to valorize the irreducible and improbable world of things we encounter over the conceptual and intellectual categories that annihilate their living presence to stabilize and domesticate them as ideas. In his essay on "Shakespeare and the French Poet," first published in French in 1959, Bonnefoy maintains that the modern poetry that aims at salvation "conceives of the Thing, the real object, in its separation from ourselves, in its infinite otherness, as something which can give us an instantaneous glimpse of essential being, and thus be our salvation, if indeed we are able to tear the veil of universals, of the conceptual, to attain to it."

One would be wrong, however, to align Bonnefoy too absolutely with the *chosistes,* or to view him as a kind of material realist with mystical tendencies, or as a pre-Socratic fundamentally uninterested in the human beings who surround him. The least sentimental of writers, the furthest removed from the cult of personality and the fascination with individuality as such, Bonnefoy will nonetheless invest his idea of presence with the human element above all others. For the presence of things imposes itself above all against the backdrop of eventual disappearance and absence, and this fact, which the poet must always keep in the foreground of his consciousness, gives special power and poignancy to human exchange. Bonnefoy's poems make this clear, but the many essays that he has written as homages to his friends—the pieces on Gaëton Picon, on Paul Celan and Georges Seferis, on Paul de Man—all bear witness to the importance in his life of those he has loved. Evoking the blue gaze that seemed to fill the room when he met Paul de Man, Bonnefoy wrote: "A presence began to make itself felt, with all the mystery this word entails."

In his essays on "The Act and the Place of Poetry" and on "French Poetry and the Principle of Identity," Bonnefoy suggests that in its most intense form the presence of a person, of a situation, of an object can be experienced so deeply as to place us outside time for an instant and to give us a momentary intuition of eternity and universality. What remains constant in the evocations of presence is the emphasis on the intensity of a real experience, of a lived experience that is first of all beyond words and that words, later, will never be able to reanimate by themselves. What words can hope for is the preservation of some hint of the original fire. At best, they are but dying embers.

The presence of things is thus absent in all forms of representation, and this is apt to be more dramatically true of French writing than of others, since, in Bonnefoy's view, the French language is a naturally "Platonic" idiom which tends to substitute eternal forms for specific realities. And in

Bonnefoy's analysis of his own tradition, it is Mallarmé and Valéry, in particular, who have sought to replace the bewildering complexity and uncontrollable contingency of life with verbal systems, considered "purer" and more real than the chaotic world we live in. The essay on Valéry explains the attraction and yet rejection of the poetry of essences through which the evocation of the sea is not so much apprehension of that foam or that brine actually before us but rather the *idea* of the sea—a glittering, unchanging form.

To the extent, then, that words close themselves off from real experience, from danger and chance, to become a world in themselves, Bonnefoy sees them as the locus of failure, of transgression, of sin. And this poet often has recourse to moral and even to religious categories when he discusses the situation of modern poetry. In the late forties, Jean-Paul Sartre praised him in his book *What Is Literature?* for the honesty with which, even as "a young surrealist," he had discerned the difference between the protection provided by all types of writing and the perils involved in all forms of living, for the sincerity with which he had insisted that the practice of words was not necessarily the best practice for living. The moral dimension of Yves Bonnefoy's poetics, however, is first of all situated on the level of an inner debate and sometimes even of spiritual warfare. "Against whom do we ever struggle if not against our own double?" he asks in the essay on *The Song of Roland*. And in the piece on Paul Valéry, one of Bonnefoy's most emphatic statements of moral reserve with respect to the enclosures produced by the play of verbal constructs, he is quick to insist that certain poets "exist *in us*."

> We must fight against them, as we must choose, in order to exist.
> It is a private struggle. It is perhaps a wager, in the rather serious
> sense this word has acquired.

This principle of doubling, which creates the sense of spiritual tension so fundamental to Bonnefoy's thinking, is reflected in a number of the essays published here: the dialectic of language and speech discussed in the piece on *The Song of Roland,* the differences between French and English proposed in the essay on "Shakespeare and the French Poet," the distinction drawn between the "readiness" of *Hamlet* and the "ripeness" of *Lear,* the dialogue between Baudelaire and Mallarmé on the destiny of poetry, the opposition between image and presence that forms the core of the inaugural address at the Collège de France.

From the beginning, Bonnefoy has used for his own purposes the Saussurean distinction between *langue* and *parole*—a distinction he invests with his own particular experience of poetry. Thus, he tends to try to discover the heart of a great poet's work in the way in which that poet establishes himself against the flow of his tradition, against the backdrop of his idiomatic norm, of the temptations posed to him by his language and his historical moment. Bonnefoy sees poetic speech—what he calls *parole*—as a special, individual animation of language, through which the governing system, or *langue,* is shaken, impacted by a particular, unique experience that seeks to preserve itself as such through the disruption of the dominant and habitual modes of expression that control not only poetic utterances but social life as well. Bonnefoy's early fascination with Surrealism began as the desire to revolutionize the world proposed by science and convention. All of his mature work, however, is placed, as many readers have noticed, in the context of a meditation on historically canonized forms—the plays of Shakespeare, the great works of Poussin, Constable, Tintoretto, to name just a few of the cultural mediations that structure and spark his own poetry. A product of history who speaks of the importance of moments outside time, speaker in a tongue that nonetheless establishes a significant dialogue with the language that a tradition has erected and embellished, Yves Bonnefoy has elaborated a poetic speech that places itself both inside and outside a long line of Western representation. In his lectures, Bonnefoy often stresses that all great poetry is born from fundamental contradictions. and that we might profitably discuss a poet's work from the perspective of the way in which he confronts and seeks to come to terms with the contradictions that divide him. The poet must at every moment both depart from the acquired and the known, thus venturing toward openness and renewal and, at the same time, remain within a recognizable system of signs in order to communicate with others. The emphasis in Bonnefoy's work is always insistently on the lived experience that poetic utterance can only strive to preserve or commemorate in something approximating its original intensity, its difficulty, its truth. One will often hear Yves Bonnefoy say that moments of sharing, of kindness, of compassion are moments of poetry—moments compared to which a written form, even the poem striving to overcome its insufficiency, is of lesser importance. The value of the poem resides only in its capacity to encourage the emergence of poetry in the life we share, in the experience we have in common.

Another dimension of the tendency toward polarization in Bonnefoy's writing concerns his attitude toward his own poetic idiom and the somewhat nostalgic view he has developed with respect to the English language through his experience as translator. "The confrontation of two languages in a translation," he maintains in his essay "Shakespeare and the French Poet," "is a metaphysical and a moral experiment, the 'testing' of one way of thinking by another." For Bonnefoy, this testing will have been to have brought into clear focus the Platonic aspect of his own idiom, its tendency to transform the rich diversity of the world into manageable intellectual categories, to conjure up not so much the thing before us now as the word that signifies its eternal form. The "otherness" of English, its greater proximity to concreteness and particularity, its "passionate Aristotelianism" thus become the object of the modern French poet's desire. In Bonnefoy's view, furthermore, the French poetic tradition lacks the indispensable Mercutio figure—conscience of the poet himself—that voice that mocks the purely mental constructions of men, the abolition of the real by the image.

The distinction Bonnefoy seeks to establish between the disillusioned "readiness" of *Hamlet* and the more accepting "ripeness" of *Lear* may, in fact, be applied to his own development. Whereas certain English and American critics (and I am thinking particularly, for instance, of J. V. Cunningham) have argued that the readiness of *Hamlet* and the ripeness of *Lear* are in fact similar expressions—of a traditional sort furthermore—of the apprehension of human mortality, of an awareness of the fact that the fruit of a man's life will ripen and grow ready to fall, Bonnefoy will use the two terms as a point of departure for a meditation on the radically different attitudes toward life each play develops and the opposing notions of poetic possibility implicit in each. For in the presence of meaninglessness and ontological instability, Hamlet feels that "a single act still has some logic and is worthy of being carried out: and that is to take great pains to detach oneself from every illusion and to be ready to accept everything—everything, but first of all and especially, death, essence of all life—with irony and indifference." The "ripeness" that emerges in *King Lear,* on the other hand, is the loving and compassionate acceptance of mortality, the understanding that finitude binds men together and that, while it strips them of their vain illusions, it can open them to their essential oneness. *Lear* thus evokes "the quintessence of the world's order, whose unity one seems to breathe," whereas *Hamlet* deploys "the reverse side of that order, when one no longer sees anything in the grayness of the passing days but the incomprehensible weave."

As I have said, this distinction has some applicability to the evolution discernible in Bonnefoy's own work. "I used to think," he said in a lecture in 1967 called "Baudelaire Speaks to Mallarmé," "that words, desiccated by their conceptual use, failed to convey presence, were forever limited to a 'negative theology.' Now I sense that some sort of archeology is possible, which would reveal, piece by piece, the essential elements of our form." In a first phase, then, when he was above all aware of the insufficiency of words, his sympathy seems to have been for the prince of Denmark, and in his essay on "Shakespeare and the French Poet" he identifies Hamlet's plight with that of contemporary French poetry. It is this first phase that doubtless also explains Bonnefoy's enduring sympathy and respect for some aspects of contemporary deconstructionism and his active defense of Jacques Derrida. Through the forties and fifties, Bonnefoy himself was

almost obsessively concerned with contesting traditional notions of the
self, of God, of history, and all that has become the core of the postmoder-
nist repudiation of stabilized, canonized forms of representation in favor
of a jubilant and disillusioned *erring* was clearly at the center of his own
initial preoccupation. "I maintain," he wrote in 1958, "that nothing is
truer, and more reasonable, than erring, for—is it necessary to say it?—
there is no fixed method for finding the true place." By the mid-sixties,
however, a change in attitude becomes evident, animated, in part, by an
increased confidence in the emergence of coherence in the poet's life—a
confidence inspired, it should be noted, by love and also by the moments
of great depth and richness spent in an abandoned, barely habitable mon-
astery he had acquired in Provence, in the country near the Vachères
mountain. Bonnefoy has often spoken of the importance of these mo-
ments for his development, and they occupy a central place in all of his
poetry since the sixties. His experience there seems to have transformed
him and to have encouraged a growing faith in the power of a few simple
words—those that speak of the fundamental human realities that all peo-
ple share, those that are so fully steeped in what they name as to become,
in the poet's eyes, more signified than signifier: no longer reality absorbed
into language but the formulas of language subsumed in a participation in
the real. "The creative act," he says in the homage to Borges he wrote in
1986, "is not in writing; it is in giving to each thing its name, and in
listening to the mystery of being reverberating, indefinitely, in it." And
this conviction is already present in many of his essays from the sixties.
"Words prove our nothingness," he writes in the piece on Baudelaire and
Mallarmé, "opening an abyss beneath our feet, but words can offer us a
home."

> For language is not originally freedom granted to words. If we
> listen to it in its depths, we hear that some words—home, fire,
> bread, wine—are not entirely concepts, can never be taken quite
> as "pure notions," for they are bound to potential presences,
> pillars upholding the vault of speech, points of condensation
> where physical needs appease the need of being, by analogies that
> structure the human place and preside over the formation of
> words. Fire and the name of fire *are,* so that life might have a
> center.

And as Joseph Frank has aptly pointed out in his Foreword, it is the desire
to share with others this sense of center, this conviction that life has mean-
ing, that has gradually become the heart of what Bonnefoy is about.

The pieces on Baudelaire and Valéry evoke death as a starting point, as
the background against which the presence of things imposes itself. The
essay on "French Poetry and the Principle of Identity," on the other hand,

reveals a more convinced apprehension of the unity of being and speaks of Oneness in a manner sometimes reminiscent of Plotinus. The essay on Valéry discusses the olive tree, for instance, in "its profound difference." And this apprehension of a particular and irreducible presence which makes its appeal to us beyond the casual observation that simply places a specific reality into a mental category is the necessary first step for poetic consciousness. In "French Poetry and the Principle of Identity"—a difficult essay, but seminal for an understanding of the metaphysical underpinnings of Bonnefoy's poetics—the same olive tree is placed in the context of a system of analogy by means of which any reality deeply experienced becomes the experience of being itself, as the essence of one thing "spreads into" the essence of all things. It is in this essay, too, that Bonnefoy returns to the use of the definite article in poetry, a subject he had treated briefly in the piece on Valéry. This time, however, he seeks to explain the way in which the definite article, though in some forms of poetry the expression of Platonic form or abstract category, may in others serve to designate the participation of the particular in the Oneness of being, the presence of the universal burning, as though eternally, in the presence of some specific thing we experience deeply and patiently. Expressing myself in this way, I know that I must appear to be robbing this idea of its poetry, since it is in the very *intensity* of our relation to some particular tree or stone, to some very real human body or place, that these realities etch themselves into forms of eternity, become expressions of the universal. Words will never say these things very well, but surely the essays in this volume will express them as rigorously, and yet as poetically, as can be.

It is customary, on occasions such as this one, for translators to remind readers of their sense of insufficiency, of their conviction that, despite all their best efforts, they have betrayed and impoverished what they most would have wished to protect and preserve. And certainly, in this case, these inevitable feelings of inadequacy are very strong indeed. It is, of course, particularly appropriate that Yves Bonnefoy be translated into the idiom he has himself so often translated from, but the tendency toward abstraction and intellectuality that Bonnefoy laments as the all too natural penchant of French is also what can constitute its elliptical elegance, and it is the remarkably sober and yet graceful density of his own prose that is most resistant to English renderings. I imagine that we will sometimes seem lumbering or unclear; the rhetorical flourish so striking in the French may at times sound flat or empty in English. Sometimes translation is sheer impossibility, indeed vanity, as Bonnefoy himself has said in his essay on

"Shakespeare and the French Poet." And yet, in another of his meditations on the problem—the essay called "Translating Poetry"—he has suggested that what is asked of the translator above all else is neither the search for equivalency, nor the deliberate abandonment of all idea of fidelity in the effort to establish some form of creative imitation, but rather the reliving by the translator of the experience that gave rise to the work he is translating. And for the many translators, from both sides of the Atlantic, who have given their best efforts to the creation of this book, it is surely the impression of life shared, of participation in a common reflection on the limitations and the power of languages that has been the immeasurable benefit of a project otherwise doomed, as we know, to be less than what inspired it.

A NOTE REGARDING THE FOOTNOTES: Symbols throughout indicate Yves Bonnefoy's own notes. Numbered notes are those of the translators.

1 Words and Speech in *The Song of Roland*[1]

AGAINST WHOM DO WE ever struggle if not against our own double? Against that *other* in us who would have us believe that the world is without meaning; who would have us turn, wounded and without hope, toward the stream where the blood of the dying day, of the battle lost, vanishes?

We collide with the forces of nature, with the malignancy of chance, with the immoderation of men, and the collision is painful. But this is not what causes us the most suffering; it is rather the indifference of the world, the hollow sound it sometimes makes, as though it were an empty jar. It is not at every moment that a presence dwells in our system of signs, so porous despite the streams and grasses to which it sometimes gives life: they both are and are not.

In *The Song of Roland* we notice those little tableaux that are maintained in the luminous form of the *laisse,* shot through with its unchanging rhythms: everything appears simple here, precise. Abstract? No, for what is universal seems to be breathing here. Orchards that become *the* orchard. Irreducible, mysterious elements that are the ultimate data—the words—that have shaped a world. *The Song of Roland* is the very space, the depths and all the brilliant layering of the Frankish world. From the trees to the emperor, from abundance to duty—through the agency of supreme, transparent words, the presence of God is enshrined. Nothing future, unexplored here. Except those "high dark mountains" down there, near the southern border. . . .

From which it follows that if one loves works of literature as structures, and loves to discover in the power of writing the power of establishing an order, this oldest of our great poems will seem one of the most modern,

1. "Words and Speech in *The Song of Roland*" ("Les mots et la parole dans la *Chanson de Roland*") first appeared as an Afterword to a new edition of the poem published in Paris by the *Collection 10/18* in 1965. The essay was reprinted in a volume of Bonnefoy's essays called *Le Nuage rouge* (Paris: Mercure de France, 1977).

more so than the many centuries of "personal poetry" that have come after it.

But would I be wrong in seeing something clouding this seemingly so unshakable and limpid crystallization? I look with joy at those Edenic trees of the first days of the world, at the "glittering" stars and the "clear" night skies—everything is at peace, or so it seems, in the depths of nature; so why this troubled voice speaking to us of an ever-renewed evil? *The Song of Roland* is an epic; its subject is war, waged at a difficult moment—and it evokes the enemy less with hatred than with horror. He is evil incarnate. If he triumphed, then, what would become of the sun and the trees? Wouldn't they be, from that moment on, "black sun" and forms of absurdity?

And here is another question that rises within me and that I cannot suppress, despite such firm coherence, and limpidity, in "sweet France"— or rather, in fact, because of them. What exactly is the evil threatening this harmony? And from what exterior place might it come? There can be nothing exterior to a form that appropriates the real, no *other* conceivable in the architecture of the *same*. Matter, certainly, and resistance, dangers, but that take shape only in the context of the structure meeting them. The obstacle of the dimensions of a form is never experienced, cannot be experienced as a competing order; it is rather formlessness, an "evil," certainly, but an inert one. So why is there this moral mobilization against an "Infidel" in *The Song of Roland*? And if evil, too, has its structure, isn't it because this structure is already lying hidden, in one form or another, in the beautiful dwelling we live in?

In fact, this is the case, I think, and *The Song of Roland,* whether consciously or not, reveals it, and precisely through its form — through what one might call the *reduplication,* or diffraction, of its structure.

Let us consider, from the point of view of its construction, the first half (up to Roncevaux) of the poem. Two things are clearly noticeable. In the first place, the Sarrasins—that is, the enemy—are constantly evoked. Intertwining with the series of tableaux that establishes, through successive evocations, the Frankish world, a second series brings vividly to life the world of the Moors. One hardly thinks of a "here" and a "there"; the enemy to be destroyed is looked at in an almost familiar way.

One might even wonder how words so clearly meant for things French could ever lend themselves so easily to what is foreign—but there is scarcely time. For the other fact, more surprising still, is that the world of the Sarrasins is absolutely indistinguishable from that of the Franks. Truly, be it the dukes and the counts, the knights, the king's nephew, the twelve barons; or the "steps," the orchard; or what constitutes beauty, valor, intelligence; or the reason for fighting or even, and especially, the desire for peace— everything, from objects to moral decisions, is the same for the Sarrasin as it is for the Frank who would destroy him.

And yet, the poem lends to the Moors' most natural kinds of behavior tiny signs that show that even the most obvious and familiar of forms becomes emptiness and negation once invested with the will of the Sarrasin. The smallest of indications, but ones that subvert all the music. Thus, certain of the most valorous Sarrasins have "silk robes on their spines, like pigs." And the son of one of the emirs is "very tall"—a remark that is all the more troubling for seeming innocent. One clearly senses that the shadowy life of evil has not been productive of form, or rather has failed to affect the economy of form. It does not, at least outwardly, produce some monstrous universe but rather envelops with an aura, like the threat of darkness, the modes of being practiced right here.

And thus it is that evil, far from having an existence exterior to the orders that prevail, and rebellious by definition to their mediations, has in fact risen up within these very orders, or tries at every moment to do so, interfering with their most precious forms and affecting them, if one might so put it, with a lesser sign, robbing them of their proofs. A dizzying moment, since the abyss opens up everywhere. What comes to mind is an image in the mirror, showing the emptiness beneath appearance—the "sinister" image—or of Mallarmé looking into his mirror at Tournon and seeing a head detached from the bright evidence of day. What is the evil that emerges in *The Song of Roland*? Not other modes of being, forever foreign to our universe—and reassuring for this very reason, since what would then appear would seem a purely natural menace—but rather something that is capable of growing *in us,* even if symbolized by the Sarrasin, since its only real terrain is what is our own form.

And again we must insist: this moment is a terrible one. For, without anything having really changed, everything could lose its value. Isn't God Himself implicated, sustained, in the mediations that teach us about Him? On what can we build, or base our actions, if the good dwells beyond what designates it most concretely, if even the orchards can mean the desert?

And of course there is nothing surprising about discovering, in the depths of a poem, these mutations we know so well.

"A world" is nothing in itself. The same key for the same door, the same work as yesterday; and all about us the same clearly defined exchanges, coherence perfectly intact; everywhere the same galaxy of values, tastes;

compliance, or conflict with the far and near; and all of it amid the rustling of presences that are closer still—and yet all of "this" can suddenly, and without a radical change taking place, become a *dead letter* when certain ties snap that held together all the others. Nothing but a machine is left, its heavy wheels spinning dolefully. And it is not that our reason has failed us— that reason whose job it is to verify that the key is really for the room and that the room is for this or that task, this or that diversion, and these in turn for life, with its open circles that seek still further off, in the infinite aeolian wells, the resurgence of deep waters: no, reason is still available, still receptive, and the internal relations are more intelligible than ever. But these have come to replace a presence it was their role to sustain. Their writing has become an end in itself. And we would have very little if we only had words. What we need are the presences that words leave in dotted lines in their mysterious intervals, and that words in themselves cannot restore to life.

How, then, can what has disappeared be found again? This power we have for bringing things together, what is it made of? Here we must content ourselves with a few approximations that are far from clear, that are difficult—that always run the risk of being, perhaps, too simple. When we attach ourselves to anything whatever, we are, by this very fact, suddenly able to leave ourselves and to break through those fatal walls that turn our finitude into death and reality into objects. When we plunge into time, we discover that its wheel does, of course, crush lives; but it also unites them momentarily in a kind of shared absolute, in a *recognition* which is, in its essence, timeless. When our eyes are all at once opened in this way, words are no longer ends in themselves, impersonal forces that set us adrift, guilty stereotypes: they now allow speech to take place, in a true exchange between people. And everything is restored when one is capable of speech, when one is capable of moving toward the other person and of drawing him toward a destiny.

Societies, however, can be empty or criminal. Ringing with the hollow pounding at the surface of words but ravaged by a deeper silence. And if poetry were nothing more than production, differentiation, the careful balancing of structures, what would it have to offer other than what is already ruining an aphasic society? It is perhaps *in poetry* that the phrase must appear, not in its meaning but in its fullness or its emptiness; and it is in the hollow spaces that the act out of which plenitude flows must be formed. Revelation, at first, of a society of "infidels" and of a war to be waged; but then of our own precariousness, of the desert threatening our own orchards—and of discord that must be vanquished at the decisive moment. . . .

And this leads me back to *The Song of Roland*. As archaic as it might be, the poem seems aware of these shiftings between dead letter and authentic speech. And it even seems to have roughly sketched out, beneath the decor of the feats of war, the act expected of poetry.

❧

"A qui le cherche, point n'est besoin qu'on le désigne" ("For the one who is seeking, there is no need to point out"). It is not the inexplicable way in which words sometimes seem "given in advance" that this line is evoking; it is the emperor. But there is a profound resemblance between Charlemagne and words. One is struck by it in the very first lines of *The Song of Roland*.

Charlemagne, with his "flowing white beard," appears infinitely old, and yet all his forces are intact; one never feels that they might some day diminish. He rises with the sun; he seems to walk with the same step as that light that differentiates among things (and that perhaps brings them all together); he holds council, providing a place for words so that they might become sentence and meaning—but on this occasion he "lowers his head," he "muses," and, traversed by his barons' speeches that can find no area of agreement, that war with one another in the silence, his presence seems more to hollow out than to assert itself. He seems vacant, inert, strangely vulnerable. Like other princes in other works. King Arthur is also defenseless when the magic powers of the forest defy him at his very table and rob him of Guinevere, his destiny. And still another sovereign is *mehaignie* or maimed on his "wasteland"—ultimate form of the reification of the real. And what are these forms of powerlessness if not a reflection of the emptiness of words, if not a sign that we can use them to work for unity or against it, words themselves not knowing how to decide. Charlemagne is the beautiful language, the material of "sweet France," but it is into the heart of its richest formulations that the "Sarrasin" night is able to cast its darkness—being neutral, it is open to betrayal.

And betrayal, of course, takes place—that betrayal of which the entire being of the poem will, in the final analysis, have indicated the imminent peril—in the council itself, through the deceitfulness of Ganelon. And what an admirable moment it is! For here are assembled the principal advisors of the nation chosen by God. The French language should, at this moment of moral tension, maintain the place of man before God. And yet, like some mysterious fatality reemerging:

> *Guenes i vint, ki la traisun fist*
> *Des or cumencet le cunseill que mal prist*

> Ganelon came, he who betrayed the King
> Then began the council that went so wrong.

(11.178–179)

And everything "goes wrong," takes shape, in fact, according to what is wrong. The occasion is that the Sarrasins have proposed to give themselves up and to pay tribute. Put another way: life organized according to the principle of nothingness—death in life—is in fact seeking to extend itself, using to this end the lure of material possessions. It is, therefore, a trap, and someone is there to cry out: "Woe to you if you believe in Marsile!" And as he withdraws, it seems that he has triumphed. Ganelon, however, insinuates that this intransigence is pride and that appeasement is necessary. And, in a way, he has our sympathy. For well we know that there comes a moment, in our relation to the real, when we must try to get the most from the objects we encounter, when we must, as a consequence, listen to them as autonomous, sacrifice them as presences to deepen our understanding of them as essences; and thus, for a moment at least, we lose sight of what is the cause of unity in order to elaborate its language. And this work would take place, furthermore, whether we wished it or not; speech must adapt itself to the changes in language, and the great symbols must submit to the evolutions of the object, if they are to avoid becoming empty forms. Ganelon, it should be noted, is not one of the twelve peers. In the midst of those who represent the order desired by God in language, in the presence of the architecture of the great symbols that so quickly turns to pride, Ganelon stands for the concept. But he also represents its dangers—the idolatry of material ends, the excessive fascination with the self—and it is this drama that the poem has chosen to relive. Ganelon, at first an ambiguous figure, protector of at least one aspect of the truth, and who has been treated with perhaps a bit too much contempt, decides to betray the cause of Presence. He agrees to negotiate with the Moors but only to set a trap for the twelve peers. And Charlemagne is blind to all this. The council, assembled to remove the contradictions of being, has discovered—and this comes as no surprise—these very divisions in its own midst.

But there is pride, or what Ganelon has called pride, and let us now try to understand the nature of the hero who will seek to restore at least the possibility of the poem and a future for beauty and transparency. From one point of view, and it is not Ganelon's alone, Roland might seem blameworthy. At Roncevaux, when he refuses to summon the army to defend the rear guard, he weakens the former and condemns the latter to certain destruction. Is this the way to serve the French cause, and is it really a Christian act to allow one's friends to perish in order to preserve one's honor? One might be tempted to think that it is the "wise" Oliver who is in the right and not Roland. And yet this is not, dare I say, the way God sees it, since he sends his angels to minister to Roland when he is on the brink of death. And this is because on the horizon of those "high dark mountains," at the borders of an empty world, and in the face of a betrayal that reenacts—and in us as well—the first revolt of the fallen angels, it no longer becomes a question of managing or administering a world according to its internal order but rather of saving it from the abyss. And it is against that covetousness, born of fear and engendering death, that Roland reinvents the notion of sacrifice that frees men and makes them eternal. "Dying," Roland destroys that boundary that shuts in the created being: the enclosure of the self, vain rival of being. He dissipates the confusions locked up in majestic phrases. He comes into contact with the stuff of life and makes it well up once again, a fountain in which every existence can find itself in every other—and it is true that there is a synthetical function in the gift of the self; Jesus, who prefigures Roland, taught him this, Jesus who, through his death, founded a communion.

But is it really Roland who has understood this, and willed it, or rather the poet of *The Song of Roland* who, through Roland, has rediscovered it and, in a measure, achieved it, since his personal commitment to a reflection on death surpasses the events that have become the myth? For while Roland is fighting, we feel that a transformation takes place, that the horizon changes, that the mountains, the armies shift into the space of a consciousness—a perfect transmutation of event into symbol, of memory into poem. The drama at Roncevaux gradually becomes eternal—the place of that "spiritual combat" of which Rimbaud would speak—and there everything turns inward, as when one creates or contemplates an icon. And thus the Sarrasins, for example, swarming on the hilltops, passing again and again like waves on the ocean, become a kind of evil infinite, the one offered by the world of appearances, by the heaps of objects, and Roland, who in this takes on the divine part in all of us, would be lost here if he accepted it as true, if, as Oliver urges him, he agreed to sound his horn. But he fully realizes now that what saves us from death is acceptance of death. When he refuses to sound the illusory appeal for help, he immediately places himself outside the reach of the Sarrasins and cannot be wounded or exhausted by them. He tears himself apart in a *beyond,* and when his horn can be nothing more than his final testimony he fills it with his breath in a universe redeemed. Roland dies, as we all know, bursting his lungs: speech consumed in order to deliver.

And Charlemagne—words reanimated by speech—emerges from his long torpor at the sound of this distant horn, seeing clearly all at once, measuring the extent of the betrayal. He returns to the place of battle, catches up to the enemy, and defeats Baligant in single combat. Countless demons scatter. Charlemagne's sword "Joyful" triumphs over "Precious," the idolatrous arm wielded by Baligant. "Ah, Durendal, how beautiful, shining, and white thou art!" Roland had said to his own sword when, just before his death, he was able to confirm its invincible power. Each thing, when placed in the context of unity, can seem to overflow with light, like water from a spring, outside time. And thus it is that the words are clear and bright in this poem, founded and not merely inhabited by its hero. For it is thanks to Roland that the darkness in the work always remains only a possibility. The decasyllable lines, with their twofold rhythms (four feet like the eternal, six like time), seem to drain away all darkness and to spread peace over the earth. The phrases possess the truest kind of simplicity, not the fruit of mournful deprivation but the resonance of the invisible. The waters of presence have come together again. But for whom, other than the distant poet and some chance reader, has the music of the world surged up once more? From the point of view of the spirit of vigilance, which must be keeping watch somewhere in the social consciousness, since this poem did appear, has there been some *pas gagné,* some step forward?

I don't think so. For *The Song of Roland* tells us that to complete his victory Charlemagne needs God to arrest the decline of day for a few hours, and this image of a sun made motionless for justice, though superb, is certainly not, in my eyes at least, the most auspicious sign among all the stars that have appeared in the skies of poetic struggle. What is this new zenith if not the cipher of unity? But in these unmoving shadows, time is only stopped and not abolished, as it should be, in the depths of its own expenditure—and eternity, true eternity, can never be dissociated from the physical sun. Once again, an image has replaced an experience. Is it, then, that sin reemerges the moment sacrifice is fulfilled? In fact, the poem tells us that Charlemagne is unable to find rest once he returns to Aix-la-Chapelle. Scarcely is he back in his room and on the point of sleep when the Angel Gabriel appears to him to tell him that the Infidel must once more be vanquished and that the battle must once more be waged. The emperor weeps with weariness. An admirable and brutal ending, this ceaseless starting over again.

Roland is gone now. Very quickly human society will lose the spiritual instruments—symbols, myths: vocabulary and syntax of Presence—that made the hero possible. But then, too, beyond the epic the first traces of personal poetry begin to appear. Through death and resurrection a new kind of Roland emerges in the form of the great poets—Dante, Villon, Shakespeare, then Baudelaire and Rimbaud—who will give new life to poetic speech. And the necessity and sense of this appears clear to us. It is not enough, in poetic speech, for words to be different or for structures to flourish; love must reconcile them to their own empty form. From the same to the same, a returning—and it is sometimes a long searching—and yet, this, and only this, is the real.

Translated by John T. Naughton

2   Shakespeare and the French Poet[1]

How MIGHT WE EVALUATE French translations of Shakespeare? Do we have a truthful image of him in French—or at least a compelling one? Have we, for instance, a French equivalent of the German translations of Schlegel and Tieck which have known, ever since the Romantic period, such favor and renown? No, there is nothing comparable, and I believe that it is useful and important to recall and to analyze this astonishing absence.

It is not that Shakespeare is unrecognized in France. We read him, as best we can, we evoke him; we have had for quite some time a general idea of his greatness, if only because an army of adaptors, coming at the work from all sides, have managed to point out this or that aspect of an opus whose essential feature is precisely its extraordinary diversity. In one sense it is probably an advantage that we have not known in France a translation comparable to that of Schlegel and Tieck—a "classic," beautiful and power-ful enough to constrict us within the limited perfection of its own particular vision. The Romantic age, in any case, was not capable of truly understand-ing Shakespeare. The fact remains, however, that to this day we still do not have in France a complete translation that is both faithful to the original and great literature in its own right—one, I mean, in which the reader can get more than an abstract idea of the dramatic elements of the work and some-thing of the substance of Shakespeare's incomparable poetry. Perfectly good translations of particular plays there are. I would mention, for exam-ple, those of Jules Supervielle, Pierre Leyris, the *Romeo* of Jouve and Pitoëff—but they seem piecemeal and inconsistent when what is needed is an organic whole, a single profound vision combining anew all the aspects

1. "Shakespeare and the French Poet" ("Shakespeare et le poète français") was first pub-lished in France in 1959 in the review *Preuves* 100 (June):42–48. A version of the text also appeared, together with the essay "Transposer ou traduire *Hamlet*," as an Afterword to Bon-nefoy's French translation of *Hamlet,* published in 1962 by Mercure de France. An English translation of the essay was published anonymously the same year in *Encounter* 18, no. 6 (June 1962):38–47. A great deal of the present translation has been taken over from the *Encounter* version, but with considerable revision by the present editor.

of the Shakespearean world—and this could only be attempted by one poet working alone with authority and decision.

In other words, the French have only been *told about* Shakespeare and, if translating means catching the original tone of voice, that fusion of personal vision and word which makes the poetic dimension, then he has not yet been translated at all. How are we to account for this? I have no doubt that it is worthwhile looking at the problem from a somewhat theoretical angle and trying to find out if there is not some basic, essential cause for this persistent frustration. But to state the problem, I shall first consider the less successful translations: what strikes me most about them, apart from any individual shortcomings, is one serious weakness they all have in common.

Although historically speaking the idea is absurd, it is a lasting pity that no one thought of extemporizing a translation in Shakespeare's own day. At the beginning of the seventeenth century, before Malherbe's influence turned the scale and while the impression of Garnier's breathless verse still lingered, something of the essence of Shakespeare could have seeped into our poetry and modified it, perhaps profoundly. But the taste for classicism soon barred any genuine understanding of Shakespeare. In an age dominated by Racine, one can hardly imagine anyone translating *Macbeth*. And when Voltaire takes it upon himself to initiate the French mind into what he called *English Tragedy* (after Corneille and Racine even the word *tragedy* is charged with overtones very remote from anything English), the rendering he offers of Hamlet's "To be or not to be," for instance, is a complete travesty of Shakespeare, and precisely because of that facile and totally unpoetical Alexandrine which was then the principal cause of the vapidity in the theater:

> *Demeure, il faut choisir, et passer à l'instant*
> *De la vie à la mort et de l'être au néant . . .*

What is surprising is that, with the intention of giving some idea of Shakespeare's "woodnotes wild," Voltaire should have followed up this doggerel with a literal line-by-line translation which has a kind of beauty of its own and, in its freedom and flexibility, is related to what we might welcome today. In rendering "Or to take arms against a sea of troubles" as "et de prendre les armes contre un mer de troubles," he shows a fine audacity, and in my own translation of *Hamlet* I have paid the unwitting forerunner of all modern translators the compliment of taking over this line. Voltaire, however, put it forward only to cut it out, as if he meant to show the kind of excesses from which the French genius had to be protected. And when in the age of Louis XVI, Ducis in turn composed "imitations" of *Hamlet* and *Othello* that were widely read and often reprinted (I remember they were still to be found in my grandfather's small library), it was from Voltaire that he had learned to cut and rearrange and simplify Shakespeare's text so that the end product was a "five-act tragedy" of the utmost regularity and inanity. "I don't understand English"—this is how Ducis begins his preface, and in fact the original plot is so distorted that Claudius, to take one example, is turned into Ophelia's father, and we can be fairly sure that this is in order to face Hamlet, like a character in Corneille, with a choice between revenge and love. From the neoclassical point of view of the "Age of Reason," Hamlet's delays had to be justified on rational grounds which were *perfectly clear and distinct*.

Nevertheless Ducis's clear-cut line is to some slight extent shaded off; he has a touch of the Gothic novel, and I must confess that I do not find his renderings altogether intolerable, if only because they illustrate with such perfect clarity the difficulties of translating Shakespeare. Indeed, after Ducis, the problems were more often shelved than solved. After the Revolution until the Second Empire, Shakespeare was continually translated, but in the spirit of a vague Romanticism. Letourneur (between 1776 and 1782), Francisque Michel, Benjamin Laroche, Guizot, François Victor-Hugo, Montégut, all published *Complete Works,* with some progress in accuracy (though Letourneur had no objection to cutting out complete scenes and bowdlerizing passages he thought coarse), and even perhaps in felicity—but with a defect which is of course present in Ducis and which is so subtle and elusive that it is not at all easy to describe.

Here is a famous passage from the first part of Henry IV, the one where Falstaff is in a black mood, repenting of his evil life:

> "Why," he says to Bardolph, "there is it. Come, sing me a bawdy song, make me merry. . . . I was as virtuously given as a gentleman need to be: virtuous enough, swore little, diced not above seven times a week, went to a bawdy-house not above one in a quarter of an hour, paid money that I borrowed three or four times, lived well, and in good compass; and now I live out of all order, out of all compass."

In these few lines, and in the background they suggest—a world of authentic bawdy houses and taverns—we are confronted with a real human being talking about himself, and any feeling of unreality arises only from the joking contrast he himself makes between his actual way of life and the impression of it he would like to create. Falstaff is completely there in the flesh, and for whatever universal meaning he attains, his starting point is the same as that of any other mortal: his individual reality, which persists in vivid unpredictability throughout the entire play. Falstaff is an archetype only because he is in the first place this particular complex and enigmatic personality that we cannot fathom any more than we can really understand any other real human being. And the words seem to lend themselves to this total *thereness*. They seem to be one with the puffing voice, and even to be reabsorbed into the world of sense they evoke, so that we are left with nothing between us and its raw assertiveness, its undiminished complexity.

But let us now look at a translation, a very meticulous one, by François Victor-Hugo.

> FALSTAFF: Oui, voilà la chose. Allons, chante-moi une chanson égrillade. Egaye-moi. J'étais aussi vertueusement doué qu'un gentilhomme a besoin de l'être; vertueux suffisamment; jurant peu; jouant aux dés, pas plus de sept fois . . . par semaine; allant dans les mauvais lieux pas plus d'une fois par quart d'heure; ayant trois ou quatre fois rendu de l'argent emprunté; vivant bien et dans la juste mesure; et maintenant, je mène une vie désordonnée et hors de toute mesure.

Certainly it is the same passage: the ideas and the references are the same. But there is a world of difference between the original text and the translation. Whereas Shakespeare's Falstaff seems actually *in the room,* in the translation he appears distant, insubstantial, dimmed, as if we were looking at him through a windowpane. He is no longer a living being, he is a character in literature, but one striving, by his exuberant language, to resemble life too closely and hence all the less convincing. In all these translations, all Shakespeare's characters lose their roundness in the same way. Even where Shakespeare's "excesses"—the puns, the bawdy—are scrupulously preserved, the characters seem insubstantial and their speech lacks life. "I feel immortal longings . . . " is what Shakespeare wrote at the end of *Anthony and Cleopatra.* "Je sens en moi l'impatient désir de l'immortalité" is Letourneur's version, while "Je me sens pressée d'un violent désir de quitter la vie" is Francisque Michel's. Where are we? The words create neither reality nor myth. This is the ghost of Shakespeare.

And yet we need not be in any doubt that these translators chose a prose rendering so as not to be led into the unreality, the unnaturalness and lack of body, characteristic of the Voltaire and Ducis translations. They used prose because it can serve the Romantic aspiration to lay hold of the real in all its heterogeneousness—not only local color and the picturesque but the inwardness of beings as remote as possible from ourselves—in short, to bring language and real life as close together as possible. Admittedly the earlier Romanticism (I mean that of Hugo and Musset) had no very profound grasp of this reality. And since Shakespeare could hardly have been less concerned with the picturesque, it is likely that one of the reasons why nineteenth-century translators were frustrated is just that they had lost touch with what is the real source of Shakespeare's truth—that vital force of human creation, that passionate depth of feeling, that his verse directly expresses. But even in the most recent efforts, that sense of the glass between, of which I have spoken, is painfully persistent: so much so that, in André Gide's translations (alas, very poor), we are left with the effect of a puppet theater—literary, artificial, and affected. Surely we cannot attribute this defect to some mere accident of literary history. Surely it is one of the inevitable misfortunes of the French language when it tries to translate poems without being able to escape from the hidden principles of its own very special and peculiar poetry.

What I wish to do here is to contrast Shakespeare's poetry with this unspoken assumption about the nature of poetry. For I am convinced that, quite apart from all the particular illustrations (I should like to have quoted more but nothing would really be adequate or clinching), the essence of this failure in translating Shakespeare lies in the opposing metaphysics which govern and sometimes tyrannize the French and English languages, respectively.

If I had to sum up in a sentence the impression Shakespeare makes upon me, I should say that, in his work, I see no opposition between the universal and the particular. In spite of scholastic tradition, he does not envisage these two poles of thought as contradictory because he does not admit them as his intellectual focus.

Is Macbeth an archetype like Antigone, or even Harpagon, or is he rather an individual caught in a unique destiny, the product of pure chance? Is Othello the type of the jealous man—or the incoherent victim of blind and senseless forces that could not be further from anything "clear and distinct"? These questions cannot be answered because they are wrongly stated. For Shakespeare deals with man's *actions,* which are never "particulars" because they participate in the universal categories of the consciousness that conceives them, but which also never—not even in the case of Brutus and Julius Ceasar—reach the fullness and clarity of the universal because they have to compromise with the brute contingent.

Human action cannot be fitted into the framework of logic because man acts only in order to contradict his own nature, to be at once both individual and universal—and the essential ambiguity in Shakespeare means that his theater is the empirical observation, without literary or philosophical preconception, of man as he actually exists. The apparent subject of his tragedy is thus just a means of capturing a possibility of human existence so that it might then be examined. The seemingly abstract setting of the action does not so much exclude, as concentrate, the real world, like a framework within which all the variations of action that human passion might conceive could be instantaneously evoked. And Shakespeare's language, too, is a means rather than an end; it is always subordinate to the external object, which is something English allows. Nouns fade before the real presence of things, which stand starkly before us in the actual process of becoming. The uninflected adjectives snap qualities photographically without raising the metaphysical problem of the relation of quality and substance, as the agreement of adjectives and nouns must do in French. English concerns itself naturally with tangible aspects. It accepts the reality of what can be observed and does not admit the possibility of any other kind, of another order of reality; it has a natural affinity with the Aristotelean critique of Platonic Ideas. And if its Latin roots, to some extent, unsettle this philosophical choice and grant a more abstract handling of experience to an intelligence brought up in this "devotion to the realm of things," they do not undermine the natural realism of the language so much as simply make it easier to express those moments in life when we are guided by a sense of the ideal. To quote again that moment of the purest poetry, those most sublime words of Cleopatra—"I feel immortal longings": on the one hand, the English is capable of seizing hold of the living actuality at its most concrete, immediate, and instinctive while, on the other, by using a word like *immortal,* which is pure Idea, it retains the capacity to reveal in this same concrete action the eternal and the universal. At a deeper level, the English language tells us that Immortality, this pure Idea, in some sense really exists and that it is a noble and veridical part of speech but also that its activity and life depend on our will to create them. English poetry, Shakespeare's at least, rejects archetypal realism but only in order to follow the inalienable liberty of man with greater flexibility.

And the greatness and richness of English poetry come from service to this liberty, as if offering it at every moment the entire range of its possibilities, so that any given word can open up a world, a "brave new world," to our perception. With French poetry it is a very different matter. Generally, with this more cautious, more self-contained kind of poetry, it is a fact that the words seem to state what they denote only to exclude immediately, from the poem's field of reference, whatever else is not denoted. The poet's statements do not set out to describe external reality but are a way of shutting himself in with certain selected precepts in a simplified, more circumscribed world. For instance, in his plays, Racine rejects all but a few situations and feelings. By stripping them of all the contingent or accidental details of real life, he seems to raise them to the dignity of the Platonic Idea, as if he wished to reduce his dramatic structure to the bare relations of

congruence or opposition which hold between these Ideas. A more co-
herent world of intelligible essences is substituted for the real world. And,
for all that, it is not an abstract world, for the Platonic Idea is profoundly
double-natured, in the sense of taking on the life of sensible appearance in
its most intense and specific form. But this world is, despite everything, *a
place apart,* where the bewildering diversity of the real can be forgotten, and
also the very existence of time, everyday life and death. Poetic creation, in
short, is hieratic; it makes an inviolable place, and while the rite of reading
continues it draws the mind into this illusory communion.

Not all French poetry, of course, can be identified with the art of
Racine. And in one case, that of Baudelaire, it went counter to Racine's
design for poetry: but even then without moving out of this magic circle by
which words circumscribe the mind. In rediscovering and reaffirming for
himself the notion of poetry which was already implicit in the work of
Villon and Maynard, Baudelaire was asserting against Racine the very exis-
tence of sensible things, the particular reality as such, the stubborn entities
that people our mortal horizon, as if giving himself up completely to the
phenomenal world and abandoning the hieratic use of language. Baudelaire
is the most consistent and determined opponent of the Racinian theory.
And yet this *principle of exclusion* I have referred to still governs his poetry.
Even though he is dealing with *this* particular swan or *that* particular wom-
an rather than with swan or woman as such—with the idea, that is, of swan
or woman—it is not, for all that, what these particular entities are like that
matters to him. What matters is simply this mystery—that the Idea should
have strayed into the very marrow of the sensible world, that it should have
agreed to undergo limitation and death and that, while retaining its abso-
lute status, it should have entered into this world of shadows and chance.
Baudelaire is not trying, at any level of penetration, to describe things as
they are: he is trying to convey the act of being, and the passion and moral
feeling that can be based upon it. An intense and narrow aim that restored
to poetry that almost obsessional detachment from the phenomenal world
which seems to be the fate of our main body of work.* It is as if words, in
French, excluding instead of describing, brought into the poem the pos-
sibility (for the poet) of entering upon the threshold of a divine world, a

---

* If Baudelaire, for instance, calls up the image of a woman with black hair or green eyes,
these are not so much personal characteristics as a definition of his own kind of sensibility.
[Y. B.]

possibility that shakes off the disintegrating diversity of things: as if they made the work of art a world of its own, a closed sphere.†

I should like to conclude by saying that in English the word is an opening: it is all surface—and in French it is a closing: it is all depth. On the one hand, a kind of word that can call upon all the rest to aid precision and enrichment; and on the other, a vocabulary as reduced as possible, so as to protect a single essential experience. On the one hand, unlimited dissociation, receptiveness to every dialectical or technical possibility, so that an alert awareness can penetrate always further into the phenomenal world. And on the other hand, all these evocations of sense entering into poetry as one enters into an Order, to be completely transformed, dying to the world, becoming one with the Idea the poem continually realizes. English poetry is like a mirror, French poetry like a crystal sphere. The French poet who is least like Racine and most like Shakespeare—so at least it is often said—is Paul Claudel. Now in *L'Annonce faite à Marie,* not only Violaine but Mara, not only Pierre de Craon but Jacques Hury speak with the same deliberate and highly stylized speech, a uniformity that symbolizes the unity of creation in the bosom of God, the nonexistence of evil at the heart of God's world. In spite of its richness, there is no poetry more organic, more closely knit than Paul Claudel's: still a sphere even if, with a medieval pre-Copernican sense of the cosmos, Claudel thought he could succeed in making it into a correlative of the Sphere of Created Beings.

English poetry, as I said, can be represented by a mirror, French by a sphere. How can these contradictory forms of poetry be translated into each other?

It may be easier now to see why so many French translations of Shakespeare are mediocre: they are nothing more than a compromise between these two linguistic structures. The French poetic vocabulary irresistibly tones down and dims the particular reality, that stubborn compound of the essential and the contingent. How then could we expect it to preserve Falstaff, who is particularity itself, emancipated from all forms and laws, even moral law? It is easier, too, to see how the majority of these translations came about historically. For Romanticism thought that it could be free of this inner law of the French language that I have tried to isolate. But the

† And that is why English poetry "means" so much more than French poetry. The former, whose words have no pretension to be Idea, will be able to put the world into words, to interpret and formulate it. The latter can only reveal the Idea, manifest beyond words and concepts. From this opposition the profound divergences of Anglo-Saxon and French literary criticism can also be deduced. [Y. B.]

Romantics, who wished to revolutionize the old dictionary and multiply its references to the real world, while still producing poetry, never achieved more than a shallow exploitation of this new territory. They were no more sensitive to the deeper stirrings of instinct and passion than they were to the dialectic of essence and existence on which Racine and Baudelaire had both pondered.

How, then, is Shakespeare to be translated? If I wished to end on a pessimistic note, I could easily make a list of all the forms this fundamental opposition might assume, or, in other words, all the points of fidelity a translation should realize and which French structure makes difficult, if not impossible. Thus the alternation of prose and verse in Shakespearean tragedy is true to reality; it witnesses to the opposing forces—the heroic and the commonplace—which are at work in the world: at the end of the cobbler's scene in *Julius Caesar,* the abrupt return to verse is a dramatic assertion of the will to nobility in a boorish world. But this plurality of perspectives is not possible in French poetry. Not only with Corneille and Racine but also with Hugo and Claudel the minor characters speak in verse and, like the Chorus in Greek Tragedy, the less they share in the nobler dimensions of the action, the more strictly they are bound to formal poetic expression.

That word-play has to be translated is another difficulty. Shakespeare's punning is genuinely "two-valued," reflecting the complex nature of the real world, but French does not take kindly to the pun, and it is unlikely to be anything better than a nihilistic (sometimes a directly subversive) assault on rational mind. Indeed, the least significant word in a poem has latent within it the entire structure of its language. Mere literal translation of the word is not enough to break down the structure. Take that one word *Sortez,* Roxane's cry in *Bajazet.* How much of its implication would we expect to survive, translated into English or many other languages? There is a great danger that this tremendous word by which Roxane severs herself from the world of sense, this word that implies a whole metaphysics, would wind up a mere theatrical effect.

But is there much point in making a long list of difficulties? It would be of more use to take note of the one remaining possibility that may, one day, give us the chance of solving the problem of Shakespearean translation—at least of raising it to a new level.

❦

If, as I have tried to show, every language has an individual structure and the linguistic structure of French poetry is Platonic while that of Shakespeare's English is a sort of passionate Aristotelianism, then every true translation—and this quite apart from accuracy of detail—has a kind of moral obligation to be a metaphysical reflection, the contemplation of one way of thinking by another, the attempt to express from one's own angle the specific nature of that thought, and finally a kind of examination of one's own resources. From that point translation penetrates far beyond the rendering of explicit discourse and of the significances that can be directly grasped, into the indirect ways of expression (prosodic usage or the handling of imagery, for instance). Translation becomes a language's struggle with its own nature, at the very core of its being, the quickening point of its growth.

Now I believe that French poetry today is much better prepared than it has ever been to wage this struggle with its own language. In general terms, we may have reached that point in Western history when the major languages have to emerge from their naïveté and break with their instinctive assumptions, so as to establish themselves in a different kind of truth, with all its contradictions and difficulties. And without attempting to deny the existence of its ever-present structure, recent French poetry is undergoing a revolution which by disturbing this metaphysical tendency, and curbing it, could make it at some time or other more possible to convey Shakespeare's artistic intention.

What is the real point at issue? I have contended that a French word, in its "classic" usage, designates what it refers to only in order to exclude the real world of heterogeneous existences. I have contended, too, that Baudelaire affirmed this reality of existences but that it was not so much these real entities as our relations with them that he took as the focus of poetic contemplation; and so once again he made a closed world out of language, the world of a being struck by the mystery of presence, yet doomed to speak but obliquely of this reality he could never really make a part of his life.

This kind of poetry is still a subjective account of the soul, it is a *psychology;* but there is another, more recent poetry which aims at *salvation.* It conceives of the Thing, the real object, in its separation from ourselves, its infinite otherness, as something that can give us an instantaneous glimpse of essential being and thus be our salvation, if indeed we are able to tear the veil of universals, of the conceptual, to attain to it.

Whether this ambition is well-grounded or not is of little importance. The essential thing we must bear in mind is the demand it makes on language—to be open to this most remote kind of object: the being of things, their metaphysical *thereness,* their pressence before us, most remote from verbalization, and receive them in their pure existence, their stubborn atomicity, and their opaque silence. While it continues to exclude the complexity of phenomena, this poetry is an attempt to lose its identity, to go beyond its own nature, to the point where the universal *becomes* the particular (the ontologically unique), an ecstatic plunge into what is. This pursuit of otherness, of absolute exteriority, is surely not so far from Shakespeare. Is it not an attempt to contemplate, in the dimension of universality, what Shakespeare lays bare in particular beings as their source and background? When, for instance, he traces through Macbeth's whole line of fate the ineluctable presence of the witches, or shows Hamlet's mind haunted by the indissoluble Ghost, or reveals, in *The Winter's Tale,* the hope—absurd but still triumphant—of a real resurrection in the flesh? Always a rational universe is given the lie; it melts away before the void, and human action projects itself into an obscure and incommunicable region. There is no great difference between the Hamlet who realizes that the reign of law has passed away (and that justification is to be found, if anywhere, in a subjective choice without ground or warrant) and our contemporary French poetry which has abdicated its age-old kingdom to take, like the Prince of Denmark, its chance with *Angst,* impotence, and silence.

To put it another way, it is at the level of their deepest intuitions that the realism of Shakespeare and recent French poetry's denial of idealism may henceforth communicate. For the one describes what the other asks to live. And what can be said directly by Shakespeare may, perhaps, be indirectly suggested in this other language that, while honoring the explicit content of each work to be translated, can now contribute a profound feeling for the very being and presence of things, which will be an unremitting testing of all of its poetic resources. Thus the necessary surpassing of classical forms, of closed types of prosody (which is not inconsistent with a concern for the real laws governing the verse) becomes one, in translations of Shakespeare, with the need to preserve the poetic line and its lofty tragic quality, without giving the impression that the English poet believed in a hieratic and unreal world. In fact, Shakespeare and many Elizabethans have become immensely instructive for French poetry in its process of finding itself. We ought to give them our most serious attention. And if we still fail to translate them properly we shall certainly have less excuse than translators who have gone before.

The confrontation of two languages in a translation is a metaphysical and moral experiment, the "testing" of one way of thinking by another. Sometimes it is sheer impossibility, indeed vanity. But from time to time, something may emerge whose consequences add another level of interest to the mere fact of translation, by raising a language to a new level of awareness through the circuitous ways of poetry.

Translated for Encounter, 1962; revised by John T. Naughton

3 Shakespeare's Uneasiness[1]

WHY CONNECT *Macbeth* with *Romeo and Juliet?* The one a drama shrouded in mist, stained with blood, pierced by cries of terror, the most Nordic and nocturnal of Shakespeare's works—the other, on the contrary, a romantic tragedy, essentially Mediterranean, a poem such as Pisanello might have chosen to illustrate in a fresco in one of those beautiful palaces where music and the dance seem to release desire from its matrix of primitive violence?

Whereas Macbeth seems to us to represent guilt in the absolute, without anything about him to arouse that compassion which to Western thought is the principle explaining our interest in tragedy, Romeo and Juliet are, or at any rate seem to be, the totally innocent victims of a conspiracy between human stupidity and their unlucky stars. They die, but as though to prove that nobility and purity are not intellectual concepts. Day dawns when the play ends.

Let us begin, however, by observing that Italy was not, for the Elizabethans, what nowadays we fancy it must have been for them. No doubt they saw it as the scene of culture, beauty, sensuous delight, but the revolutionary thought of Machiavelli had spread through Europe like a threat to be defeated, and in Protestant countries this opposition took a complex form, entailing a suspicion of culture even while its benefits were acknowledged. Machiavelli was likened to Satan, together with the Jesuits, agents of the Counter Reformation and tools of the Devil, and Italy was consequently identified as the land of treachery, poison, and murder. Iago is Italian, and in *Hamlet* the "play within the play" that tells the sinister story of a nephew's murder of his uncle by pouring poison into his ear while he sleeps is "writ in choice Italian." The Gothic novel is prefigured. The South provides as apt an occasion as the North for meditation on the darker sides of the soul, in jeopardy since the Fall.

1. "Shakespeare's Uneasiness" ("L'Inquiétude de Shakespeare") was published as a preface to Bonnefoy's French translations of *MacBeth* and *Romeo and Juliet* (Paris: Gallimard, Collection Folio, 1985).

Such meditation occurs in *Romeo and Juliet,* an early play, and in *Macbeth,* the work of Shakespeare's maturity, in not too dissimilar a fashion, so that a comparison of the two plays sheds fresh light on each of them. Is Macbeth evil incarnate, while Romeo represents love unjustly, mysteriously victimized? But Shakespeare has shown from the opening words of *Macbeth* that his hero is the victim of an attack as hard to combat as it is pregnant with consequences. He was, we are told, the essence of loyalty and valor, but the forces of evil decide, then and there, on the stage before our eyes, to involve him in a plan that reaches far beyond his personal lot, since it concerns the fate of a dynasty that was still in power in Scotland and in England when the play was written. And for Shakespeare's contemporaries, these forces existed; one and all felt threatened by them. That they should attack Macbeth, that his was the soul they had to capture and that they were able to persuade him to his criminal projects by proving that they had the gift of deciphering the future was surely a singular misfortune for this obscure clan chieftain.

It is true that the three female demons who thus caught him in their net could only prevail over his will because it was potentially or noticeably flawed: in spite of the vestiges of paganism that Shakespeare can discern in Scotland, we are still in the Christian world of free will where the devil has great power, but within precise limits. Macbeth, who yields so readily and is so soon to become so black a figure, cannot originally have been a truly righteous man, a pure soul. But the choice that has been made of him, enhancing his peril, turns our attention from one level of guilt to another, more inward and less easily perceptible—even by the man within whom it dwells—than simple vulgar ambition or a taste for rapine or murder. Macbeth is not innocent, but his soul was so insidiously affected to begin with that he was unaware of his own guilt.

This is confirmed moreover by a whole series of indications that Shakespeare gives us from the start, or rather perhaps that he sees developing, sometimes indistinctly, in the figure that rapidly becomes so concrete, through the sympathy he feels (and this is the essence of his genius) for everything that lives and dies. What he first shows us about Macbeth—and only a genius could have had such an intuition about a warrior famous for his courage in battle—is fear, omnipresent fear. Macbeth does not dread his adversary's sword, but an old wives' tale sets him trembling. Hardly has he envisaged his crime when visions terrify him. Banquo's ghost signifies his remorse, no doubt, his natural dread of the wrath of heaven, but it frightens him far more than any flesh-and-blood judge because it comes from that world of the unseen by which he has always felt terrifyingly surrounded. This fear is metaphysical in essence, and shows Macbeth as subject to that insidious, almost covert alienation that we had begun to sense. In face of

Nature, where others might only see cause for praising God, this uneasy spirit is on the alert. He is not so much a being lucidly choosing evil as one in constant dread of it, like a dizziness that paralyzes his capacity to love and over which his will has little power.

And furthermore we realize, from the first dialogue with the witches, that Macbeth has an obsession which is also unconscious, although it is the source of many of his thoughts and actions. This is the obsession with fatherhood, a joy denied him (since for all his apparent virility he has no children), and jealousy of others' progeny. "Your children shall be kings," he says to Banquo, as the witches, those Fates, vanish into the mist. This thought already spoils the future promised him, and later drives him back to the priestesses of Hecate, to the very door of Hell, because he wants at all costs to hear them repeat what he already knows but refuses to admit. And his wife, on two occasions, refers with singular violence to the children she has apparently had but in any case has lost. In terrible words she sets her murderous intention above the child she has suckled. We realize that the assassination of the King, with the usurpation of power, is to be the new progeny of this man and this woman: born in the anguished hours before the dawn and soon becoming the sole link between the couple.

Now one of the more important features of the medieval mind, and one that still prevailed in Shakespeare's day, was the sense that God's world was a vast and perfect form within which every creature had its place in the whole structure, an emanation of the Divine; and each was expected to compensate for the damage done by his death to the plenitude of the cosmos by procreating other lives to take his place. The destiny of Being is thus entrusted to the ardor specific to every creature, and this is particularly true of man, who has been endowed with freedom of choice. If he has children, that is a positive sign in his favor. If he has none, he must feel indebted and rise through mental effort to that participation in the form of the Universe he is debarred from physically.

Macbeth shows no signs of such a capacity for contemplation; on the contrary his fear reveals that earth and heaven are alien to him, and his jealousy shows that other beings are rivals and enemies rather than kindred spirits. Whether his sterility is the cause or the consequence of his terror in the face of existence, in any case this lack of children intensifies it, making the created world into a hostile and enigmatic place. And thus in two furtively convergent ways, Macbeth is shown to be in a state of severance from the whole, of retreat into the self, which can be recognized as that vague but very deep and dangerous badness of which the Evil One takes advantage. Does Shakespeare portray a creature of unbridled violence and ambition, whose crimes result simply and directly from obvious and dominating impulses, such as in other tragedies motivate Richard III or Edmund in *King Lear?* No; he has probed more deeply, at the unconscious level where desire becomes corrupt almost at the moment of its birth: when the wrong choice is made without a clear awareness of its consequences, so soon to become criminal. Whence the astonishment of Macbeth, overtaken in his own fate by some unknown power. Lacking desire at the outset, terrified of a world to whose beauty he is indifferent, then carried away by a dark wish which is perhaps only a mask for that emptiness, he remains to the end a man who fails to understand. Remember his reflections on learning of his wife's death. They clearly display that incomprehension of the created world which, for a Christian of the Renaissance, was the most radical sin of all:

> "Out, out, brief candle!
> Life's but a walking shadow, a poor player
> That struts and frets his hour upon the stage
> And then is heard no more: it is a tale
> Told by an idiot, full of sound and fury,
> Signifying nothing."

When alienation has reached this point we are no longer dealing with the common sort of violence and treachery. We sense here the ache of a longing for love: however much this sinner has accumulated misdeeds, however far gone he is in crime, yet Shakespeare perceives him at so deep a level, so close to the painful recesses of our original being-in-the-world, that in spite of everything this man Macbeth embodies our universal condition: grasped at that mysterious point where one can still choose what to be, but where it is late, terribly late in one's relation to oneself.

In *Macbeth* Shakespeare is undoubtedly the playwright depicting visible violence and its explicit intentions: but he is also, without using specific words for this but by means of brief notations based on intuition, the theologian probing the most secret area of the soul—this of course being defined according to the Christian doctrine which is its frame of reference.

And if we now return to *Romeo and Juliet,* what we have learned from *Macbeth* sheds light upon the earlier play, which predates the period when Shakespeare was to deal directly with the question of evil; and a greater complexity of meaning is revealed. The problem of *Romeo and Juliet,* at first sight, is that of the sufferings of the righteous, or the silence of God. The Elizabethan thinker admits that the fall of man disturbed the workings of the world, that the very course of the stars lost that harmonious coordination which should have ensured for mankind, through a play of influences involving the elements and the humors, an untroubled destiny. Nevertheless, there are too many setbacks in the fate of these two lovers, who had apparently only sought to conform to the great law of life which is also God's law and that of the heavenly bodies. Should one say that the hard but noble task of the just man afflicted by misfortune is to rise above adversity? And yet this unfortunate pair have scarcely had time to prepare for such a life, let alone live it: it seems as if heaven had ordained that the best people by sheer force of love should succumb to total despair and have recourse to suicide, which leads to hell.

But just as in *Macbeth* the protagonist's guilt is fully revealed only by a profoundly searching insight, which discloses the metaphysical vice underlying crude impulses, it may be that in *Romeo and Juliet* the misfortunes that ravage two lives are caused not by mere chance but by the difficulty one of the two finds in adapting to the world he has to live in. Is Romeo really that lover whose emotion, in harmony with the will of all creation, is so pure and so intense that Shakespeare takes it as a point of reference, standing out like a bright color against blacks and grays? In fact, as the first act insists, he is the melancholy character as studied by the Elizabethans, the sad youth who before becoming enamored of Juliet fancied himself in love with a certain Rosaline who was nothing but a mirage, an excuse for him to shun the world. At this point Romeo lived only by night, avoiding his friends, and all his words expressed only a great dream that substituted a simplified image for the practical experience of everyday reality. And this may seem like intensity and purity, but it means being oblivious of people as they exist in ordinary life, and hence a lack of compassion, which is potentially evil.

It may be objected that this is only the beginning of the play and that the evil vanishes later with the meeting of Romeo and Juliet and the discovery of mutual love. But a careful reading of the tragedy reveals that, on the contrary, when Shakespeare dramatized the story told by Bandello or Arthur Brooke he introduced into it a suspicion which brings out and enhances a number of facts that preoccupy him. Romeo only goes to the house of his enemies the Capulets with a foreboding of misfortune, as though he feels driven by a baleful power, already at work within himself. He has "dreamed a dream last night" which Mercutio's interruption prevents him from relating: so that one is tempted to believe that what he was going to tell is what takes place that night or next day, already half envisaged by his subconscious mind. Surely he is the kind of man who can only love if some obstacle intervenes, distancing the beloved object, haloing it with transcendence. Notice that Juliet is still far off in the great hall when he is dazzled by her beauty

　　　　too rich for use, for earth too dear

and it is still as an image that he sees her at her window at the beginning of the balcony scene. The ecstatic words in which he greets the lovely nocturnal vision do not suggest a real person but a cosmic form, where two bright eyes are about to take their place among the stars, and this silent apparition seems to emit a disturbing light, anticipating the dream-visions of Poe. Ill-omened, too, is the secret marriage, which will render impossible any meeting in ordinary reality. Sexual possession is not incompatible with dream when it is confined to the mere physical act by the furtive character of the lovers' meetings. For this kind of lover, Juliet may well be another Rosaline, a proof that one can reject the world for the sake of beauty, and meanwhile fail to understand the true nature of the person one thinks one loves at other moments of her existence.

Now this is a psychological experience which, even if it involves no sense of guilt, resembles that negative disposition that Shakespeare shows to be underlying Macbeth's wrong choices; and here again it can have fatal consequences. To stake everything on a dream, to bank on the semblance instead of facing the presence, is to involve oneself between reality and mirage in a difficult quandary, where impatience lays down the law, where actions are more risky and where consequently risks are more dangerous, and disaster strikes at last. "He was asking for it," proverbial wisdom says in such cases. And we may suspect that Romeo, in the depths of his being, was asking for what he thought he was simply enduring. We can see in his decision to kill himself, taken like a flash of lightning, as sudden as his love had been, the consequence not so much of his misfortune as of the alienation that had always warped his view of the world and submerged action in dream.

We must realize, too, that he is responsible not only for his own misfortune but for others that occur in the play, primarily for Juliet's. Married in secret and thus exposed to such dangers as the marriage planned for her by her father, which involves her in terrifying, traumatic experiences, she seems to us robbed of her destiny, and Romeo may thus be thought to have seduced rather than married her, to have raped a willing victim: whereas an alternative solution was possible, as several hints reveal. Repeatedly, Shakespeare lets us understand that the quarrel between Montagues and Capulets was dying down, kept alight only by the folly of servants and the arrogance of young Tybalt, whose high-flown fantasy echoes on a more vulgar note that refusal to accept reality which is characteristic of Romeo. The head of the house of Capulet, who wants to marry his daughter, speaks in praise of Romeo ("a virtuous and well-governed youth") and accepts him in his house. Romeo might have remembered the words that express the essence of Christianity: "Knock and it shall be opened unto you." Antagonisms, at that period, were often brought to an end by marriages. Romeo's better self, with greater trustfulness, might have brought about that great reconciliation that Friar Laurence anticipated, and which was achieved by his death, too late and at such cost.

In *Romeo and Juliet,* Shakespeare raises somewhat the same problem as in *Macbeth,* responding to a similar enigma in the same kind of way. The question in each case, the dilemma that disturbs a mind accustomed to the idea of heaven's vigilance, is that of chance, which seems to contradict this, less because of the manifold vicissitudes it inflicts on the innocent than through the traps it seems to lay in their path, of which the Devil takes advantage. And the answer is not only to recognize in these victims of chance the fact of a preexistent fault, which exonerates Heaven from the reproach of indifference, but also to disclose that fault in a remote recess of the soul, where lesser writers, satisfied with the virtues and vices current in ordinary behavior, would not have thought to search. Shakespeare, in short, is held back neither by horror nor by compassion, although he experiences both. By the power of his sympathy—which is denied to none of his characters, whence the impression of universality he conveys, although he has a highly personal sensibility and asserts his own opinions—he is aware of frustrated longings, naive aspirations, latent alienations, and morbid tendencies however slight; and like a theologian, although his language is not philosophical, he discovers in these indications of man's relation to the world the mysterious root—the still voiceless mandrake—of that which later in life, in altered circumstances, will take the form of evil. Like a theologian, but also like the devil who, let us remark in passing, does exactly the same thing. But in the latter case the aim is evil, whereas Shakespeare holds a mirror up to society only so that the Christian soul, more readily aware of its own failings and consequently of its danger, might in fact escape the grasp of the great adversary. Shakespeare knows the appalling consequences as well as the imperceptible origins of evil; in *Romeo* and in *Macbeth,* he does not trace the intermediary stages of its development. The language of inner experience was not yet sufficiently diversified or admitted on the Elizabethan stage to make readily available to him those monologues that are like windows opening on to the relations between action and the unconscious mind. In *Hamlet* and *Othello,* however, it is on these moments of groping deliberation that he focuses his attention, moments of weary ennui when the time seems out of joint, or of sudden eruption into madness or crime.

Whence one final observation. In contrast with Marlowe, whom he had closely studied, Shakespeare seems an optimist, since tracing back the sources of crime or injustice to states of mind that are difficult but not impossible to localize, to study, to understand, he refuses to admit the radical senselessness of any human condition. It may seem odd to use the term optimist about a poet so conscious of the black depths of which mankind is capable: who puts Iago beside Othello, and imagines Richard III, of whom one wonders whether he has ever been capable of choosing between good and evil. But Shakespeare is obviously unwilling to see these few monsters as other than exceptional, a sort of countermiracle to be explained by some anterior fault or a design of Providence, and whenever he can, Shakespeare tends toward the idea of liberty, recognizing the original fact of man's fall and its consequences, the weakening of the human will, but describing subsequent lapses only against the background of virtues that can persevere and new beginnings that mean hope. How often in Shakespeare's plays the action ends as day breaks, when order, which has been shaken and ravaged, is finally restored, when positive values are reasserted, either suddenly as in *Romeo and Juliet* or, as in *Macbeth,* by the action of the forces of good, ever more clearly at work toward the end of the play! Evil, for Shakespeare, is always at the basis of his study of destiny, but it is a relative evil, outlined against a background of divine light and circumvented by Grace.

Optimism? Yet not without genuine disquiet, shown throughout his work by certain frequently recurring signs. Is evil only a sort of dizziness before the plentitude of being, to get rid of which one simply has to arise and walk? But how swiftly some barely perceptible psychological twist may sometimes spread, and with what vast consequences for the individual and society, even sometimes for nature itself, which in *Macbeth, Julius Caesar,* and *Lear* we see thrown into a disorder that reflects the turmoil in human consciences! Shakespeare does not pause over the intermediate stages, as I have said, but in fact his sources all tell him that the disaster happens, immediately, without a lingering trace of the moments that preceded it in the deterioration of his characters. And yet so many of these had seemed, at the beginning, so rich in virtues and gifts! Leaving aside Macbeth, who was never more than a brutal warrior in a still-barbarous age that seems pre-Christian and thereby almost reassuring, consider Romeo, the fine flower of a Christian society in which art, music, and rhetoric could sustain a troubled conscience. His good intentions, his will to love are manifest, as is that physical beauty which to the Renaissance mind represents the outward sign of moral quality, of purity of soul. It is surely disquieting to see that the taint is in him, too, and will spoil everything in two days, like the canker in the rose.

Shakespeare is certainly disquieted. This is proved by the insistence with which, fascinated by such a contradiction, he speaks both of Romeo's melancholy and of his rich virtues, calling to witness Mercutio, another melancholic but a clear-sighted one, whom we may take to represent the author at the heart of his creation. And it is proved, too, by Shakespeare's increasing concentration in subsequent plays on the problem of the rift between the mind and the world, of the repudiation of life, of excarnation: which was already suggested in the Sonnets, where the fair young man's perfection is valueless since his refusal to marry and beget a child suggests metaphysical avarice. Then, shortly after Romeo, we find Brutus, in the harsh Roman world, and soon there will be Hamlet. The prince of Denmark, melancholy, skeptical, sickened by life, is a more self-aware Romeo who knows the flaw in his love of which Ophelia, however, will be as much a victim as Juliet. The most famous and modern of Shakespeare's tragedies openly tackles the problem which was as yet only latent in his most romantic one; and does so with an anguish—in spite of the end, which restores order—metaphorically conveyed from the start by the cold night, the deserted battlements, the warlike preparations, the threat of the unseen.

Remember we are in the Renaissance. Artistic creation, beautiful objects, poems revivifying old myths, the fuller acknowledgment of physical beauty, are liable to ensnare one with charms that may prove illusory. The dream spreads, it permeates life itself, it seems victorious. In philosophy, in moral life, even and above all in forms of mystical experience, neo-Platonic thought, which Shakespeare knew through Spenser, seemed to justify a preference for the mirage, though this resulted in the melancholia of those young men who sit silently, chin in hand, their shoulders draped in their inky cloak.

And if, as the century drew to its close, there was Shakespeare—so deep a gaze scanning so wide a realm—it was not only because a mirror had to be held up to virtue so that it could see itself without complacency—the danger now being only a failure to recognize those initial moods of dejection which could so quickly lead to despair, madness, and crime—but because the trust that medieval man had placed in the world had now been undermined and so had to be restored; and this required a probing investigation of all the enigmas the poet perceived, all the dramas developing under his gaze, every sort of dream. The great writer is the one who senses the weakening of that faith in the meaning of the world that ensured the survival of society, if not its happiness; and who makes this decline his sole concern, unafraid of its very monotony, which enables him to take in the immense diversity of situations and of human beings.

Translated by Jean Stewart

4 Readiness, Ripeness: *Hamlet, Lear*[1]

JUST AFTER HE AGREES to fight with Laertes—but not without a sense of foreboding that he tries to suppress—Hamlet concludes that "the readiness is all." And toward the end of *King Lear,* Edgar, son of the Earl of Gloucester, persisting in his efforts to dissuade his father from suicide, asserts that "ripeness is all." And shouldn't we suppose that Shakespeare established consciously the opposition in these two phrases that are so closely related and that come at two moments so dense with meaning—and that they therefore speak of one of the tensions at the very heart of his poetics? I would like to try to understand more clearly the "readiness" in *Hamlet* and the "ripeness" in *King Lear*.

But first a preliminary remark which, though it has been made before, seems nevertheless useful to bear in mind when we raise questions about Shakespeare's work. As one studies the history of Western society, one discovers at one moment or another, and on every level of life, especially on the level of self-awareness, a deep fissure whose line marks the point of separation between a previous and now seemingly archaic era and what one might already call the modern world. The time "before"—that was when a conception of oneness, of unity, experienced as life, as presence, governed every relationship one could have with specific realities. Each of these realities thus found its place in a precisely defined order which in turn made of each a presence, a kind of soul alive to itself and to the world, among the other realities endowed with the same life, and assured to each a meaning of which there could be no doubt. The most important and the most fortunate consequence of this fact of an order and a meaning was that the human person, who knew himself to be an element in this world and who sometimes even thought himself the center of it, also had no occasion to call his own being into doubt or the fact that he stood for the absolute. Whatever may have been the high and low points of his existence, in which chance

1. "Readiness, Ripeness: *Hamlet, Lear*" was first published as a preface to Bonnefoy's French translations of these two plays: *Hamlet, Le Roi Lear,* Collection Folio, © Editions Gallimard 1978. The English translation of this essay by John T. Naughton first appeared in *New Literary History* 17, no. 3 (Spring 1986): 477–491.

often came into play, the human person still could and had to honor his essence, which preserved a divine spark—herein is the whole substance of the teaching of the Christian Middle Ages with its theology of salvation. But a day came when technology and science began to mark out—in what as a result became simply objects—features that could not be integrated into the structures of traditional meaning. The established order fell into fragmentation, the earth of signs and promises became nature once again, and life matter; the relation of the person to himself was all at once an enigma, and destiny a solitude. This is the fracture I was speaking of, the final settlings of which have not yet been determined.

And it should also be noticed that the first truly irrevocable manifestations of this crisis out of which was born the civilization—if this word still applies—that today we oppose to the rest of the planet, this first manifestation took place, according to the country and according to the social milieu as well, at various moments of the end of the sixteenth and beginning of the seventeenth century, which in England corresponds to the years during which Shakespeare wrote his plays. The fracture line that broke the horizon of atemporality and gave over the history of the world to its ever more uncertain and precipitous development, this fracture line passes through *Hamlet*— this is obviously one of the causes of the play—and I would even say runs right through the heart of the work. Without attempting a detailed analysis, for these few pages would hardly be the place for it, I can at least emphasize, as an example of what I mean, the central importance of the opposition of two beings who clearly represent the succession of the two eras, a contrast which is all the more striking for being established between a father and son who bear the same name. On this scarcely realistic stage, where aspects of the high Middle Ages are boldly combined with others that reflect the life of Shakespeare's own time and even its philosophical avant-garde—the references to Wittenberg, for instance, the stoicism of Horatio—the old Hamlet, the king who furthermore is already dead, although he continues to make himself heard, the old king represents, and this is obvious and even explicitly expressed, the archaic mode of being. Not only does he wear the dress and bear witness to the customs of feudal society, even his need for vengeance signifies his adherence to the dying tradition, since this demand that is so full of the conviction of sacred right, implies, among other things, the certainty that the entire state suffers when legitimacy is violated. And beyond this, his status as battling and triumphant sovereign of being is an excellent metaphor for the domination that the Christian of the era before the new astronomy thought he exercised over a world on the peripheries of which the devil might nonetheless be prowling. And finally, the first Hamlet is a father, without the slightest apprehension, with hope even—which means that he has confidence in established values, in continuity. Claudius, who puts an end to the reign, has no children.

And as for the other Hamlet, as for this son called upon to reestablish the traditional order and thus to assume his royal function, it is easy to see that if he is the hero of Shakespeare's tragedy, it is because the values evoked by the Ghost, which Hamlet tries at once to inscribe in the "book" of his memory, have now almost no reality in his eyes. His goodwill is nevertheless quite real; he burns with the desire to vindicate his father, and he admires two other sons who do not hesitate to take their place in the society they believe still exists; and if for a moment he thinks of marriage, he who had been filled with disgust for things sexual by his mother's new relationship, in my opinion it is in the hope that the very real love he feels for Ophelia might reconcile him to life as it is, and to the idea of generation, which in turn could help him to vanquish the skepticism that saps his energy and turns him from action. But this desire to do what is right sets off even more strikingly the extent to which his vision of the world, like a paralyzing, if not completely destructive fatality, no longer recognizes its once perfect organization—that organization which is, in fact, already in disarray in the comportment of the "Danish" court, prey to a symptomatic corruption. One remembers his moving words on the earth, that sterile promontory, on the heavens, that foul and pestilent congregation of vapors. Similarly, if he fails as he does with Ophelia, although there is nothing really wrong with their personal relationship, it is because he has not managed to spare her from that vision that seizes everything and everybody from the outside—as is indicated by his mocking cry, "words, words, words"—and he therefore can see nothing but opacity and lies in every manner of thinking and speaking, including those of young girls. Even if one feels obligated to try other keys—the oedipal motivations, for instance—for understanding the suspicion with which Hamlet persecutes Ophelia, it remains nonetheless true that this suspicion betrays, in its difference from the simple faith of Hamlet's father, the presence of an alienation, of an isolation, a vertigo which the earlier, more united society could never have imagined and would not have tolerated. And it is, furthermore, in his ambiguous relation to his father, who represents—who is, in fact, the former world—that Hamlet's revulsions most clearly appear. He does not want to doubt that he admires and even loves his father; but when he calls him the "old mole" or thinks he sees him in his nightgown the second time he appears, or lets himself be carried away by the thought of those sins which keep him in Purgatory—the reference to him as "gross" and "full of bread," for instance—aren't these simply more signs of his inability to understand the ways of the world and the beings in it, as the old way of looking at life would have allowed him to?

This inability to recognize his father for what he truly is, although he will affirm his worth at every chance he gets, is doubtless one of the most painful of Hamlet's secrets and one of the unacknowledged elements with which he nourishes what is obviously his sense of remorse, and it explains a number of the most obscure aspects of the play, beginning with the other great obsession that structures it. There are certainly many reasons that explain Hamlet's rages against Gertrude—and once again I am not attempting for the moment anything like a systematic analysis—but it seems obvious to me that if the son accuses his mother so violently of betrayal, it is because he himself has betrayed—although he does not realize it—the very person whom, according to Hamlet, she should have kept without rival in her heart. He always insists that it is the majesty of the old Hamlet, his twofold greatness of man and prince, that has been insulted by the new marriage; he vehemently denounces Claudius's vices, especially as they show him to be unworthy of the role he has usurped; but the whole scene of the "two pictures," during which Hamlet would prove to Gertrude the grandeur of the one and the ignominy and even the ridiculousness of the other, serves only to show that rhetorical device plays a large role in the emotion he tries to feel. Once again in this play we are at the theater, and perhaps much more so during these moments of accusation and introspection than when the player recites those rather bombastic, if deeply felt, verses on the death of Queen Hecuba. Hamlet tries to live according to the values which have been handed down to him from the past, but he can only do so on the level of "words, words, words," the obsession with the emptiness of which one now begins to better understand. He who, in order to wreak his vengeance, in order to restore the threatened order, in short, in order to proclaim meaning, feels it necessary to disguise himself for a brief interval that in fact becomes endless, is merely an actor on this level as well—so that his true double in the play is, alas, neither Laertes, nor Fortinbras, nor even Gertrude, who is only guilty of weakness—and Hamlet knows this, as does his father who reminds him of it with insistence—but rather the character who says one thing and thinks another, and merely pretends to respect and observe values in which he certainly no longer believes: Claudius, the destroyer, the enemy. . . . This is the true core of *Hamlet,* as well as the necessary consequence of that crisis in society of which the murder of the king is only the symbol. Those who appear now, and who can be seen to exist beyond the boundaries of the broken social order, are more deeply imbued with reality, more fully steeped in the denseness of life than their fellowmen, whose obedience to the categories of former times seems only backward and obtuse. They live in anguish and confusion; their survival reactions are cynical and ignominious—as is certainly the case with that opaque being, Claudius, for such a long time the shadow of his brother. He is an undeniably covetous man, as there have always been covetous men, but he is also one who has consciously transgressed the strictest social codes.

All through *Hamlet* there are a thousand signs of the fascinated interest—sometimes bordering on the equivocal, it seems so affectionate—the nephew has in his uncle. One senses that something attracts him in the very person he thinks he detests, without it being necessary to infer from this strange obsession, at least as its essential reason, some ambiguous extension of the complex algebra of the oedipal relations to be deciphered by the psychoanalyst. I would say that Hamlet less loves, than he simply *understands* Claudius for what he is, and that he understands him more intimately than he can understand others, because it is his contemporary he is encountering, and his only contemporary, in these changing times that have suddenly become a thundering storm, a sinking ship. He feels for this man who is nonetheless his adversary according to the reasoning of days gone by—and certainly his enemy according to values that are eternal—that instinctive solidarity that binds together shipwrecked men.

In short, *Hamlet* is clearly, deeply, specifically the problematics of a consciousness awakening to a condition that was undreamt of and unimaginable only the day before: a world without structure, truths which henceforth are only partial, contradictory, in competition with one another—as many signs as one would wish, and quickly far too many, but nothing that will resemble a sacred order or meaning. And it is from this perspective that we have to try to examine the idea of "readiness," as Hamlet advances it, at a moment, it should be noted, that is late in the play—in the fifth act—when Hamlet has had the chance to measure the extent of a disaster that he experiences at first as an endless tangle of insoluble contradictions. And what about Claudius? Hamlet had been so filled with the desire to kill him, and yet here he is still hesitating to do so, apparently resolute, as resolute as ever, but distracted in every situation by some new consideration—this time, for instance, by his interest in Laertes. And Ophelia? It is certain now that he did love her, the news of her suicide has given him absolute proof of it—he loved her, he says at the time, more than forty thousand brothers, and more in any case than Laertes whose grandiloquence is clearly open to criticism; and yet this strange love, poisoned by suspicion, disguised in insult, has only thrown her into despair and death. It is clear now that he is suffering deeply from an evil the cure for which is beyond him, and that he has lost all hope in his ability to arrest the collapse of meaning. Hamlet is acutely conscious of his own powerlessness as he gives expression to his deepest thoughts on the last day of his life in the presence of Horatio, who always seems to incite him to profound reflection and exigency.

What does Hamlet say to Horatio in this scene—preceded, it should be remembered, by their long meditation in the cemetery beside the skull of Yorick, the king's jester, he who knew better than anyone the falseness of appearances? He says that even the fall of a sparrow is ruled by Providence, that "if it be now, 'tis not to come; if it be not to come, it will be now," and that if it be not now, let there be no doubt about it, "yet it will come." And as we do not know this moment, and never can, the important thing is to be ready. . . . One might suppose that Hamlet is talking about death here, and in a way that does not seem in contradiction with traditional teaching, since the medieval mind loved to insist that God had the final decision about the fate of man's undertakings. Should we draw the conclusion that Hamlet—who has obviously thought a great deal during his trip to England, and after it as well—is in the process of rediscovering the truth of the ancient precepts and is referring, in any case, to those fundamental structures of being of which they were the expression? But Christianity confided to Providence only the final result of an act and not its preparation which, on the contrary, it asked one to subject to careful consideration and to bring within the bounds of established values. Hamlet, however, is taking advantage of what seems fatalistic in the traditional way of looking at things in order to dispense with the necessity of examining what he has been compelled to accept in this situation which could be decisive for him—his swordfight with a master duelist—an encounter which could easily be refused, especially as it clearly seems to be part of a trap. Why does he consent to risk his life before having brought to successful conclusion his grand scheme to reestablish justice? Neither the ethics, nor the religion of the Middle Ages would have accepted this way of behaving that seems to suggest that a prince is indifferent to his cause, a son to the wishes of his father.

In spite of how it might seem, therefore, Hamlet has not really taken up for himself an adage which in its true significance—"Heaven helps those who help themselves"—gave such apt expression, in fact, to the old universe with its contrasting poles of transcendence and chance. If he has recourse to a traditional formula, it is to turn it toward aims of an entirely different nature, and this time authentically, totally, fatalistic. The "readiness" he proposes is not reliance on the will of God as the guarantor of our efforts, the protector of our meaning, it is rather cessation of what the God of former times expected of us: the fearless and unflagging exercise of our judgment in the world He created, the discrimination between good and evil. In place of the discernment that tries to organize and provide, and does so through awareness of values, he substitutes the welcoming acceptance of things as they come along, however disorderly and contradictory they might be, and the acceptance of chance: from the perspective of this philosophy of pessimism, our acts seem as thoroughly devoid of a reason for being as the necessity that comes into play with them. Our condition is in non-meaning, nothingness, and it is just as well to realize it at moments that seem moments of action, when normally our naiveté is summoned. In a word, a single act still has some logic and is worthy of being carried out: and that is to take great pains to detach oneself from every illusion and to be ready to accept everything—everything, but first of all, and especially, death, the essence of all life—with irony and indifference.

And yet it cannot be denied that the Hamlet who proposes this surrender is, as the whole scene will show, also a man who is now much more alert than at other moments of the play, and much more attentive than he once was to the ways in which others behave, for example, even if his observation leads only to mocking and scorn. He can even be seen to prepare himself for a sport which nothing in his past has allowed us to expect from him, a sport that demands swiftness of eye and quickness of hand—and also the encounter with the other, in that true and not entirely heartless intimacy which can exist in hand-to-hand combat. These characteristics, so unexpected in the one once covered by the inky cloak, act, of course, to pave the way for the denouement of the play which must pass through the battle of two sons who are, as Hamlet himself remarks, the image of one another; and yet, so striking and so present are they, that they must be said to play a role as well in the implicit characterization of the ethics that is developed, and thus it would be a mistake to think that this *readiness,* which is a form of renunciation, is so in a passive or discouraged way. Doubtless because the conclusion reached by Hamlet has freed him from his earlier self-absorption, from his recriminations and his endless reverie, his new mode of being seems also to take on a body, a capacity for sport, an interest, if perhaps a cruel one, for those things in the world he once had fled. This is now an all-embracing consciousness, an immediacy in the way the world is received that is already response, return: and this "readiness" is in truth so active, one can feel so intensely the need to bring together everything in the experience of the void, that one is tempted to compare it to other undertakings which, though they too seem pessimistic, are nonetheless of a spiritual nature and another form of the absolute. Is the "readiness" of Hamlet an Elizabethan equivalent of the Buddhist discipline, of the way in which the samurai, for instance, prepares himself—another swordsman at the end of another Middle Age—to accept the moment of death without a shadow of resistance? A way of recovering positivity and plenitude in the very heart of an empty world?

But with the Oriental—be he warrior or monk—the critique of appearances, of the manifestations of illusion, is also, and even first of all, brought to bear on the self, which has appeared to him, not without good reason, as the supreme form of illusion, whereas Hamlet's lucidity, however radical it may wish to be, is the reaction of a man who has considered himself the depository of the absolute, who hasn't as yet resigned himself to the dislocation of that heritage which remains centered on the self; and I see it therefore as the ultimate response of an unrelenting "personality," a kind of doleful, yet not entirely hopeless meditation on the meaninglessness he himself has tried to prove. Hamlet's "readiness" is not the Oriental's effort to go beyond the very idea of meaning to attain to the plenitude of immediacy—the person who recognizes that he has no more importance than the fleeting blossoms of the cherry tree; no, it is rather the degree zero of a meaning, an order, still vividly recalled—the fundamental structures of which, though lost, are still considered desirable, and the need for which is still secretly acknowledged by that very complexity of consciousness in which all the language existing only for the purpose of hoping and organizing still remains in reserve for the possibility of some future miracle. The new relation to the self of this king without a kingdom is therefore not a peaceful one; it is not the great bright burst of laughter that tears apart ancient woe. What should be seen, on the contrary, is a sharpening of unvanquished suffering, its reduction to a single shrill note—almost inaudible and yet ever present—a form of irony not unlike that of which Kierkegaard will write, in which the moments of spiritedness or laughter are always chilled by nostalgia. Not the liberation, but the celibacy of the soul—taken on as a last sign, a challenge full of desire, offered to the God who has withdrawn from his Word. An appeal, and in this sense a recognition of the existence of others, a sign that he who pretends to prefer solitude is in fact lying to himself—in all of which is prefigured, as the enormous vogue of *Hamlet* throughout the entire nineteenth century bears witness, the dandyism of Delacroix and Baudelaire.

I therefore see the "readiness" that emerges in *Hamlet* as quite simply a negative strategy for the preservation of the soul, a technique useful at all times when humanity strives to recall what its hopes once were. And I think it necessary, of course, to try to understand whether this state of mind applies only to the prince of Denmark and to a few others like him in Shakespeare's bountiful and polyphonous universe, or whether one should ascribe it, in one way or another, to Shakespeare himself and therefore consider it as one of the possible "solutions" proposed by the poetry of the Elizabethan era for the great crisis in values it was beginning to analyze. One could easily imagine it as such—*Hamlet* is so obviously a personal play, and one can feel so intensely, in phrase after phrase of his hero, a poet's effort to stand in place of rhetorical conventions. But let us be careful to notice that nothing has really been definitively undertaken, even in the play itself, when Hamlet, at the very last moment, affirms and assumes his new philosophy. That he takes it seriously, that he would like to truly live it, can scarcely be doubted, since it is to Horatio, to whom he never lies, that he confides his deepest thoughts on the matter. But mortally wounded an hour later, it is to Fortinbras that he offers his "dying voice"—and beyond him to traditional values, or at least to the attitude that wills the preservation of their fiction. One therefore has the right to wonder if "readiness" isn't for Shakespeare simply one phase of psychological insight and in Hamlet the whimsical stance that masks the even more disastrous reason that has led him to accept Laertes's strange challenge so lightly, and with it the possibility of dying.

But let us not forget that it is in *Lear,* not more than five or six years later, that one sees clearly designated that "ripeness" which Shakespeare seems to have wanted to place against the "readiness" of the earlier work.

The historical context of *Lear* is not without certain resemblances to the earlier play, since the work is set in an England at least as archaic as the Denmark of Hamlet's father—it is even a pagan world, closely watched over by its gods—and yet here, too, one discovers signs that seem to announce new modes of being. And in *Lear* there also emerges a character one can sense from the outset incapable of recognizing that the world is an order, rich in meaning—Edmund, second son of the Earl of Gloucester. A son, then, like the prince of Denmark, and one who has, like Hamlet, reasons for doubt about what will be his heritage. But the resemblance between Edmund and Hamlet stops there, for the painful plight of the son, which Hamlet has lived through with honesty and with the burning desire to do what is right, is now studied in one who is clearly evil, and with conceptual categories that remain essentially medieval. One might, at first sight, consider modern this certainly nonconformist personality who scoffs at astrological explanations, at the superstitions of those who surround him, and even at the values of common morality. But it should be observed that Edmund's speeches are accompanied by none of those indications—such as the actors, Wittenberg, the presence of Horatio—which in *Hamlet* serve to mark, by outward sign, that one is approaching the modern era. What makes Edmund an outsider, far from being seen as symptomatic of crisis, is rather set very explicitly by Shakespeare in the context of one of the convictions advanced by the medieval understanding of man: if Edmund would usurp his brother's place, if he longs to see his father dead, if he thus shows how far he is from the most universal human feelings, it is because he is a bastard, born out of wedlock, the fruit himself of sin. And it is in complete agreement with traditional Christian teaching that *King Lear* asks us to understand that this sin, this adultery, is precisely the occasion that evil, ever unvanquished, even if always repelled, has been waiting for—the chance to invade once again the order established by God, which order will nonetheless in the end emerge triumphant once more, thanks to the intervention of a few righteous souls. And this being the case, if Edmund evokes nature as his one guiding principle, as the law to which his services are bound, one should not see in this a reflection of the Renaissance humanist for whom the study of matter is unbiased activity of mind, but rather the revelation of the baseness of a soul, influenced, on the contrary, by black magic—a soul that feels at home nowhere so much as amidst the most frankly animal realities. Edmund's actions do not disclose the ultimate crisis of sacred order but rather its innermost weakness. And one knows from the very outset of the action that he will perish—unmistakably, without a trace of uneasiness or regret, without a future in the new forms of consciousness, as soon as the forces of goodness he has caught offguard have reestablished their power.

Far from signifying, then, that Shakespeare's attention is focused on the problems of modernity as such, as was the case in *Hamlet,* the character of the son in *King Lear* serves rather to reinforce the notion that the old order remains the uncontested frame of reference in the play, the determining factor in the outcome of the drama, the truth that will be reaffirmed after a moment of crisis. And it is clearly for this reason that there emerges in the foreground of the play a figure missing in *Hamlet,* since neither Laertes nor Fortinbras ever attains truly spiritual stature: the figure of the child—girl or boy, since it is as true of Cordelia, third daughter of Lear, as of Edgar, firstborn son of Gloucester—whose purity and moral determination find the means of thwarting the traitors' schemes. In fact, more even than Cordelia, whose somewhat cool and arid virtuousness keeps at a certain distance from those violent, contradictory words, mingled with both love and hatred, through which the action of the play is developed and resolved, the agent of redemption for the imperiled group is Edgar who, at the very moment when he might have yielded to despair or given in to cynicism—hasn't he been falsely accused, attacked by his own brother, misjudged, without cause, by his father?—gives proof, on the contrary, of those reserves of compassion, of lucidity, of resolute understanding of the darkest depths of the souls of others, that can be found in anyone, even quite early in life and without special preparation. Struck in a completely unforseeable way by what appears to be the purest form of evil, this still very young man, who only the day before was rich, pampered, assured of a future place among the most powerful of the land, chooses at once to plunge into the very depths of adversity, taking on the semblance of a beggar and the speech of a fool to shatter at the outset the too narrow framework of his own personal drama and to bring his inquiry to bear on all the injustices, all the miseries, all the forms of madness that afflict society. He understands instinctively—and here is clearly a sign that this world is still alive—that he will be able to achieve his salvation only by working for the salvation of others, each man needing as much as another to free himself from his egotism, from his excesses, from his pride so that true exchange might begin once more.

In spite of everything, however, the hero of *King Lear* remains the one for whom the play is named—the old king—since unlike Edmund who has been marked from the outset by the sin involved in his birth, and in contrast to Edgar who emerges into his maturity through the crimes of another, Lear is thrown into his troubles by his own free act, and thus his punishment and his madness, his gradual discovery of those truths and realities he had neglected before, become a succession of events all the more deeply convincing and touching. Lear begins, not with something rotten in the state, as was the case for Hamlet, but rather with a mysterious sickness in the soul, and in this case, with pride. Lear admires himself, prefers himself; he is interested in others only to the extent that they are interested in him, and thus he is blind to their own true being; he therefore does not truly love others, in spite of what he might think: and so the ground is laid for the catastrophic act that will refuse to recognize true value, that will deprive the righteous of their due, and that will spread disorder and sorrow everywhere and give the devil the chance he has been waiting for in the son born of adultery. Lear—even more than Gloucester whose only sins are sins of the flesh—has relived, has reactivated the original sin of men, and thus he represents, more than any other character in the play, our condition in its most radical form, which is imperfection, but also struggle, the will to self-mastery. When, on the basis of those values he has never denied but has understood so poorly and lived so little, he learns to recognize that his kingly self-assurance is pure pretension, his love a mere illusion, and when he learns what true love is, what happiness could be, one feels all the more deeply moved as his initial blindness belongs to all of us, more or less: he speaks to the universal. And yet, even though he occupies the foreground from beginning to end of the play, Lear cannot and must not hold our attention simply because of what he is, or merely on the basis of his own particular individuality, since his spiritual progress comes precisely from having rediscovered the path toward others and from having thereafter forgotten about himself in the fullness of this exchange. It is in the modern era, the era of Hamlet, that the individual—separated from everything and from everybody, incapable of checking his solitude, and trying to remedy what is missing through the proliferation of his desires, his dreams, and his thoughts—will slowly assume that extraordinary prominence, the end point of which is Romanticism. In *King Lear*—as on the gothic fresco which is always more or less the *danse macabre*—no one has greater worth merely because of what sets him apart from others, however singular or extreme this difference might be. The soul, studied from the point of view of its free will, which is the same in every man, is less the object of descriptions that note differences than it is the very stage of the action, and from the outset the only stage: and what appears in the play, what finds expression there, are the great key figures of the society, such as the king and his fool, the powerful lord and the poor man, and those categories of common experience such as Fortune or charity, or the deadly sins that Marlowe, in his *Doctor Faustus*, scarcely ten years earlier, had not been reluctant to keep on stage. In short, behind this character who is remarkable, but whose uncommon sides are above all signs of the extent of the dangers that menace us—and the extent of the resources at our disposition as well—the true object of Shakespeare's attention, the true presence that emerges and runs the risk of being overwhelmed, but triumphs in the end, is that life of the spirit to which Lear, and Edgar as well, and also to a certain extent Gloucester and even Albany all bear witness—what is designated by the word *ripeness*.

Ripeness, maturation, the acceptance of death as in *Hamlet*, but no longer in this case because death would be the sign, par excellence, of the indifference of the world, of the lack of meaning—no, rather because acceptance of death could be the occasion for rising to a truly inner understanding of the real laws governing being, for freeing oneself from illusion, from vain pursuits, for opening oneself to a conception of Presence which, mirrored in our fundamental acts, will guarantee a living place to the individual in the evidence of All. One can only understand *King Lear* if one has learned to place this consideration in the foreground, if one has come to see that this is the thread that binds everything together, not only the young man with the old one whose soul is ravaged but intact, but with them the Fool, for instance, who represents in medieval thought the outermost edge of our uncertain condition; and this consideration must be seen to dominate even in a context in which the forces of night seem so powerful, in which the Christian promise has not as yet resounded—although its structures are already there, since it is Shakespeare who is writing; one can therefore sense in them an indication of change, a reason for hope. *Ripeness* emerges in *Lear* as a potentiality for everyone, as the existential starting point from which the protagonists of this tragedy of false appearances begin to be something more than mere shadows; and from the Fool to Lear, from Edgar to his father, from Cordelia, from Kent, from Gloucester to their sovereign, even from an obscure servant to his lord when the latter has his eyes plucked out, it is what gives the only real substance to human exchange which is otherwise reduced to concerns and desires that are only hypocrisy or illusion. This primacy accorded to the inner life of men, with the inevitable shaking of the foundations that comes with it, is what gives meaning to the most famous scene in *Lear* in which one sees Edgar, disguised as a fool, with the fool who is a fool by profession, and Lear, who is losing his mind, all raving together—or at least so it seems—beneath the stormy skies. Those blasting winds and bursts of lightning, that cracking of the cosmos, might well seem to suggest the collapse of meaning, the true state of a world we once had thought of as our home; but let us not forget that in that hovel, and under the semblance of solitude, misfortune, and weariness, the irrational powers that tend to reestablish truth are working much more freely than ever they could in the castles of only a moment before. It is here that true reflection begins again, here that the idea of justice takes shape once more. This stormy night speaks to us of dawn. The brutality of the gods and of men, the fragility of life, are as nothing against a showing of instinctive solidarity that brings things together and provides comfort. And let us also remember that nothing of this sort appears in *Hamlet*, where, if one excepts Horatio, who in fact withdraws from the action, and Ophelia, who, unable to be what she truly wants to be, becomes mad and kills herself, everything in the relationship between people is cynical, harsh, and joyless: let us not forget, for instance, the way in which Hamlet himself gets rid of Rosencrantz and Guildenstern—"They are not near my conscience." It is not the universe of *Lear*—however bloody it might seem—that contains the most darkness. This "tragedy"—but in an entirely different sense from the Greek understanding of the term—is, in comparison to *Hamlet*, an act of faith. We meet in an arena of error, of crime, of dreadfully unjust death, in which even the very idea of Heaven seems missing; and yet, "the center holds," meaning manages to survive and even to take on new depth, assuring values, calling forth sacrifice and devotion, allowing for moral integrity, for dignity, and for a relation to oneself that one might term plenary if not blissful. Here we learn that the structures of meaning are but a bridge of thread thrown over frightful depths; but these threads are made of steel.

    Ripeness, readiness. . . . Consequently, the two irreducible attitudes. One, the quintessence of the world's order, the unity of which one seems to breathe; the other, the reverse side of that order, when one no longer sees anything in the grayness of the passing days but the incomprehensible weave.

And the most important question that one might raise about Shakespeare's entire work, it seems to me, is the significance that this absolutely fundamental opposition he has now formulated took on for the playwright himself, in terms of the practical possibilities for the future of the mind and spirit. In other words, when he writes *King Lear* and speaks of *ripeness*, is it simply a question of trying to restore a past mode of being that our present state dooms to failure, and perhaps even renders unthinkable, at least past a certain point: the only path for people living after the end of sacred tradition being rather the *readiness* conceived of by Hamlet, the Elizabethan intellectual? Or, taking into consideration the emotion and the lucidity that characterize the play—as if its author did in fact know precisely what he was talking about—should we ask ourselves if Shakespeare doesn't, in one way or another, believe that the "maturation" of Edgar and Lear is still valid even for the present, the order, the system of evidence and value which is the necessary condition for this maturation, having perhaps not so completely or definitively disappeared in his eyes, in spite of the crisis of modern times, as it seems to his most famous but scarcely his most representative character? An essential question, certainly, since it determines the ultimate meaning of the relation of a great poetic work to its historic moment. The answer to which must doubtless be sought in the other plays of Shakespeare, and in particular in those that come at the end, after *Hamlet* and the great tragedies.

One will find there—at least this is my hypothesis—that in spite of the collapse of the "goodly frame" which the Christian Middle Ages had built with heaven and earth around man created by God, this poet of a harsher time felt that an order still remained in place, in nature and in us—a deep, universal order, the order of life, which, when understood, when recognized in its simple forms, when loved and accepted, can give new meaning through its unity and its sufficiency to our condition of exiles from the world of the Promise—just as grass springs up among the ruins. One will also find here that Shakespeare has understood that, with this recognition, the function of poetry has changed as well: it will no longer be the simple formulation of an already obvious truth, already tested to the depths by others than the poet; rather it will have as task to remember, to hope, to search by itself, to make manifest what is hidden beneath the impoverished forms of everyday thinking, beneath the dissociations and alienations imposed by science and culture—and thus it will be an intervention, the assumption of a neglected responsibility, that "reinvention" of which Rimbaud in turn will speak. Great thoughts that make for the endless richness of *The Winter's Tale,* that play which is, in fact, solar, and which may be superimposed on *Hamlet* point by point—someday I would like to come back to this idea—like the developed photograph—zones of shadow becoming clear, the bright reality as opposed to its negative. The great vistas, also, joyfully dreamt of in *The Tempest*—luminous double of *King Lear.* And grand opportunities, of course, for a resolute spirit, which explains, retrospectively, what has from the outset constituted the exceptional quality of the poetry of Shakespeare—first in the West to measure the extent of a disaster, and first also, and especially, to seek to remedy it.

Translated by John T. Naughton

5   Baudelaire's *Les Fleurs du mal*[1]

LES FLEURS DU MAL is the master book of our poetry. Never has the truth of speech, a higher form of truth, shown its face so clearly. I see it as light. All the whites, blacks, and grays of a Hamlet by Delacroix with, in the background, some impossible redness. The truth of speech is beyond all formulas. It is the life of the spirit, no longer described but in action. Original, sprung from the dwelling place of the soul, stronger than words and distinct from their meaning.

And it is this true speech alone that makes it difficult to talk about Baudelaire. What can we say of it, indeed, that is not a disappointment, a mistake, or a lie? The most penetrating criticism admits defeat before it and acknowledges the absoluteness of the poetic fact. The best-armed ill-will is fooled by it and makes a ridiculous spectacle of itself. As for Baudelaire, who suffered, let us leave him in peace. His longing was for the universal. Grant him the right to fade into it, like a phrase of music, to vanish in the cloud.

But it sometimes happens that the spirit really becomes flesh, when a man who allows himself no other aim than the truth is able to endure decisive violences. Then he is cut off, by the incomprehension of his time, from vulgar opportunities, from mediocre ends. He is reduced to what is best—what is most obscure—in himself, sculpted in the form of the spirit. Forced to be the essential, for the benefit, soon enough, of all.

Such was Baudelaire's destiny. He is now common property. His exemplary life has won him the privilege of being endlessly questioned.

I will ask myself why true speech appeared in *Les Fleurs du mal*. If we can define the book otherwise than by its perfect strangeness, the extremity of its negative theology, then I would say that it is an *acceptance*. A

1. "*Les Fleurs du mal*" first appeared as a preface to the poems of Baudelaire in his *Oeuvres complètes,* published in Paris in 1955 by Le Club du Meilleur Livre. The essay was reprinted in the volume *L'Improbable et autres essais* (Paris: Mercure de France, 1980). The English translation of this essay is of the version published in the 1983 edition of *L'Improbable et autres essais* (Paris: Gallimard, Collection Idées, 1983).

different voice, a voice deep within his own, joins with the person speaking. Though it delights in words, it is purer than they. For a moment, what is and what should be are no longer opposable worlds. A remission occurs in an eternal fever.

But why does this appeasement occur so often in *Les Fleurs du mal,* that is, at the height of a violent and discordant project, in which so many contraries exhaust themselves in vain pursuit of each other—in which nothing ever rests? I will set aside at once the notion that it is the result of some religious adherence. No faith is expressed or really experienced by Baudelaire. No heresy is embodied in *Le Reniement de Saint Pierre* or *Les Litanies de Satan.*

Yet the fact remains that nothing peculiar to Baudelaire—his language, his avowed ambitions—seems to have produced the truth he utters. In the essentials of their form, *Les Fleurs du mal* belong to the realm of discourse. Bold descriptions, logical thought, emotions expressed with precision—it is all a conceptual development as little concerned as possible with what surpasses words. What did Baudelaire invent, in art, that distinguishes him from Victor Hugo? It is the same instrument in the one as in the other, though the consciousness at work and the ends pursued have no common measure.

Such is the enigma of Baudelaire. Discourse, that verbal place which Mallarmé wanted to flee, that place too much frequented in our poetic tradition, remains his. It holds the most dangerous pitfalls and, with regard to truth, offers no help. I would even call it immoral, though it is really only a game. Starting from attentive silence, it gives emotion a simple means of producing itself. But becoming a poem, it affords it an equally simple means of spending itself without harm to the one who has spoken.

And he may well be sincere, who is not? Truth, however, before it is rest, is a long violence. And discourse without peril is essentially rhetoric, that is, falsehood, a failing for which poetry has been all too justly reproached.

The falsehood of discourse is that it prohibits excess. It is bound to the concept, which seeks in the essence of things their stability and certainty, purified of nothingness. Excess is the splitting open of essence, forgetfulness of self and of everything, joy as well as suffering in nothingness.

The concept conceals death. And discourse is false because it removes one thing from the world—death—and thus it nullifies everything. Nothing exists except through death. And nothing is true that is not proved by death.

If there is no poetry without discourse—and Mallarmé himself admits it—how, then, can we salvage its truth, its greatness, if not by an appeal to death? Through the stubborn insistence that death be spoken; or better still, that it speak? But for that it is necessary first to denounce all recognized joys and sufferings. And then, that the speaker identify himself with death.

Baudelaire took this unlikely step.

He named death. And what was this death? A spiritual concern? A risk, but a limitable risk, to the flesh? Often—especially since Baudelaire—poetry has been merely dangerous. Then, too, physical death has always already begun in man. It is only a question of knowing it.

But sometimes poetry has cast off too much of its own knowledge and duty for a simple spiritual exercise to be still possible. Too much laziness has guided the word. It has been soiled too often by too much profane facility. The mind no longer suffices to preserve its nobility, and it begins to seem that in order to purify it real blood must be shed.

There are moments when poetry needs an act of courage. Such was the case in the desert of 1840 when, with Port Royal closed, with Phèdre dead, there was only falsehood left—apart from those exiled voices, those faint and far from serene voices of Chateaubriand or Vigny.

Baudelaire understood. The death he took upon himself was real.

Jean-Paul Sartre has shown that Baudelaire made, very early in his existence, a choice that he never went back on. But he is mistaken about the object and the raison d'être of that choice.

Baudelaire chose a fatal path, a path leading to death. It was a series of decisive events, bound one to the next, and each one hastening his death. Along this way, the illness he contracted, and the debts, the willfully harsh moral constraints, the trial, etc., are pictures of decadence. Over them from the very beginning—ever since Baudelaire began writing, since Sara-la-Louchette—speaks the voice of poetry, imperious and fateful. It was poetry that asked and was given.

Baudelaire chose death, that death might grow in him like a conscience, that he might know through death. A severe, sacrificial decision. And hazardous for poetry as well. Not only would he go unrecognized, so deep was his difference, and with no friends to confide in, which brings the danger of demoniacal mutism, but Baudelaire could also see his own intelligence foundering, after he had risked so much for it. That that was possible, the great difficulties he had in working and his final aphasia prove. That he was aware of it, he tells us in *Fusées*. There is worse. The supreme danger is that the poetry obtained from death, which might stand at last, and ring true, will be incapable, in the intensity of its trial, of uttering more than words of woe and lamentation.

But we know that the truth was not denied to Charles Baudelaire.

Death in action is at least the ground of *true discourse*.

Poetic discourse, which changed its role for Baudelaire—it is no longer a theater of emotions, it is the insinuation of a voice that aims at loss; it traces and intensifies the mortal course—also changes its nature thanks to him. This discourse that once concealed death casts off the poor tricks it used for that end. The picturesque, the ornamental. Affective babbling. The Romantic eagerness to say, to invoke everything in the world, to grasp everything—only, more profoundly, to say nothing at all, because the essential is silenced. Baudelaire replaces this theater of the world, to which Hugo summoned his shades, Napoleon or Canute, with a different theater, a more matter-of-fact theater: the human body.

Body, place, face. Grown to stellar proportions once they are recognized as mortal, these are the new horizon of *Les Fleurs du mal* and the salvation of discourse.

The body enacts nothingness and discourse expresses it. This is the pure, reciprocal act of *Le Beau Navire* or *Les Bijoux*. Death in its chosen place and attentive speech together compose the profound voice that is capable of poetry.

There are no Olivias or Delias in *Les Fleurs du mal*. No myth comes to insert its distance between speech and the world. The truth of speech, conscious and unadorned for the first time in our letters, issues directly from this meeting of the wounded body and immortal language.

One could describe at length—if speaking of the sensible aspect of a work were not a kind of paraphrase—the new world that Baudelaire won from death. Its objects, colored as in Chardin or Manet with the simplest truth. Its exchanges, under an absent sun or by night. Its opening of hearts to the penetration of a cold mist.

Better to read *À une passante* or *Le Balcon*. Above all, Baudelaire produces what I mentioned at the start: light. It cannot be described. It allows for a truer existence, elsewhere, in a world always yet to be named.

But to grant too much to this light would be to simplify *Les Fleurs du mal*. Besides the purity of death, there is in this book a dull suffering, a different voice, forsaken and despairing.

To be sure, Baudelaire's satanism is only a stage set. Pierre Jean Jouve is right to say so. In a society that detested the eternal, Baudelaire loved evil as a shock of the absolute. But something other than this provocation may have contributed to his satanism. An anger or resentment against a too-powerful religion, which grew in his work to the point of changing its meaning. Baudelaire had submitted mainly to the moral exactions of a God he accepted without genuine belief. And these exactions conflicted, if not with the beginning of his experience at least with its final success.

Baudelaire suffered greatly from being less of a rebel than he thought.

He saw the values of mortal life contradicted by accepted values. The good brought forth by death collided with the Catholic good. And the richness of the former, the pure joy, the iron of his lance, was as though shattered. Joy turned into enjoyment. It is under the sway of the idea that our world appears guilty. Nothing pure remains in it after sin and damnation. Even death, in this light, may be good or bad. Death has lost its purity. And it has lost its being, since it is no more than a threshold beyond which we glimpse damnation, the only true death. Baudelaire did not follow the Christian argument to its end. But often, on the stage of his theater of the body, we lose sight of physical death. It takes on the drab colors of a chastisement of this world, it disappears behind the spectacle of illness, old age, and poverty, thus denying itself, and turning tragedy into melodrama, destiny into suffering, the exaltation of essence into its degradation in the long travail of time.

As a result, daylight disappears from Baudelaire's poetry. This is the underside of his work—where misfortune declares itself and wins out over beauty. The latter is sometimes even mocked, or cruelly portrayed in its decadent forms. Baudelaire is far, then, from his early vigor. Under a sky of ash and iron (the sky of *La Béatrice*) he falters, disposessed. He expected strength from death. He got only a sullied world. He feared then, in his pride, that he had been only vain speech: a *beggar,* as he says, a *buffoon.*

An essentially poetic disappointment. It is perhaps here that Rimbaud too fell silent. Furthermore, it may be that some obstacle from the world must bring a necessary destruction to poetry. It may be that poetry is only a hope without issue.

But, despite all, the most constant quality of *Les Fleurs du mal,* that is, of Baudelaire, is energy.

And in the extremity of his confusion, Baudelaire recovered himself, in strange scenes of a dark, mixed truth, where the death sprung from sin is on the point of a pure rebirth: double images—I would give *Une Martyre* as an example—paradoxical thought. The profoundly Dionysiac is combined with a sort of Jansenism. But, also, in despair, the still shadowy idea of salvation takes shape again. Baudelaire senses that truth is at hand. He *burns,* if I may put it so, he is the greatest of poets, untamed, exact. . . . And yet he cannot tear the sad veil. His great object, worthy of the most splendid torches, remains covered with a sort of mud.

And now he utters a grave sarcasm. But doing so, he still loves this empty world. He is saved, like Villon or Maynard, by the truth of love.

❦

It may be that Charles Baudelaire saw himself much deteriorated by his great spiritual effort. The impulse to self-loss and the loss of that loss—it is a double passion, the second symbolized by the collapse of his mind which he recognized a year before his actual death.

Nevertheless these *Fleurs du mal,* these "morbid flowers,"[2] are a quasi-sacred book. In it our yearning for transcendence finds its unquiet rest.

Baudelaire revived the great sacrificial idea inscribed in poetry.

When God had ceased to exist for many, he invented the idea that death can be efficacious. That death alone will re-form the unity of lost being. And, in fact, through the work of Mallarmé or Proust, of Artaud and Jouve—all spiritual heirs of *Les Fleurs du mal*—we can well imagine death as a servant of souls: in a world at last free and pure.

Death would fulfill the destiny of the word. It would open to religious feeling—at the end of its long wandering—the dwelling place of poetry.

Translated by Richard Pevear

---

2. "Fleurs maladives" in the original French. The phrase is not a translation of Baudelaire's title but comes from his dedication of the book to Théophile Gautier.

6   Baudelaire Speaks to Mallarmé[1]

WHAT CAN POETRY ACCOMPLISH? But on the other hand, what does mankind need? On what plane can the potential of poetry and the future of our civilization—now questing, now passive—meet, perhaps unite, in any case benefit from one another? We must attempt to answer these important questions when we consider the role of art in contemporary society. But I shall not seek to do so directly. It seems to me better to examine certain works which, on the very threshold of our own time, have helped to shape it; which contain in embryo both our aspirations and that which is capable of satisfying them; which represent lived experience and thereby have the advantage over mere speculation. And which sometimes have come into conflict, revealing in the inmost depths of their opposition an alternative which still divides us today. I am thinking here of a specific event in the history of poetry: the dialogue between Baudelaire and Mallarmé.

A dialogue? The term may seem surprising. Baudelaire in his last years felt a deep need for solitude. And although by 1860 his poetry was appreciated in a new way by young poets in Paris, he still chose to leave—to turn toward the shadows. The "sacred conversation" of which we may so often have dreamed—Mallarmé questioning Baudelaire—never took place in any "chamber of time," before the folds of any real curtain. The young Mallarmé never read his first exercises to the closest of his forebears.

But it is true nonetheless that he dreamed of doing so, and may indeed have done so indirectly, and that Baudelaire may have heard him from a distance and replied in his own fashion. And it is this fragment of an important unrealized conversation that I shall try to reconstitute and understand.

The first fact—in itself a decisive one, from which everything else proceeds—is Mallarmé's ambivalent attitude, at this period, toward

---

1. "Baudelaire Speaks to Mallarmé" ("Baudelaire parlant à Mallarmé") was first given as a lecture in Geneva in 1967 under the title "L'Art et le sacré." The lecture was subsequently published in the volume *Entretiens sur la poésie* (Neuchâtel: Editions de la Baconnière, 1981).

Baudelaire. He admired and loved him to the point that in 1866, after the fateful visit to Namur, he wrote to his friend Cazalis: "Don't be too distressed about my depression, which may be due to my grief at Baudelaire's state of health. For two days I thought he was a dead man (oh, those two days! and his present misfortune still appalls me)." A few months later he refers to "notre pauvre et sacré Baudelaire" ("poor Baudelaire whom we revere"). It is clear that the author of *Les Fleurs du mal* is more for him than just a great poet. Baudelaire, like Poe, stands almost alone for a kind of saintliness which compensates for the coarseness of the age, restoring one's confidence. And yet in 1863 Mallarmé had written (again to Cazalis): "A modern poet has been foolish enough to lament that Action is not the sister of Dream." This obviously refers to Baudelaire's lines in *Le Reniement de Saint Pierre:*

> *Certes, je sortirai quant à moi satisfait*
> *D'un monde où l'Action n'est pas la soeur du Rêve . . .*

> I shall leave without regrets
> A world in which Action is not the sister of Dream . . .

Thus, in the eyes of the future author of *Hérodiade,* there was something in *Les Fleurs du mal* contrary to the true interests of poetry.

What was this? But before venturing to define it we should consider another text of Mallarmé's, written just a little later, *Symphonie littéraire,* the three sections of which pay tribute to Gautier, Baudelaire, and Banville. Speaking of Baudelaire, he tries to recreate for us the "surprising landscape" he discovers in the "beloved pages" of *Les Fleurs du mal.* And what is most immediately striking is that what is depicted is a barren land, as though to portray Baudelaire all notion of human presence had to be banished. Moreover, it is suggested that the deserts we know are too natural to correspond to the *oblique* spirit, "l'âme détournée," that Mallarmé is seeking to describe. "Above, and on the horizon, the sky is livid with ennui. . . . Along the road the only vegetation consists of a few wretched trees whose tortured bark is a tangle of nerves laid bare: their *visible* growth is endlessly accompanied, despite the strange stillness of the air, by a heartrending lament like the sound of violins, which at the end of the branches shivers in musical foliage." Nature is a prison in which the soul is held captive. And so there is another world, which one may attempt to conjure up, but for this one must choose, among the conditions of human existence, those most alien to the purposes of life: "I see gloomy pools laid out like the flowerbeds of an endless garden: within the bleak granite of their rims, inlaid with precious Indian gems, dead metallic waters sleep, with heavy copper fountains lit mournfully by a strange gleam full of the grace of faded things. No flowers on the surrounding soil. . . ." In fact real flowers are imperfect and our homeland is a world of pure forms, which can only be imagined beyond the twilight realms we inhabit. "A bitter feeling of exile." This Baudelaire is one who distills the crude data of the senses; the Prince of Dream, to quote a friend of Mallarmé's. And it is only because of this that he has become the "poète savant," the cunning poet, the mediator, who gives way to angels in the last lines of the portrait. One cannot even be sure ("I have closed the book," Mallarmé says) if this lofty figure is still Baudelaire or a poet of the future before whom the *Fleurs du mal* would express no more than "the hysteria of exile." A light of deliverance surrounds the "cunning poet." And just as the gardens of Arnhem formed the background to this landscape, so Ligeia and Morella can be glimpsed beyond the sea in the "hymn" where this desert land, this nightmare, fades away.

And yes, Edgar Allan Poe is present, too, in the *Symphonie littéraire*, so much so that in spite of the admiration Mallarmé appears to show for the "beloved" pages of Baudelaire, this text seems to transpose rather than to contradict the injurious words of 1863. For this Baudelaire, now seen as a book ("my scarcely opened Baudelaire," Mallarmé writes), could hardly seek to unite action and dream without profound inconsistency. That he is still caught up in the drabness of the world, a prisoner of its temptations, a living being with all his painful weaknesses, this Mallarmé does not seek to deny: and this is why sin is everywhere present beneath the livid or blood-streaked sky. But the merit of Mallarmé's Baudelaire is to have made of sin, of a rejection of the existing world, the key to a higher Beauty. And any longing for action hence becomes a betrayal of that supreme quest.

The context confirms this implication. Nowadays we no longer have much respect for Théophile Gautier; we are tempted to pass rapidly over his lightly sketched portrait in *Symphonie littéraire*. But Mallarmé praised him in emotional terms in *Toast funèbre*. Gautier is the poet who, because he *looked* ("which others do not," as Mallarmé stresses in a commentary on his poem), endowed each thing with a "lucid contour, a gap" separating it from the chaos of individual existences, presenting its essence and thus making it available for Art. Gautier's impeccable descriptions in fact speak of the emptiness, or rather the uselessness, of the world. And essences thus freed from "action" form, as Mallarmé had already said in the *Symphonie*, "an ensemble of such marvelous rightness that sheer lucidity results from the interplay of its elements. . . ." Here Mallarmé has already moved far from the extraterrestrial mirages of Poe, but at the same time farther than ever from involvement in this world. Now Baudelaire also loved Gautier, to whom he dedicated his whole book. By associating Baudelaire with the "perfect magician of French literature" of that dedication, Mallarmé reminds him of his allegiance to pure Beauty and asks whether he can remain faithful to it.

❦

And we must now note that the question did not remain, this time, concealed in a private letter. Here begins, indeed, what I called the "dialogue"—at any rate the effort of the younger poet to gain the ear of Baudelaire. One of his poems of this period, *Plainte d'automne,* bears the dedication "To Charles Baudelaire. . . . ." Although the latter was already in Belgium, he remained an accessible presence. Banville and Glatigny were in contact with him, and they were friends of Mallarmé's. May not Banville have shown the *Symphonie littéraire* to the poet who usually met with nothing but mockery or indifference? As for *Plainte d'automne,* this poem appeared in the *Semaine de Cusset et de Vichy,* a journal Glatigny edited for a while and which had just published Baudelaire's *Vocations.* (Since 1861 he had been publishing his prose poems, a genre much neglected since the time of Aloysius Bertrand). Writing *Plainte d'automne* meant attracting the attention of Baudelaire and at the same time raising afresh the question asked in the *Symphonie.* For, while recalling the attraction of the "beloved poems," *Plainte d'automne* compromises the theme of *Spleen de Paris* by placing it in various crepuscular connections, the decline of the year and that of Latin poetry, associates it with the noxious groves of *Ulalume,* and consigns Baudelaire to the library of the decadent aesthete Des Esseintes. Mallarmé at twenty-two must have been in great anguish, faced with a work that fascinated and yet eluded him, that shocked him sometimes and may perhaps have inspired him with unease and remorse. Would Baudelaire allay his distress by accepting the ambiguous hommage of the *Symphonie littéraire?* by appreciating *Plainte d'automne?* Would he say anything in reply?

I myself, given the circumstances, have felt the need for such a reply. Reading the *Symphonie littéraire,* I wonder, How can anyone see Baudelaire like that? But when I turn again to the "beloved pages" of the *Fleurs du mal* I am forced to recognize in them that great livid sky at the edge of another world, and all the signs—jewels, perfumes, or cats—of a potent sterility. Baudelaire the dandy—the artist?—wrote, it is true, those *Hymnes à la beauté* which praise Beauty for its "mineral" qualities, its immobility. And he spoke of the "exclusive love of the Beautiful." And above all he specified: "The Poetic Principle is strictly and simply man's aspiration toward a higher Beauty, and this principle is manifested in an enthusiastic excitement of the spirit—an enthusiasm quite independent of passion, which is the intoxication of the heart, and of truth, which is the food of reason. For passion is natural, too natural. . . ." Yes, that was Poe's way of thinking, and also Mallarmé's. But is it the whole of Baudelaire? Isn't there a secret within this unqualified assertion that alters its meaning? How we should like to have Baudelaire's answer on this point! And yet he probably said nothing, sent no message. Was he perhaps too mistrustful? "Ces jeunes gens me font une peur de chien," I'm scared stiff of these young men, he told a friend. Mallarmé got nothing but that silence.

In fact—and this is the essential thing I must point out—if Baudelaire said nothing, he nonetheless reflected, directly and specifically, about Mallarmé's view of poetry, and he even wrote his answer, which is now available to us. In Brussels, as we know, Baudelaire made notes for one or more future books. All *these* have now appeared under the misleading title *Pauvre Belgique,* and here we see him take his stand, as we had wished. Baudelaire notes: "A young writer has recently had an ingenious notion which is not quite right. The world is nearing its end. Mankind is decrepit. A showman of the future displays to the degraded men of his day a beautiful woman from ancient times, artificially preserved. 'What!' they say, 'can humanity have been as beautiful as that?' *I say this is not true. Degenerate man would admire himself and call Beauty ugliness. . . ."* This "ingenious notion" was obviously the *Phénomène futur,* a prose poem by Mallarmé, and these lines of Baudelaire's confirm, to begin with, that Banville or some other had acted as intermediary, since the *Phénomène futur,* written in the autumn of 1864, was not published until 1875. Baudelaire can thus have seen only a manuscript copy of it. But if Mallarmé had sent it to him, or had a copy conveyed to him, it was also because his "ingenious notion" asked once again the question implicit in *Symphonie littéraire.*

I shall not attempt a resumé of the "Future Phenomenon" since Baudelaire has done this so clearly. I shall merely note one detail that it contributes to Mallarmé's poetic theory, on a point that possibly caused him the greatest anguish, and its secret connection with Baudelaire's criticism. Doesn't woman represent that *other,* that possibility of incarnation, of life here, of the future, the very existence of which is denied by the poetic cult of Dream? Has she not the power to reconcile us with the earth, the right to preserve our "ancient concern" with it? But the woman displayed by the Showman of Bygone Things has "eyes like rare gems." And even if she combines all the most sensual attributes of the female image it is in each case with such intense perfection that she removes them from the world, adding a kind of death to such opulence. Her hair is a golden ecstasy, her lips have a "blood-red nakedness." This beauty is immobile and profoundly indifferent, like some stone vision. She is certainly not *the other,* but rather the supreme embodiment of absence, requiring above all that severance of all bonds with the simple processes of life, the illusions of individual existence, for which Mallarmé prays, naming it *impuissance,* that is, impotence or powerlessness. "Muse moderne de l'impuissance"—these are the opening words of the *Symphonie littéraire*. And this too might have attracted Baudelaire's attention.

For *impuissance* is one of those themes of *Les Fleurs du mal* that seem to confirm Mallarmé's reading of the book. As something inseparable from the poet's condition, it is the subject and the claim of *L'Albatros,* in which the poet is compared to that "prince of the clouds" who cannot walk because of his huge wings. Often, elsewhere, it is associated with Ennui, mingled with pleasures to intensify exigency, with sensations as a factor of refinement, and this too suggests Mallarmé. But anyone who has read Baudelaire knows, too, what distress this causes him, and indeed the sense of guilt he associates with it, as though it were a sin and not the necessary condition for spiritual lucidity. Why should he celebrate it if its only value is in its association with that higher Beauty which he is capable of rejecting?

That rejection is indeed the meaning of his comments on the "Future Phenomenon," and we can return to these now, having verified that it is the center around which all converges. If there is such a thing as Beauty in itself, then Mallarmé is right, impotence is the supreme duty and a longing for action a form of folly. But Baudelaire, recognizing in the future man of Mallarmé's poem a symbol of man today, says without hesitation that man can imagine nothing save on the basis of his own experience, and that if he dreams of any form of beauty it will only be a projection of his own ugliness—mangified. Who knows, perhaps ugliness itself is actually a consequence of his dream, the price of the vain pursuit of Beauty? In any case, it implies an effect of illusion, a *petitio principi;* an intensifying—as a result of poetic idealism—of the degradation into which man has fallen, whatever its ultimate cause.

Clearly, Baudelaire has given a direct answer to Mallarmé. And by so doing he has authorized our rejection of *Symphonie littéraire,* encouraged our revolt against a certain view of poetry, proposed a different reading of *Les Fleurs du mal,* which its redoubtable interpreter sees only as a book but which may perhaps constitute a wholly different world of signs, another realm.

❦

And first of all, backed by such authority, we can the more readily understand his apparent contradictions—which are in fact dialectic, a movement in search of true Beauty. Undeniably Baudelaire loved the Beautiful as understood in the *Symphonie littéraire,* but that is no longer the essential point; we feel intuitively—and in fact we always knew—that his real concern is to study this attraction and integrate it into a wider field of thought. Many passages suggest this, from the earliest to the latest of his verse. For instance, in one of the poems on *La Beauté,* he says that Beauty inspires "a love/eternal and mute, like matter," which is a strange reversal, since Beauty is supposed to cure man of material reality. The truth is that Baudelaire always showed a marked ambivalence. In the *Hymne*, if Beauty's gaze is "divine" it is also "infernal," and Baudelaire stresses its destructive effects. And if in the end he yields to its power, saying "Qu'importe!"— what matter!—the fact remains that the tone of the poem is predominantly a moral one, and we sense that his commitment is contradicted by other values or factors at the level of a kind of life the cult of Beauty should have rendered beneath contempt.

Moreover in the very series of poems on the Ideal which opens the book, Baudelaire includes one that unequivocally denounces that illusion which so often attracted him. *Le Masque* is one of the finest poems in the *Fleurs du mal*, precisely because it traces so vividly the passage from acceptance—as Baudelaire gazes with delight at a statue in which "elegance and strength abound"—to alarm when he discovers the secondary characteristics, which are actually moral ones, the vanity, insincerity, and sensual self-satisfaction discernible in the face of the statue, and even wonders whether these human, all-too-human aspects of Ideal Beauty don't after all add to its charm for him:—but finally to horror, because the allegorical figure has behind its beautiful smiling face another, which corresponds only too well to his darkest apprehensions.

> *Mais non! Ce n'est qu'un masque, un décor suborneur,*
> *Ce visage éclairé d'une exquise grimace,*
> *Et regarde, voici, crispée atrocement,*
> *La veritable tête, et la sincère face*
> *Renversée à l'abri de la face qui ment. . . .*

> No! This face with its exquisite false smile
> is but a mask, a cheating make-believe!
> And see, here, horribly contorted,
> is the real countenance, the true face
> hidden behind the lying face. . . .

Behind Beauty there is at best only suffering, and once again life—only life wasted, a defenseless prey to time and death. In other words: the basis of beauty is sense-perception, and this ignores the true condition of existence—time—which thrusts choices on us, forces us to have a destiny; and the more subtly we study colors and forms, the less we shall understand of our true task. *Rêve parisien* says the same thing. In this poem Baudelaire gathers together in the evocation of a "terrible landscape" all the elements that Mallarmé was to reproduce in his portrait of Baudelaire in *Symphonie littéraire*. He seems to contrast Art with the "irregularity" of life, the power of genius with the incompleteness of this world, but suddenly he becomes aware that the scene is *for the eye alone.* A "terrible new phenomenon," the "silence of eternity," overwhelms him. And then his eyes open again to discover that this vision was merely a dream, and his paralyzed ear revives, allowing him to hear again what had been stilled, the funereal ticking of the clock, the sound of time, real time.

Baudelaire, separating the misleading power of the eyes from the reproachful warnings of the ear, stresses metaphorically the image-making character of aesthetic creation. He would never have added to the background of his marble landscape the sunset that suggests the existence elsewhere of some glorious noontime of essences. No, beauty has two faces, one of illusion and the other, consequently, of lost time, of suffering. And if one does not look beyond the first, if one lets oneself be fascinated (like too docile a lover) by those "great eyes" with their seemingly eternal light, one is caught in a trap. Baudelaire loves Beauty, but as a drug, out of weakness, and the more avidly because it has already weakened his will and courage. He writes:

> *Ne me suffit-il pas que tu sois l'apparence*
> *Pour rejouir un coeur qui fuit la vérité?*
>
> Is it not enough for me that you be mere appearance
> To rejoice a heart that shuns the truth?

And his realm is this very weakness, and the facts of his life are the stuff from which his poetry is made.

❦

But we should betray Baudelaire were we to confine his understanding of Mallarmé's question, and his answer to it, to this criticism of a too obvious beauty.

In fact, the true problem has not been formulated, except that a word has now appeared—Time—through which the principal categories of the problem begin to emerge. If human beings are shaped by Time, bowed down by their finite nature, does this not mean that, whatever they do, they are still mere nothingness, and that Beauty, even if dangerous and destructive, can thus provide a way of escape? In the universal emptiness, why not a sort of supreme game? And behind the dream of some higher Beauty, is there not a more substantial intuition of the function or the privilege of Art, which would justify Mallarmé's criticism of the moral attitude I may seem to have been defining? Mallarmé himself was not so naive as to lay much store by the idea of a higher or preexistent Beauty. From this point of view the *Symphonie littéraire* must be taken for what it is, the writing of a very young man with a still confused vision. And in a very short time Mallarmé was to undergo a crisis through which his real thought would emerge.

It is as though he had heard the criticism hidden within the rough drafts of *Pauvre Belgique,* since he came to renounce certain forms of the Dream; but in one sense one can truly say that Baudelaire spoke to him. Not with any direct answer, but with one last message: his own death. In 1866 we see the author of the most beautiful of modern poems paralyzed, aphasic, striken directly in his admirable intellect. The "Prince of Dream" can only utter an expletive, *Cré nom.* "Yes, I know," Mallarmé wrote a few weeks later, "we are merely vain forms of matter." And in the same breath he admits: the Dream does not exist. Now the vision of a spiritual world, like the rose-window of some ancient church, is finally shattered, together with any notion of temporal decadence, which would imply (like a cast shadow) the original brightness of Being. The dream of some more perfect Else-where was pure fantasy. The only angel that appears at the windows of the Ideal is the reflection of the approaching seeker. Reality has asserted itself, with all its inflexible motivations. But here Baudelaire's death restores Mal-larmé to his true self. To understand the vanity of the dream means recover-ing the right to love reality. The love of nocturnal marble, of inert and metallic pools of water, did not come naturally to Mallarmé. If he gave himself over to it, it was from a sense of that exile by which the finite, individual human being is kept far from the rejoicings which the best of our sensations seem to promise us. The limitation of our powers means that our being is unfulfilled potentiality, our condition is prior to its dawn. But henceforward Mallarmé will no longer doubt the nothingness of this indi-vidual existence; he has succeeded in detaching himself from it. "Fortu-nately," he writes, while Baudelaire is dying, "I am utterly dead." And since he can outlive his personal interests through his boundless intelligence and his sensations, he has only to let the unfulfilled world achieve reality through his voice, the light of day shine through his shadow, and the Universe, still concealed by the truncated perspective of our futile action—and hence still unaware of itself—finally achieve its proper form.

To find the Beautiful by probing the void—"en creusant le néant"! Let man sacrifice his personal interest, his vain pursuits in the world, and each thing will take on its absolute quality, its essence, its "pure notion"—and its capacity for uniting with others in the Universe according to its "correlative phases." Being pure notion, indeed, things can attain transparency by iden-tifying with the elements of language. Reality is dissipated in language, yet language reveals it, indeed establishes it, allows it to be itself and see itself. Language explains the earth in an orphic manner, provided of course that it speaks in the supreme and useless fashion that is Verse. Mallarmé did indeed renounce his earlier dreams, "ennemis de sa charge," hostile to his mission, those that were unduly remote from the evidence of the flowers and from the "gardens of this planet," yet it was certainly not to replace them by Action, but to abolish them amid the "true groves" of the great Dream which is Being, inaccessible to human acts but conceivable through Speech, which is the conditional absolute. Thus Poetry is founded, "avaricious silence" is overcome at the same time as "massive Night." And Baudelaire's Time is expelled from words, where there was no real place for it. The poet's task is to fade out of this world in order that Being may exist.

Mallarmé may well have remained haunted by the feeling that he cannot in fact quite obliterate in his speech traces of his personal ambitions, of the element of chance in his life. These lingering traces of subjectivity will cloud his gaze, will prevent the cast of the dice from turning up a double-six, will mean that despite all intellectual efforts the poem will remain subject to "the rule of passion and reverie." Then the poet's work will be no more than a "glorious lie." But even so it will remain the supreme Game to be played, the only act worth accomplishing. "My entire admiration," Mallarmé writes in 1885, "is due to the great Seer, the inconsolable and stubborn seeker after a mystery which he knows does not exist, and yet which he will pursue forever, for this very reason, mourning from the depths of his lucid despair, *for it would have been the truth.*" He is speaking of Redon, but may perhaps have been thinking of himself. There is no outside world. The delusion of the work of art is better than the misery of Time. Such is the core of the affirmation Mallarmé wished to convey to Baudelaire. And it is doubtless the meaning of his final word in the "dialogue," when incidentally, as a postscript to one of his great letters of 1867 (to Cazalis, May 14), he writes of Dierx, a disciple of Leconte de Lisle: "Will he part company from him, as I have done from Baudelaire?" With Baudelaire, subjective poetry—or at least the right to it—come to an end.

And yet Baudelaire's poetry still appeals to us with a sound that Mallarmé's Harmony cannot diminish: a sound he sometimes heard involuntarily and uncomprehendingly, but which at all events obsessed him—sometimes in the form of remorse, sometimes as a kind of hope.

One proof of this mysterious interference with the more conscious elements of Baudelaire's poetic creed is the new definition of Beauty, which came to him as a whole, irresistibly, as though dictated from within. In the *Journaux intimes* he writes: "I have found the definition of my own sort of Beauty . . . I don't maintain that joy cannot be associated with Beauty, but I say that joy is one of its most commonplace ornaments—whereas melancholy is, so to speak, its illustrious partner, so much so that I cannot conceive of any type of Beauty (is my brain a bewitched mirror?) in which there is not an element of unhappiness. . . ." It is most moving to overhear the poet asking such questions, suffering such distress. Baudelaire is driven on, he doesn't know where. But this shows the power of that obscure conviction that disturbs the beautiful image in the mental mirror. And this is what appears. First a trace, as it were, of that loftier Beauty, since the presence of melancholy seems to speak of frustrated aspirations, of an unattainable ideal. It is perhaps the inaccessibility of aesthetic Beauty, or the dangers incurred in pursuit of it, that are the cause of this unhappiness. But the essential fact is that unhappiness is now an element of Beauty in its new aspect. Now, unhappiness is a mode of being of the human person, not of essences. It denotes a presence, and thereby poetic dignity is conferred upon *the other*. Our finiteness terrifies Baudelaire when it is manifest in the blank time of the clock; he seeks to escape from it through aesthetic reverie, precisely when it tells of the aesthete's wasted time. But when it appears in the form of a human presence, if it still disturbs him—and he does withdraw, or try to flee—at least it fascinates him. A presence can be beautiful. It may seem to hold a promise.

And it is noteworthy that the presence of another person constantly haunts Baudelaire's poems, even those most burdened with aesthetic preoccupations. In fact, he seldom tries to imagine a higher beauty in itself, in its perfection and isolation, and should he sketch its features he immediately integrates them into his own life-situation. Baudelaire's diamond does not glitter on the tiara of some Hérodiade, but on the body of his *très chère,* his beloved Jeanne Duval. And after all that diamond may be a mere trinket, that beauty a piece of cardboard scenery in some *théâtre banal:* his real object is the woman, whom Baudelaire rejects and yet acclaims, denounces for her playacting but celebrates for her magic power, through the illusion he creates around her. The author of *Les Bijoux* is by no means the showman of *bygone* things! He is striving to attenuate the excessive power of a *presence*. And the same sudden vision, the same ambiguous rapport appear in the sonnet *À une Passante*. As a living person passes by, something is promised and then lost. We can imagine Baudelaire in the crowd, staring at other people eagerly, with ardent curiosity. Is it, as he says, in order to analyze their defects scientifically, to produce an etching of the human face, to provide Ideal Beauty with its antithesis, the singular "Beauty of Evil"? But this is not what we feel when we read *Les Petites Vieilles*. And this is not what *Le Cygne* seems to be seeking. When Baudelaire, wandering through a "changing" Paris, thinking as ever about the passing of time, meets:

> *Un cygne qui s'était évadé de sa cage,*
> *Et, de ses pieds palmés frottant le pavé sec,*
> *Sur le sol raboteux traînait son blanc plumage . . .*

> A swan which had escaped from its cage,
> And rubbing the dry pavement with its webbed feet,
> Dragged its white plumage along the rough soil . . .

what experience does he initiate? What does he expect of the swan, which *had been* the symbol of Ideal Beauty, but which is now merely a poor creature? And why in the very first lines of the poem does Baudelaire think of Andromache, "Hector's widow, alas!"

Writing about *Melmoth,* he said, "Any man who does not accept the conditions of his life sells his soul."

And it is time now to gather together a few simple ideas which Mallarmé's poetic theories have not yet succeeded in devaluing for me. The first is that existence—our actions—is the only reality open to us. We may have an idea of the Universe: in fact we only know it from outside, abstractly, as though in profile. But we inscribe thereon signs—the tree, the spring, the storm—by which we recognize our existence, express ourselves, and these signs, these words—truly a whole world—are our home. Furthermore, our existence is finite in its means and in time. I simply mean that, as individuals, our own particular actions or even our knowledge cannot "cover" our world, although language entitles us to call it our space, our realm of possibilities. We see around us all our footprints on the great shore: and how many regions are still untouched! My third remark is also based on experience: sometimes this network of footprints seems like a chaos of contradictory intentions, of trampling or wandering steps. And before these scribblings, this formless achievement, we feel alien, everything appears as desert and night to us. But sometimes, too, the prints are distributed according to what seems indeed some mysterious order, a crude mandala which the sea has already begun to obliterate but cannot distort. Here there seem to be paths, there centers, here there must have been a fire, and elsewhere the "sailor abandoned on an island" has gone to reconnoiter his shore and locate the points of the compass. An order that simplifies things and gathers them together may develop in our actions; then both existence and reality will have taken shape, and we become that structure and can no longer think of ourselves as exiles.

For this ordered structure—mightn't one call it the Intelligible?—implies an ignoring of place, a suppression of limits, a release from time, in order to establish itself as meaning. Being is now no longer the purely external pattern of our tracks but the achievement of an inner music. Saying this makes me no doubt seem close to Mallarmé. And from this point of view I can acknowledge the cogency of his concern with the Idea and with music, his desire to subordinate futile lyrical lamentation to the knowledge of relations within the whole. But in order that this alchemy should be more than a dream from which one awakes irreparably; in order that the form that thus develops should allow no part of our being to proliferate beyond its limits and so decay—is it not essential that each of these incessant operations be related to our actual conditions, "the conditions of life," as Baudelaire reminds us, to the element of "chance" in existence we must not seek to abolish? A great danger threatens us. The animal in nature is bound to its condition and develops in a form it never recognizes. But words have freed us from this yoke of the first Eden. Beyond the possibilities open to our actual conditions, they allow us to envisage many others which we are free to construct and inhabit imaginatively without having to subject them to the burden of experience. These are exciting voyages of exploration; our freedom might inscribe its intentions here, that we can then try to decipher as we would a dream. But some inner motivation that had been overlooked, some accursed and too readily forgotten limitation had meanwhile continued to constrain our ordinary behavior; and henceforward unity will be shattered by the obscure working of these forces. While imagination grants us worlds, we cease to belong to the world, we shall awake as strangers.

The key to our being, the only path toward wholeness, thus seems to me the acceptance of chance. One might call such acceptance a *sacrifice*, since it implies that the individual should renounce infinite possibilities and choose to venture toward his absolute. One might call it consent to death, since it fixes our eyes on finitude. And one may call it love, for only love with its imperious decisive choices enables us to consent to what has been given us. Thus love is a consequence of language: the mode of being that words compel us to discover within ourselves, and to protect, so that their free associations should not rob us of what is present. And so we find—a paradox according to Mallarmé's logic—that we need *the other*, so profoundly different, so free, if our own form is to acquire full meaning. Awareness of the other is the way to incarnation, the decipherment of reality. Respecting another's presence and thereby, before long, that of all others, as individuals, this awareness recognizes needs, reexperiences necessity, is converted to the weight of things, *la pesanteur;* it understands the way the particular is inscribed in the whole. This means, too, the deciphering of language. For language is not originally freedom granted to words. If we listen to it in its depths, we hear that some words—home, fire, bread, wine—are not entirely concepts, can never be taken quite as "pure notions," for they are bound to potential presences, pillars upholding the vault of speech, points of condensation where physical needs appease the need of being, by analogies that structure the human place and preside over the formation of words. Fire and the name of fire *are,* so that life might have a center. The treasury of analogies, whose blank page is destiny and whose syntax is our needs, lies beneath the algebra of differences. And our quest for a destiny enables us to understand that language was, to begin with, only the depository of speech inscribing man in Being: the means of an initiation, the instrument of a mystery.

"In certain almost supernatural states of mind," writes Baudelaire, "the depth of life is revealed in the spectacle that lies before one's eyes, however ordinary it may be: it becomes symbolic. . . ." This experience, which Goethe too has described, is supported by a whole network of words—of symbols—whose interconnection, whose mutual generation serves only to maintain that unity; and poetry will recover these. I used to think that words, desiccated by their conceptual use, failed to convey presence, were forever limited to a "negative theology." Now I sense that some sort of archaeology is possible, which would reveal, piece by piece, the essential elements of our form. Nevertheless, it is not so easy to shed an inhibition— which brings us back to the problems of our own day. When Baudelaire writes, "Vous êtes un beau ciel d'automne, calme et rose" ("You are a lovely autumn sky, calm and rosy"), we understand, from the very boldness of his simplicity, that he knows the art of those great metaphors through which presence glows. He knows the *meaning* of autumn, of the "echoing ports," of the "eternal heat," he knows that eyes *are* light, he anticipates the return of sensation to its full significant value. And yet he is compelled to add: "Mais la tristesse en moi monte comme une mer" ("But sorrow surges like the sea within me"). Drawn toward presence by a vocation of his whole being, bound to it by his physical pact with sickness and death, he becomes at the last moment of many of his states of consciousness the unforgettable stranger of the sonnet *A une Passante,* tottering, "crispé comme un extravagant"—crazily tense—a few impossible steps away from the "fugitive beauty" passing by.

Why is this? Because of an alienation that afflicts us all. There have indeed been societies in which, through a collective act, the circulation of symbols was maintained within language. Sacrifice, that earliest of institutions, reminded the individual of his actual conditions, kept the imaginary—what Plato called poetry—outside language. Then everything had its place in a single form which was that of existence incarnate: the olive tree was seen not as a plant among others but against the horizon of the sea, because together they made up the place of life. Inventions took place in accordance with the rhythms and valences of this great figure. And poetic speech meant participation in this shared place, acceptance of time as circular, as cyclical as birth and death. But words have crossed the barrier of sacrifice. They have sought to speak of things in themselves, independent of the finite nature of the one who bears witness to them.

The olive is no longer the complement to bread and wine but has joined the chain of concepts. The *tel quel* or raw material of our realities has served to build a world without death, and this thereby has become noth-ingness, which we dread and seek to evade in the practice of appearances that seem free but whose perfections are illusory. With Descartes this exte-riorization of reality is generalized, if not accomplished. And that is why the danger of which I spoke—that of creating "worlds"—has become in *modern* times far more than a mere possibility over which any one of us could triumph. Concepts have submerged symbols. And henceforward words are our opium, our ceaseless invention of purer worlds, our "higher beauty," like that of which Baudelaire's poetry represents both the practice and the painful denunciation.

Poetic writing is, in fact, the realm where the power of excarnation will first work its ravages. Are not three words enough to suggest "a whole world"? Now that the sense of the sacred has disintegrated, now that the notion of duration—felt as something to be simply endured—obliges us to choose between impulses and needs that appear as either incompatible or frustrated, there is an irresistible temptation to take refuge in this pure space, where the powers of that "latent ruler" struggling futilely in us toward "becoming" might freely be displayed. And then that monologue will occur in which all beings evoked are abolished as real presences (as Mallarmé shows is the case in *Hamlet*), to become no more than functions in some illusory celebration. A form will be achieved in which part of our experiences may be engaged, but whose value lies in itself alone, and which remains forever extrinsic to our destiny: the consecration will have crowned only an image, and meanwhile loneliness will have increased, social func-tions becomed devitalized, and the tyranny of anonymity and emptiness may have grown. There is an ancient tradition of thus evading death, as classicism bears witness—it is *rhetoric,* a form of language in which words no longer presuppose a speaking subject. Mallarmé had subsequently only to decide that this language was the real and had nothing to say but itself. And indeed this is quite logical and perfectly befits the modern age. For our languages, ever more steeped in science, incline ever more to the side of "pure notions." Modern man is deprived of the understanding of time by his education and almost all his occupations. How hard it would be for him to imagine that this fragment of duration might be the voice of Being itself! Beclouded by pure notions, he even begins to think that his own self, determined by the "correlative phases" of these notions, is only an illusion.

And that is indeed the *ultimate truth*—"la vérité suprême"—at least if concepts alone are true. But does one need that sort of truth to realize that one is one's own cause—and to arise and walk? Cannot one counter the concept of a universe whose identity to itself implies our dissolution—

"nothing will have taken place but the place"—with the reality of a humanity which, having overcome its vertigo, is *on the move?* There is a choice. Words prove our nothingness, opening an abyss beneath our feet, but words, as I said earlier, can offer us a home. We are all, more or less, disciples of Mallarmé. He has a hold on our minds, and thus it is quite possible that the Universe seen as a *supreme dream* may ultimately triumph. Yet, in this centenary year of the death of Charles Baudelaire, I cannot but reassert that a poetry without a sense of passing time, and purely impersonal, is *la faute,* the great sin, the temptation suggested by that "unknown Hermes" or that "Satan trismegistus" of whom Baudelaire says that he turns the poet into a Midas and "vaporizes" and so ruins the metal of man's will.

"Poetry is a consecration," writes Mallarmé. "Every poet must be an incarnation," Baudelaire says somewhere. Between these two aims the human drama is played out, and this drama persists today.

Translated by Jean Stewart and John T. Naughton

7   Madame Rimbaud[1]

I SHOULD LIKE TO reconsider Rimbaud's relation with his mother, adding greater precision and certain qualifications—and sometimes, perhaps, rather more than that—to what I tried to suggest in my book on Rimbaud.[2]

I should like, in particular, to examine the connection between purely psychological data and spiritual experience. For the fact that in Rimbaud's case this experience, from its onset, was so closely involved with his family situation and with problems of an oedipal nature should help us to understand, from the example of a great poet's writing, how such a connection, which is at the very heart of poetry, can become established. After all, Madame Rimbaud's character, her tendencies, perhaps her neuroses can be and have been defined. There is general agreement, in particular, as to the decisive importance in her life of that isolation which became her lot when, as a quite young woman with no experience of the world, abandoned by her husband, she felt bound—and unfortunately it was almost obligatory in that sort of society—to assume a father's role, educative if not indeed repressive, toward her children. This did not come to her as easily as I once believed. As certain of her letters show, Vitalie Cuif as a girl had been timid and romantic, or at least given to daydreaming and quite unlike the brusque and unimaginative mother she became, especially as her sons grew up. Her stern expression was a construct as much as, or perhaps more than, an innate tendency. And much of Arthur's disturbed state was the direct result of the strain she underwent as she achieved this androgynous role, trying meanwhile to conceal from others—above all from the son who understood everything only too well—her moments of panic or weakness. If the rules of everyday behavior, those of his social milieu, had been presented to Rimbaud in a less clumsy, less inconsistent manner, if he had had the daily example of a man's self-assurance at a period when prejudices still had the

---

1. "Madame Rimbaud" was first published in *Etudes sur les "poésies" de Rimbaud* (Neuchâtel: Éditions de la Baconnière, 1979).
2. Yves Bonnefoy, *Rimbaud par lui-même* (Paris: Editions du Seuil, 1961).

force of dogmas, he could have had easy access to the Thursday evening concerts in the square; which does not imply that this uncompromising character would have deigned to sit there. And on the other hand the fact that the symbol of authority wore female dress, however austere, and was liable to flush with anger at masculine arrogance or coarseness, must have contributed to the child's longing for a law that was more dialectical, closer to life—which means grace as well as strength; whence that "mysterious delicacy" which was to remain his charm as well, of course, as his weakness in the most painful circumstances. Even in his moments of violence as he was developing physically, when he sought to assert his uncertain virility by brutal actions, he still conformed to certain feminine values and manners, which were to make it difficult for him to approach women sexually, in a society where the male took courage above all from the sense of being master, and he armored himself with contempt, which of course did not help a timid partner to take the first step toward such an unusual and forbidding young man. It is distressing to see a youth of such promise, since he is incapable of directing that contempt a priori to the girls he meets, seeking out those who are immediately and actually contemptible, such as Nina, the supposed innocent, who has her *bureau*, her office, and is kept by an official! Rimbaud would only be able to achieve union with women who, in one way or another, were willing to sell themselves—as in fact his mother had done when she became engaged to man she scarcely knew. He was indeed that "crippled creature" who dreamed of brutally acquiring the services of a female slave on returning laden with riches to his native land. . . . Surely in this as in many other ways Rimbaud can be defined and explained on a level where psychological or sociological analysis can shed a clearer light than any speculation about being, language, or the spirit's quest for unity.

But in this way we define and explain him only too well, since by enclosing his existence in so tight a net we soon cease to understand, even if we still seek to understand, whence he derived that hope—of which we know his mind was capable, a hope not so much formulated as lived, and with such uncompromising violence. Nor yet why Rimbaud's poetry, which presumably should be accounted for by inhibitions and deprivations, scarcely ever seeks to compensate for these by dream. Granted, the author of *Coeur volé*, *Déserts de l'amour*, and *Honte* tells in these poems of frustration, discordance, and powerlessness, and in so doing seeks to triumph over them. But has it been sufficiently noticed that, except in the case of a few pages that precede the awakening of his genius and five or six of the *Illuminations* that anticipate its close, he does not seek to achieve this mastery in the way psychological criticism might expect, by compensating for a lack, by sublimating appetites through the only means available to those who are too deeply disturbed, namely, through the process of dream, through symbolic transpositions? There are no heroines like Mallarmé's Hérodiade—however androgynous the latter, however fitted to resolve the conflicts between sense and soul—in this spontaneously visionary poetry; no fiction, save in brief flashes that quickly give place to incisive assertion, to criticism and conflict. This dispossessed creature, who tells us that he is dreaming, that he is looking at "marvelous images," seems to need no "beloved image" when he is writing; and his "girls," his "queens" belong only to a "dark side" which he rejects from his work. Should desire surface in his writing, he promptly diverts it to situations of lived experience, by methods I have already tried to describe. And on the level of unconscious symbolism, where even the most firmly suppressed desires cannot remain inactive, it is striking to see that by the end of 1870, when his character is fully formed, Rimbaud, whenever he catches a glimpse of what is going on deep inside himself, promptly seeks to discredit fine images, to denounce his fantasies, to mock the idealism that gives rise to them—"I live sitting down like an angel in the hands of a barber," he writes, so much does his need for truth surpass his longing to escape. Undoubtedly a force was at work, in this unusual experience, quite different from those that account for the behavior of so many people who have had absent fathers and dominating mothers.

I return therefore to that relationship with his mother which seems to me essential but not to be interpreted by psychology alone. And I shall try to pinpoint more exactly those characteristics, and other data of the family situation, of a component whose function, from the outset, was not necessary and yet was so intense that in its metaphysical aspect it served as a provocation to the spirit, and as an incitement to that rebellion we call poetry. Madame Rimbaud! When shall we reach agreement about what she was at that deeper level, and in the first place toward herself? In my earlier essay, a long time ago, I wrote that Vitalie Cuif was "a being full of obstinacy, avarice, concealed hatred and aridity," and I have somewhat regretted since then that I painted her in such black colors, since some letters from her which we understand better now show her capable, even in old age, of recovering her youthful aspirations: a hint of romanticism she must merely have buried hastily when her life had become one long "patience" (a favorite word of her son's), those gray years of doing her duty. She, too,—on a particular day or on successive occasions—must have renounced the happiness of the *années enfantes*, the years of childhood. And when, at an advanced age, she describes to her daughter her meeting in church with a cripple who reminded her of her dead son, a loving thought seems to overwhelm her. "In spite of all my efforts I could not restrain my tears," she writes next day to Isabelle, specifying moreover, "tears of grief, of course, but there was something deep down that I couldn't explain." On another occasion, in 1907, when she is eighty-two, she tells her daughter that "a great many soldiers have been passing through, and this disturbs me very much, remembering your father, with whom I could have been happy," adding immediately, and even underlining (which she does nowhere else), *"if I had not had certain children who caused me so much suffering"*; which remark brings us back to other realities. What had her two sons done to her that she should thus proclaim that they had ruined her happiness? And how could it be only when they clashed with her—which could not have been before Rimbaud's *sept ans* or even his adolescence—that her married life, which had ended long before, took on its definitive direction?

But this time, leaving aside for a moment what Mme Rimbaud was, or appeared, to Arthur as a child or as a rebel, I shall examine another period, that of the last important conflicts that divided them, which reveals unambiguously, I feel, the most peculiar aspect of her nature. In May 1891 Arthur had come back to France and was lying sick in the hospital at Marseille; his leg had been amputated, and his mother came to visit him. But on June 8 she left again—despite his tears—for her distant home. She may have been worried about the health of Isabelle, who was alone there, but in this case she should at least have explained her feelings with a certain patience or tenderness to the son who was so obviously tormented by physical suffering and anxiety about the future. Yet she did no such thing. "I was very upset when maman left me," Rimbaud wrote to his sister a week later, "I couldn't understand why. . . . Tell her I'm sorry." In fact Mme Rimbaud cannot even have allowed her son to try to detain her, since she left him feeling thus remorseful and was to refuse any further communication: from that moment until his death Arthur was to have contact only with Isabelle, who thus assumed the mother's role. Never a note from "Madame" to the son who lay sleepless in the stifling heat, weeping day and night. And in two letters we have from Isabelle—June 30 and July 4—there is nothing that can be interpreted as a message from Vitalie. "Goodbye, dear Arthur, I send you my fondest kisses," writes Isabelle. Only on July 8, when she expected her brother to return shortly to Roche, did the girl venture to replace that *I* by a *we*, which disappears again from the letters of July 13 and 18, although on the latter occasion the mother makes her voice heard. "A message from Maman: take good care of your money, or your securities if your money is invested. . . . "

Indifference or resentment? In the first place, no doubt, at the conscious level, the conviction of having been right—"I do everything for the best," she had written on June 8—so that the other person has only to understand and submit to the law. But let us consider now another set of facts, this time from Rimbaud's very last days. He had finally reached Roche on July 24, but barely a month later—for fear of winter, he said—he left again for the sunnier lands he longed for. In fact, his condition was appalling, and, assisted by an increasingly devoted Isabelle, he could only collapse on arrival at Marseille for what were, quite obviously, to be the last moments of his existence. Now on September 22 his sister, respectful and devoted as she was toward her mother, ventured to speak out in remarkable fashion. "My dear Maman, I have just received your note, you are very laconic. Have you really taken such a dislike to us that you no longer wish to write to us or answer my questions?" And later: "Although you seem not to care, I must tell you that Arthur is very ill." On October 3: "I beg you on my knees, please write to me or send me a message. . . . What have I done that you should hurt me so?" In fact, Mme Rimbaud had written to her the previous day; the letter (now lost) reached her, but it seems to have been concerned chiefly with the doings and problems of the farm, for Isabelle replies on the fifth: "Yes, I'm asking a lot, but you must forgive me," and "I know how busy you are, you must be patient and brave with the workpeople," fol-lowed by a long disquisition on milk, cows, pigs, horses, and their well-being, on oats and wheat, before the deeply distressed sister feels entitled to speak of her dying brother. To him, not a line of sympathy had been vouchsafed: that is obvious, for how joyfully Isabelle would have acknowl-edged it! By now he was considered merely in terms of money that must be collected and invested as profitably as possible, and Isabelle, still on October 5, had to reassure her mother about the commercial ventures Arthur might undertake; she promises to lie to him if need be, to prevent this, which does not seem to have pacified Vitalie, since we find questions of inheritance reappearing in Isabelle's letter of the twenty-eighth in which she expresses her great joy at that conversion which has since become notorious.

These few lines must be quoted, since they unequivocally support a verdict that cannot be accused of hostile bias. "With respect to your letter and Arthur: don't count on getting any of his money. . . . I am absolutely determined to respect his wishes and even if there is nobody but myself to carry them out, his money and his business concerns shall go to whomever he likes. What I have done for him was not out of greed* but because he is my brother, and when he is deserted by all the world I will not let him die alone and without help. . . . " That money! It only amounted to some 40,000 francs—the booklet *Les Poètes maudits* was then selling at 3 fr. 25— while Mme Rimbaud was already "worth 300,000 francs" according to her other son Frédéric. . . . These details may seem tedious, but we need them to understand things fully.

* A reflection that suggests that Vitalie had already (perhaps even in this lost letter) pointed out to her daughter, or reminded her, that "Arthur's money" might constitute her dowry. [Y.B.]

❦

And that we can now do, it seems to me, for the sight of such suffering so self-righteously rejected, so promptly relegated to the category of the irrevocable, so unfeelingly enshrouded in financial respectability, confirms my conviction that Mme Rimbaud may actually have loved her son, indeed did love him—she was fonder of him than of her other children, it has been pointed out, and for a long time he was the only one of them who addressed her as *tu*—but it was within the limits, or rather through the prism, of her own concept of law, of duty, of what was Right, so that— since such abstractions stifle our impulses, dictate curt answers to our anxieties, repress our deepest personal concerns—this love was literally bound up with death, a love of the other as though dead, as being sacrificed beforehand to his "good death," perhaps indeed a love of nothing else but death, death being preferable to the terror of living. Mme Rimbaud may well have felt unconcerned about her dying son: he would die, he would at last be wholly transmuted into the image to which, in her love for him, she had always sought to reduce him—an image in which a little money, conscientiously brought back from foreign parts and paid into the family account as reparation for former misdeeds, would surely make an excellent impression. Oh, of course it would have been better to marry him off, on his return, to somebody respectable, but the present solution was after all of the same order. And those he left behind, with no joy in their hearts, would be able to safeguard the honor of one henceforward safely protected from himself, who ought already to have realized the advantage of such an arrangement. . . . If this concept of a love obsessed with pride and death seems excessive to today's more fortunate reader, let him remember the scene of *A la Musique*, where the ritual display of wealth, substantial or meager, stifles with its dreary repetition all vagrant possibilities, so totally reifying the act of living that one could have put an end to it, at Charleville, without great loss, unless one were a hypocritical epicurean—though this, too, would have been a sin for Vitalie Cuif and so many like her. And we must not forget, either, Rimbaud's own words in *Une Saison en enfer*: "How old-maidish I'm growing, lacking the courage to love death!" This means that by not facing death in the absolute, which gives life its true value, making of it a unique opportunity, a fruit with its irrecoverable savor, we make of death an impasse where consciousness stagnates: we retreat, with Mother and sisters, into the waste land of prudence, abstraction, and law. Make no mistake about it! To love death as I have said Mme Rimbaud loved it, does not imply—in spite of stony calm beside a deathbed, familiarity with tolling bells, tombstones, locks of hair fading in lockets—an intuition of death's significance, a lucid apprehension of our true condition; no, it is a kind of dream in which suffering, the end, the last looks exchanged, the last farewells, are so many shadows among others when one has accepted the radical substitution of a few rigid values for the primitive joy of being in the world.

Mme Rimbaud, in short, is one of the extreme examples, one of the most unbending, fanatical devotees of that cult of convention and propriety that has cast its shadow—and this is a lesson to be deeply pondered—over all realms formerly subject to the commandments of the law of love. In that very civilization that still pays lip service, at Charleville or elsewhere, to the God of the Incarnation, she stood as priestess, among a pious crowd, of a creed of excarnation, cold and gloomy as a crypt, which devotes life to the service of the law and finds its peculiar joy in thus reducing the unknown to the known, the inexhaustible to mere repetition. When in church the cripple came to sit beside her—he had sought that place, he had looked at Vitalie with "extraordinary sympathy"—she had seen in him merely "a very pious young man who seemed familiar with every part of the service"; exactly the opposite of what her son, as he grew up, had chosen to be, but one of the ways of living that she would have found acceptable—if supplemented by work—and the "something else" that she could not explain, but which mitigated her pain, was a sudden conviction that Arthur, of whose serious nature underlying his rebelliousness she was well aware, his violence being akin to her own, his motivation as religious as hers, had returned to vindicate her. At the time of their conflicts she would scarcely have cared, I am sure, that he had the "pale, grayish skin" of the stranger in the church, or his broken step and his disquieting weakness, provided she had been able to know that at such a cost Arthur's reconversion had been achieved; and his death would have mattered just as little, since for her real existence meant the feeling of a life well spent, of duty done. When on June 1, 1900, a few months after that meeting with a ghost, Mme Rimbaud wrote to tell her daughter that she had had a place prepared for herself in the renovated family vault between her father's remains and her children's (a strange letter I have quoted in my earlier book), she asserted with satisfaction that her worthy father was *un parfait honnête homme*, a perfect gentleman; and perhaps as a result of that experience in church, she went on to make specific reference, before God and man, to "my poor Arthur who never asked me for anything, and who by his hard work, his intelligence and his good behavior amassed a fortune. . . . " This was not vanity, I hope I have said enough to make that clear, and it was not even avarice, as her obsession with Arthur's inheritance might incline one to believe, no; such self-reassurance after what must have been a long period of anguish came from the need to be accepted by others—since an existence governed by dogma only acquires a semblance of life through the gaze of others, provided this can itself be identified with the laws of society—on the basis of principles and values of which money is one form, whenever it implies, through its slow, painful accumulation, the pious sacrifice of all joy.

This can be expressed otherwise by a single concept that, moreover, will suggest the basically religious nature of such mental processes—even if it be a religion without hope or any deep faith. If this "descent into the tomb" symbolized so clearly the attitude of Vitalie (inappropriately named indeed) toward existence, if it portrays in such convincing colors, or rather shadows, what this woman chose to be, it is because it is almost a schematic representation of the act (if that is not too big a word) on which all her behavior was based, and that I should like to call, provisionally, the sealed-off image, the entombment within an image. For what I have been considering is the process by which an existence sacrifices its manifold possibilities of intenser life, of wider knowledge, to take refuge, through the acceptance of determined and inflexible values, on a plane which is thus, in relation to those lost possibilities, an unreal, fictional one. I may therefore call it an image, since, whether we like it or not, any image, however inspiring, contains a network of arbitrary assertions, of reductive formulations it would be dangerous to consider absolute. This particular image is a meager one, but it compensates for its intrinsic poverty (and was chosen for that very reason) by its clarity of structure, its emphatic denial of any other sort of truth, its simple principles of action, by everything that enables its devotee to cease doubting, to repress anxiety, to escape from the dizzy bewilderment aroused in him from the outset by the vastness of that universe into which, but for inherited constraints and inhibitions, he might have flung himself boldly. The image, in short, is a flight forward into alienation, with tomorrow's ever-increasing constraints mitigating yesterday's frustrations, until the whole sum of desires, behaviors, satisfactions becomes stabilized in a system of representations and values sufficiently closed to function autonomously. The image—and I do not say the ideology, which word might seem more appropriate here because it would imply more precisely than any other the closed structure, dominated by abstract ideas. For, as was still evident in the muted life of the provinces until quite recently, Mme Rimbaud's world, her choice of a destiny for herself and for others, was less a matter of explicit thought than of practice, feeling, sense experience, even aesthetic preference—all that is concrete and yet, in a sense, suggestive of the infinite, in that bunch of dried flowers laid underneath the globe, that picture of St. Rosalie slipped between the pages of a missal. So much is asked from the image, so much is given to it that it quickly becomes far more than a guide for conduct; rather, and this is the important point, something transcendent to be celebrated, an absolute, however lacunary, into which one can pass as easily as Mme Rimbaud passed into the earthy dankness of her marble family vault.

So, in a study whose ultimate object is a poet, I stress the terribly concrete character of the image, and the way it ensnares religious aspirations thereby, giving the impression of salvation granted here and now. A "formula," but also a "place,"† the image draws to itself all the energies present in the personality, using such qualities as strength, stubborness, even fervor— only to restrict their field of action, while the more prudent qualities take precedence—and it maintains a semblance of plenitude in many things, provided this does not encourage a dangerous quest for freedom. Rimbaud's static province was a land of preserves, of cider and milk, of mild ham, and, occasionally, of dry wine. A land where, after all, some forms of sensuous richness were all the more active and resonant because so few of them were accepted—which served to ensure the necessary expansion of deep sense experience through the lapse of days, in a strange but engaging fashion, like embroidered sheets too neatly folded in a cupboard. When Rimbaud writes *Sensation*, we must above all not think that he is discovering the depth of the material world as such; no, he merely sees it under new aspects, the meaning of which disturbs the traditional system. And we need not even suppose that sensuality was absent or forbidden from the world of his childhood: it was tolerated and even carried quite far, on condition of having satisfied certain preconditions, which is unfortunately possible, as I shall illustrate.—Analyzing *Les Poètes de sept ans* in my earlier *Rimbaud*, I stressed Vitalie's harshness toward the adolescent schoolboy, what he may have thought of as her indifference and coldness. But writing *Jeunesse*, toward the end of his work, he retained—and was probably to retain until the last day of his life—a nostalgic longing for the *années enfantes*, the years of childhood, when, as he says, the flesh was like fruit in an orchard, implying plenitude, a factor of equipoise between nature and the mind. It was clearly from the resources of that brief moment that Rimbaud derived the extraordinary energy that he devoted, between the ages of sixteen and twenty, to his quest for *la vraie vie*, true life, the intuition of which thus came to him from the very depths of his relation with his mother. And at the age of seven, at the precise period when he tells us he revolted against her, indicting her, we know too that he emerged from these earliest years as *un bout d'homme*, a scrap of a man, with enough love for her, enough determination to protect her in her new husbandless state, for there to be no doubt about the intimacy that had united mother and son until this time of crisis. . . . Certainly one can wonder at the contrast between the two periods. But it is better to recognize therein one of the most remarkable, as well as the most dangerous, features of image-dominated existence, at least in our Christian world.

† See Rimbaud's "Vagabonds": "le lieu et la formule." [Y.B.]

We know, in fact, that according to the intuitive view held, only yester-day, in small provincial towns, neither overrich nor very poor, and accord-ing to the theology of that vast church of humble, decent folk to whom the Apostle ought certainly to have written, there was a belief that the newborn infant, and then the small child, is an "angel," still on the safe side of that sexual maturity that is known to be hard to control and therefore generally dangerous; and thus that one may love the child without anxiety during this brief early period, love him unconstrainedly, even with an almost avid sensuality, while harboring maybe a secret thought that, since he is living now in goodness and truth, he ought to die soon, perhaps even tomorrow. The argument is made clear in the Latin verse that Rimbaud had to submit for a competition in June 1869; the text set was a poem by one Reboul, *L'Ange et l'enfant*, "The Angel and the Child," an apt example of spiritual conditioning. The angel bends over the cradle:

> *"Sweet child who art so like me,*
> *He said, oh! come with me. . . . "*

explaining to the human infant how impure life is and how much better it would be to leave it. When her son was seven and had ceased to be a "cherub" or anything like one, Mme Rimbaud surely did not consciously ask God to let an angel take him away. But she began to see him as a man, and, with her feelings denied their former outlet, she transferred to a severe and jealous method of education all the still considerable intensity of her own desires, too early and too harshly repressed.

This brings us back to *Les Poètes de sept ans*, the great autobiographical poem I have already discussed: but now we begin to understand how these conditions of existence—about 1861, when Baudelaire and Flaubert had recently been standing trial—could have led a child to want to become a poet and to discover himself a Rimbaud. On the one hand, that constraint of the spirit, that awe felt by the poor and timid that affected every behav-ioral option, but so coherent and so concrete, from one aspect, as well as so senseless, that it has become difficult to discern its presence. This being the norm and therefore taken for granted, we should not regard Vitalie as the exceptional source of pride and harshness that might be inferred from some of her attitudes and letters but rather as a victim among others, driven by her qualities as well as her undeniable failings—her courage, let us say, as well as that gloomy temper with its permanently underlying tendency to vio-lence—to an extreme degree of dogmatic self-assertion which probably concealed an equal degree of despair and anguish. His mother's case must have enhanced the natural appeal, for a young creature avid for love and richly endowed with memories, of the world image her later coldness was to incite him to shatter: one should not underestimate these contradictions and ambivalences, which mark the start of his entrapment. And on the other hand this new, exacting consciousness, the serious and intense nature of which (itself inherited) would lead it to challenge, angrily and rebelliously, the whole mendacious order of things that Vitalie Cuif on the contrary passionately justified and upheld. Clearly, we are concerned here with a relation to the very essence and meaning of the world, to living either negatively—under the protection of the image, but with one's freedom paralyzed—or positively, which implies, for a start, rejection and risk taking. And if traits of character and oedipal tensions played their part too in this birth of a soul, it was only (as we know from hindsight) insofar as they were involved with the deeper conflict, which provoked suspicions, resentments, hostile reticences that aggravated them and made them fester. Of course it matters little in a life, for an attitude toward the world, that the mother should be masculine, the father absent, the son destined thereby to some deviation from the sexual norm: that can always, and could even then in Charleville, have been accepted otherwise, had there been warmth and a vision of the truth—and to be a homosexual, if that is what the Oedipus complex leads to, certainly does not mean that one has a "horrible crippled heart." What matters, at the real level which is the spiritual one, is whether there is true communication, living human contact within the group, and love that is more than a mere word. Or whether words have in fact stifled the possibilities one so eagerly foresaw in people and in things when one's own life was beginning.

Having said this, we need to retrace more precisely, and with certain specific details, that confrontation that, in my opinion, reveals the origin of poetic feeling in a young mind.

One such specific point may already be expected, since I have been speaking about poetry while describing modes of existence which may or may not be subject to paralyzing dogmatism—and the form of protest against orthodoxy which many people must consider the most natural, if not the only authentic one, takes place on the very plane where alienation first occurred, namely, action, political, religious, or moral, far removed from the obscurities and ambiguities that abound in writing. That such a project of direct involvement is the right answer to the challenge of closed structures may indeed have been in Rimbaud's own mind, since from his *Forgeron* to the *changer la vie* of *Une Saison en enfer*, by way of his enthusiasm for the *Commune* and his sketch of a Communist constitution, he clearly sought on many occasions to move on from his daydreams to political action. Yet it is an obvious fact that this apparently sincere partisan of immediate upheaval was, from the first day he thought seriously about things and at the very moment when he was talking of direct action, occupied almost exclusively by the practice of writing; and it is patent that writing did not seem to him the mere ephemeral diversion that would leave intact the social structure its rhetoric denounced. There obviously existed for Rimbaud an intimate, indeed an organic relation between his great refusal of Western alienation and that practice of words that is consciously and deliberately many-leveled, autonomous, uninvolved with any short-term imperative other than verbal, which we call a poem. Whether or not that search eventually provided the answer he needed to the question he was asking, it was in any case his first unequivocal resource as well as the experience that was to dwell with him until the twilight of his dreams, without ever having satisfied him. Thus, whatever our initial notion of authentic revolt, it is important, to my mind, to take advantage of the opportunity Rimbaud offers to examine whether poetry, too, may have its part to play in social change; whether indeed its role may not be the most important one, challenged and suppressed only by that which represents another form of alienation, even among those who seek to change the world.

And we shall see that to ask these questions does not mean losing sight of Mme Rimbaud or closing this chapter. For, once again, it is by looking deeper into the relation of the child-poet to his mother that we shall find the answer connected with the twofold aspect of what Vitalie represents: avowed dogmatism on the level of meaning, ambiguity on the level of the words that express it, and thus an enigmatic indication of the true nature of the sign. From this angle, which I shall now try to examine further, Mme Rimbaud will be seen as the origin of a vocation for poetry as much as the cause of a revolt. We shall see her cult of the image triumphing, but so much in contradiction with terms used to express it, with all their potential still latent, that at one point a fissure appears which allows her son to glimpse a connection between alienation and speech. So that I almost wonder if it is not often from the mother's behavior that the child—*infans*, one who is still unable to speak properly, who has yet to learn the true potential of words—derives the wonder, or doubt, that henceforward set him forever reflecting on the mystery of signs, on the enigma of their weakness but also on the hope of their inherent powers.

Let us turn again to the *Poètes de sept ans*, in which Rimbaud describes, in an admittedly simplified fashion, as though in the form of a myth, but all the more significant thereby, his first awareness of an image-dominated existence. He first records his refusal of the condition he is required to accept, then the daydream practices that enable him to escape, but suddenly, just after referring to the "visions" for which he used to press his *oeil darne*, his dazzled eye, he surprisingly exclaims "Pitié!" Then follow lines that express another aspect of the emotions that disturb him:

> *Pitié! Ces enfants seuls étaient ses familiers*
> *Qui, chétifs, fronts nus, oeil déteignant sur la joue,*
> *Cachant de maigres doigts jaunes et noirs de boue*
> *Sous des habits puant la foire et tout vieillots,*
> *Conversaient avec la douceur des idiots!*
> *Et si, l'ayant surpris à des pitiés immondes,*
> *Sa mère s'effrayait, les tendresses, profondes,*
> *De l'enfant se jetaient sur cet étonnement,*
> *C'était bon. Elle avait le bleu regard,—qui ment!*

> Pity! His only real friends were those children
> Who, stunted and barebrowed, eyes fading on their cheeks,
> Hiding lean fingers yellow and black with mud
> Beneath clothes reeking with excrement and all old looking,
> Would speak with the gentleness of idiots!
> And if, having caught him at these moments of filthy compassion,
> His mother grew frightened, the child's deep tenderness
> Would leap toward that astonishment.
> Everything was all right. She had the blue gaze,—that lies!

Elle, the mother herself, that seemingly loving gaze which he accuses of lying—it's an important passage, and I have already discussed it in my earlier study, but without sufficiently stressing the different levels of its significance. Yet there are at least two that are essential, the second of which sheds light on the origins of Rimbaud's poetic vocation, while the first seems rather to reject its philosophy. For it is obvious—or seems so—that Rimbaud's explicit expression of his revolt turns immediately toward action, at the opposite pole from writing. To feel "pity" for these poor children, but above all to *live* that pity as we see him doing, joining in their games and having long talks with them, listening to their low voices, represents more than just the rejection of an existence clamped down by a few rigid values; it means an attempt to *dérégler*, to disturb such an existence by embarking on the very action of which it most disapproves: listening to those who do not accept its values or whom it has judged contemptible. This time, Rimbaud does not escape from the system indirectly, by means of the silken ladder of visions which leave the outside world intact: he openly crosses a clearly defined and watched-over boundary, which is what horrifies his mother when she sees him in such danger, while his own pleasure lies in imagining for a moment that her alarm springs from love, from real love. We can clearly see what thought, what illusion has crossed his mind. If Mme Rimbaud has been frightened, it must surely be because trivial and indeed somewhat ridiculous dangers—the vermin, the scabies attributed to other children by the petit-bourgeois myth—have impelled her after all to worry about him, about himself as a person, whose health may be threatened, whose well-being is affected. Whence it follows that she must love him for what he is, so that her attachment to principles and precepts is modified, takes second place. On the humblest level of daily life, within the narrowest limits—and all the more moving on that account—there may reappear that concern for another person, which is the great force that undoes orthodoxies and establishes speech. But in fact, as Rimbaud realizes and must quickly have told himself, his mother is afraid only of bad examples in language or ideas that he may have acquired from his undesirable acquaintances, thus revealing yet again that what matters for her is her idea of what he ought to be, not what he is. During the months recalled in the poem Mme Rimbaud was, as we know, discontented at having to live in a district inferior to others, to which her financial situation made her feel entitled. She was preparing to leave it for the Avenues, and to send her sons to the highly orthodox *Institut Rossat* until they should go to the Collège. Her alarm, which ought to have implied love, was motivated solely by conventionality; and that is why her gaze is, as Rimbaud says, a "lying" one.

But it is remarkable that at the very moment when he identifies so clearly the main object of his deep concern, Rimbaud does not *name* it, does not even mention it directly, merely indicating the sign of it that he believes he has discerned, that "blue gaze" which, as the context tells us, is a frightened one. And must we not recognize, in this concentration on what is merely the outward sign of a feeling, a concern with something other than a child's expectation of his mother's love—a concern no less important perhaps since after all it takes precedence over the latter in actual expression? In fact, the mother's gaze—the only real thing his own hungry gaze takes in—is not a simple thing and deserves careful analysis. Let us say that it is at the same time an indication and a sign, either directly or by means of a metaphor. Insofar as it shows fear and emotion, the mother's gaze is merely an indication of the anxiety she feels, just as a flush or a rapid pulse indicate an unexpressed emotion. But, as Rimbaud stresses, the gaze is *blue*, its blueness is essential to his illusion about it, and this involves quite a different interpretation. Why does blueness affect the child? Why does it seem to add to the indication of fear this suggestion of an indubitably emotive presence? Evidently because *blue*, which is light, which implies illumination, transparency, calls forth by an immediately perceptible and eloquent metaphor the idea of the dispersal of clouds and storms, and of the mind's troubled self-searching, which is achieved by love when it makes its voice heard. Blue, then, suggests or seems to signify that "open" speech I have already defined. And now particularly, when the emotion that has disturbed that color seems to anchor this suggestion in actual experience, now that this living speech seems an established fact, a whole system of signs—whether words or meaningful gestures—shows itself capable of breaking free of the burden of constraint and dogmatism: of what I have called the worship of the image, the devotion to orthodoxy.

Briefly, the "blue gaze" was for Rimbaud the manifestation, or the dream, of a sign that means life. And when after, or beneath, the dream he was forced to remember or to understand that those eyes were "lying," that Vitalie's love, here again, was just an illusion, there can be no doubt that this disappointment and this anxiety extended also to our whole system of signs, which had appeared to be redeemed. Had there, then, been no emotion but the habitual aridity, in spite of the gaze being blue? Can one keep repeating, at home and in church, phrases about love and charity, while at the bottom of one's heart desiring merely the perpetuation of an image? Proving that words, whether or not they may once have had a full meaning, can in their relation to one another lose that meaning without altering in appearance— can "lie"? Isn't there something really disturbing about that strange duality or duplicity of language; about that mysterious weakness, that danger threatening all living speech? This is the other, the more secret, of the two themes whose origin is recorded in *Les Poètes de sept ans*. To a reflection about a lying word, about the discovery of emptiness where one expected to find a presence, this great poem adds the no less painful question suggested to so many of us by the strange propensity of words to serve that emptiness: the original sin, so to speak, of language.

And it is precisely this discovery that explains why, as I suggested earlier, this resolute partisan of "changing life," who would not have been afraid of violence, did not throw himself directly into revolutionary action. For action, however sincere, ardent, and well-intentioned to begin with, is steeped in language; speech inevitably decides and governs it: must we not then assume that, once its "moment of awakening" is past, it too can lie, lie without realizing it and without even having to alter its words? What can one do, then, except work first of all, and for a long time, at language itself, in which all is at stake and all can be lost? Which is at the very origin of our being, when it is open, but which can allow a profound meaninglessness to destroy the noblest causes? Certainly, Rimbaud wanted the Commune to triumph, the constitution to be changed, social evils to be combated—but he knew that for himself, at any rate, having achieved full awareness, other needs were more urgent, other questions had to be asked, other problems solved.

He was, in particular, to ask himself—and this takes us to the heart of his personal thinking, to the threshold of his poetic credo—whether this tendency of words to disintegrate and lose their strength, which he had noticed, might not (on a first, optimistic hypothesis) be a historical accident, thus leaving our hopes for the future intact. And actually, at this moment in Western history and at Charleville in particular, Rimbaud could find, close at hand, certain reasons for believing this. Christianity, he held, was the *voleur des énergies*, the thief of our energies: it was the unrealistic utopian mental attitude that deprives us of nature, of our bodies. In the languages formed and controlled by Christianity, essential realities are no longer named, our true needs are thus deprived of them, and others take their place that being unreal in character, leave the body unsatisfied, the soul empty, thus nurturing that appetite for power and that perverse predilection for abstractions which enables someone like Mme Rimbaud to be content with an existence governed by an Idea, an image. We have only the wrong words, and that is why we are in danger of speaking wrongly. These are the thoughts or fancies that haunt the letter to Paul Demeny, written at the same time as the *Poètes de sept ans* or only slightly earlier. And this great manifesto of absolute renewal also tells us what possibilities are left us. We are trapped, that is undeniable, since our system of representations, our values, our behavior are bound up with our words in a whole that our criticism can only penetrate in a weakened and diminished form. But if we renounce the meagre pleasures left to us by this system, the half-knowledge it grants us, if by an act of violence we shatter within ourselves all its categories, all its customary ways of feeling, making a clean sweep, something fundamental will reappear, our future harmony. At this time Rimbaud was envisaging a universal language of the future. He thought that such a language, binding words to reality, would ensure their indubitable truth, would allow their sap and strength to circulate unhindered: "a language of the soul for the soul," firing us irresistibly with "universal love." And such a task he attempted, as we know from the disclosures of *L'Alchimie du verbe*, to the very verge of madness.

But he had also wondered, when first he started thinking about society and its speech, whether the latter's instability, the readiness with which it can fall into the sudden void of words that have lost their meaning, are not inherent in *any* verbal system: which would explain as being a mere reflection of itself the original transgression of man which is disclosed by Christianity, thus making the latter simply a consequence and not a cause of the degradation of language. . . . The proof that Rimbaud's thoughts also followed this second course is that at the very moment when he was about to undertake that *dérèglement de tous les sens*, that disordering of all the senses, in preparation for a new language which would call a halt to any sort of writing that did not serve that quest, he was still using in his poems, in utter seriousness, the language he had to hand: thus saying that one must endeavor to speak without waiting for the *dégagements rêvés*, the dreamed-of release, of the future.—And this issue brings us up against the problem of the nature of poetry and Rimbaud's relation to the experiment that he carried through so daringly, to our enduring benefit.

But how had he come to feel that poetry was the only way? Discovering the inadequacy of the sign should surely, on the contrary, arouse one's mistrust of a use of it which is, to say the least, scarcely determined by the needs of mutual communication. The "fault" or deficiency of our speech clearly lies in the fact that words, just when we are trying to make them serve the purpose of really listening to another, or to ourselves, or to the world, tend to regroup themselves in structures—a necessary moment of formulation, but one which is in danger of becoming fixed and remaining in that state, thus blocking our field of exploration: of turning into a language and an answer, instead of leaving the acquired and established language free to develop, to become less absolute. Now poetry presents the same risk, indeed almost aggravates it. True, it infringes the codes of ordinary speech, but by multiplying thereby ambiguities and irrational images it becomes a jungle offering abundant occasions for the symbolic expression of our unconscious desires, which, being no less exclusive and egocentric than those of Vitalie Cuif, will yet again bring the slightest words under the domination of the image. Poetry complicates and thus obscures the structural inevitability that governs speech, but at the same time enriches it with the substance of our innermost being—which was repressed by Vitalie Cuif—and thus is liable to reinforce it. This moreover is what Rimbaud himself declared quite openly, in *Ce qu'on dit au poète à propos de fleurs*, for instance, where with angry irony he attacks the lyrical tradition which claims to express what *is* but conceals, within this professed love, needs and interests that are exclusively personal. Finally, it should be stressed that this criticism could also apply to those who, as I have already mentioned, think that one cannot be concerned with poetry if one is anxious to overthrow or reform the social order; forgetting that action, like all else that is human, is just as much bound up with speech and language as is writing in the strict sense, they indict the latter for keeping the poet enclosed within a network of figures and images that represent only his differences and are of interest only to himself.

But that was not how Rimbaud understood the way poetry works. And it is now time to examine precisely how, in his mind and heart, the desire to "change life" was reconciled with the process of writing: and what light this concept of his throws on the origin and essence of the poet's vocation. It is true that all writing becomes "closed," witness Rimbaud himself. In *Les Poètes de sept ans*, the very text that tells of his beginning, the nature of poetry is implied by reference to the poet as a solitary dreamer who only *thinks* of action. He may want to fight—he listens to the laughter and the murmur in the nearby streets of the working-class crowd that, in Paris, has taken up arms—nevertheless he has to admit that he is *vaincu, stupide*, defeated and stupefied, "lying prostrate" subject to the senseless visions called up by his inward eye or to long dreams duly organized and recurring. These, significantly, lead him to the desert where freedom will "gleam"—like low water in the distance, something purely physical—only in and by means of solitude. As for the closing scene, which we see gradually expand to the dimensions of the world for which it is the substitute, it is the child's room with its blinds drawn so that the daylight from outside should not disturb his hallucinations. And in the meantime there has appeared a figure quite unlike the poor children whose company he sought defiantly: the "daughter of the working people next door," who also invites him to play. Her dark eyes, like those of Spanish and Italian women in picture papers, suggest sexuality and pleasure: love, but of a sort quite distinct—at least in Rimbaud's day—from the great spiritual impulse he looks for in the clear light of the blue eye. This child is the "comrade" he was to meet, or dream of meeting, at different stages of his life, and always for brief periods only; she could never have been the *Epouse*, the mate, the search for and the choice of whom, under conditions of true reciprocity, would have ensured victory over the maternal prohibition. And in return Mme Rimbaud could tolerate the dark-eyed girl in spite of her somewhat unseemly behavior, since such games remained furtive. !t is remarkable moreover that her son later recalls the brief visits of his slightly older playfellow only to stress: "Eight years old! And she bruised him with her fists and heels"—a hint of masochism in the experience, which to my mind betrays the dependence he feels and perhaps even accepts toward his mother and his mother's law.

Nevertheless, these various representations of solitude and dream are not simply signs of a repressed truth seeping out from under words that say something quite different, but hints Rimbaud has himself thought over and conveyed to us through a process of elucidation that goes infinitely further, in introspection and memory, than anything achieved by most observers at that time, thirty years before Freud. In this poem there is a split between the dreamer and the observer; and the poetic quality, that sum of impressions that we get from rhythms, from the music of the words, the freshness of the imagery, here seems to belong to the seeker after truth, who with clarity, simplicity, and resolute seriousness allows the alien glance to penetrate his shuttered room. In the *Poètes de sept ans*, as in the *Premières Communions* and two or three other poems of spring 1871, the prosodic regularity, particularly through the alexandrine, which had contributed so considerably to insulate the great utterances of the Romantic poets—think of Hugo's monologues, of Vigny's soliloquies in *Les Destinées*, of the surface shimmer of the beautiful self-enclosed lines of Nerval's *Chimères*—suddenly presents itself as the standard meter, whose conventional but flexible measure, with its rational implications, would help to cut through the tangled complexities of dream, rejecting suspect alliteration or unduly autonomous imagery, thus communicating to the reader a hypothesis of meaning that is honest as well as deep, together with that ardor and enthusiasm that are born of great rhythms and carry great hopes. Perhaps we have in these lines the example of what an alexandrine "begotten of the Rights of Man" might have been, Republican in spirit, capable of moral experiment and of anticipating psychoanalysis by observing the subconscious and outwitting its egotism: assuming an active role with respect to those imaginative excesses to which traditional poetry merely submitted passively. This form was never realized, since in an era of dissociated orthodoxies there is scope only for individual personalities, each restricted to his own vision, his own anxieties. But with Rimbaud we can envisage such verse, we can glimpse the possibility, even within the field of multiple meanings, of a determined quest for light, an attempt to make contact with one's fellows through speech; in a word, we understand that the poet's work is governed by other rules and motivations than the blind acceptance of the ferments, the coagulations and crystallizations and the sudden chemical changes of dream-writing.

Now we cannot fail to recognize this principle, this second law of poetic creation—albeit struggling and endangered, yet distinct and fired with a kind of energy—if we now examine Rimbaud's subsequent poetic writing, since as is well known this consisted entirely of breaks with earlier achievement, of fresh starts, of what he called *départs*, departures; and clearly it was precisely the need for truth, truth to oneself and to others, that on each occasion caused the impatient severance. This stringent exactingness had already cut short the raptures of *Soleil et chair* in favor of the self-knowledge, individualized and with a greater awareness of history, that developed in the spring of 1871. But it was the same spirit that soon led him to fear lest this sort of introspection should remain bound by the categories of an inadequate language, against which he decreed the necessary "disordering of all the senses," only to realize in 1872 the imminence of "terror and certifiable madness" and to resume that lucid questioning by which, through the ford of *Mémoire*, amid the glittering silt of memories and dreams, he was to reach the firm bank of *Une Saison en enfer*. Time and again Rimbaud, having ventured into some field of writing, seeks to shatter its enclosing fence. And thus each time he leaves behind him in the violence of his writing a trace which is light.

Let me give an example: that of the portrayal of another person, which one might expect to undergo insidious distortions in the process of writing, with its apprehensive censorship. This was the case with the *Forgeron*, the blacksmith, where seeking to represent, in all generosity of spirit, the outcast from that society whose child he was and for which he felt responsibility, Rimbaud takes as spokesman a worker who, under a semblance of polemic eloquence, merely echoes that society's idealistic and unreal morality. This *positive* image of the other, with features clearly outlined, is always naive and possibly untrue. Without any real dialogue, it endorses the mental categories that have been used to conceive it. But the outcasts of *Les Poètes de sept ans* are described by Rimbaud only in terms of their deprivation of what matters to him, or of what is ascribed to him. In particular, his own forehead is *plein d'éminences*, full of the bumps that for phrenologists, implied all those gifts that Verlaine recognized in him, and which his education was to develop; the outcasts, on the contrary, have bare brows, *fronts nus*, being those "*idiots*" in the sense of *idiotus* which, as Rimbaud the Latin scholar was well aware, means one who is uneducated, doomed to remain ignorant because he belongs to the poorer class. These children have nothing, they are nothing, a page of the human species that society leaves blank. But for that very reason, the thought may occur to one that they remain as untouched by the limitations of society as by its benefits, and one starts brooding about them, for they seem far more significant in their frightened silence than the fine facile picture of the blacksmith in the earlier poem. . . . We must not forget that the period when Rimbaud was writing his poetry marked the triumph of that new industrial development that destroyed so much of the world's past. In the new unstructured suburbs there began to accumulate for the first time that *twofold destitution* which added to material penury and the ugliness of surroundings—*dans l'épaisse et éternelle nuit de charbon*, in the dense and eternal blackness of coal—the cultural poverty of human beings torn by the demands of the factory from their villages, where the religion of the soil still lingered briefly. But when we look today at the distressing photographs of the late nineteenth century, with those haggard, frightened children against walls of grimy brick or black plaster, we react not only with a pessimistic awareness of universal blindness and violence; there is somehow a light shining under the bushel, one senses that the future of the spirit at its purest lies hidden under those rags. Such was Rimbaud's intuition, watching the flight of his "Genius" through the sky, amid modern migrations and suffering. And having met those eyes in which anguish or resignation have obliterated the thoughts and convictions that enriched—but also limited—earlier periods, he speaks of the "eyes fading on the cheeks," the iris of the "untouchable" or the sacrificial victim, which seems colorless in radical contrast—though without far-fetched details or any projection of his own dreams—with the mode of being predominant in his day: the lying "blue gaze" of all those, men and women, who accept as absolute, however absurdly, their own narrow field of spiritual life. But I did not wish to stress only Rimbaud's awareness of the point at which societies can open on to something other than themselves; and I must now draw attention to the effect of this upon the poem, from the point of view of the poem itself and of the way poetic creation develops in Rimbaud. There is a broadening out, by virtue of which the *thing signified* which I have tried to describe—the *other* of the social group, who can give fresh impetus to its collective development—becomes the *signifier* of something that is even more radically *other*. The presence of others, in *Les Poètes de sept ans*, is obviously restricted to the children's "bare brows" and "thin fingers," since the "mother" referred to in the opening words has, as we have seen, re- nounced her role as subject, while the little dark-eyed girl appears and counts only in the context of play which she specifically represents. "The other" is thus denoted only by an empty space in the social structure, by an absence, while the actual language used hints at something beyond itself, inexpressible: and it's surely that inexpressibleness as such, this apparent enigma, so rich in promise, that is now to assume significance as the neces- sary form of all authentic manifestations of the essential being of *another* in the speech of the "self"—permanently depriving the latter of that supreme proof of its absolute value which resides in the formula one substitutes for a dreaded unknown. Somewhat as in certain iconoclastic theologies, one's intuition of what is outside a language has ceased to take the simple and positive form of a coherent representation, which could never do more than confirm the categories that describe it; it will henceforward only reverberate among these concepts and words by disturbing their sense of being able to say everything. But in so doing it *acts*, instead of simply being an object; it becomes, within the depth of the language, an incitement to listening and mutual communication, and in poetry a convincing reason for renouncing the beautiful illusion of those overconfident structures set up by the poem.

In a word, if we say that Rimbaud shut himself up in his dreams, dedi- cated himself to solitude, as he himself seemed to believe, it was not in any case, in *Les Poètes de sept ans* and in many other poems, without shaking them to their very foundations as representations or symbols, introducing that fissure that lets in the unknown, making of that fissure the sign beyond all signs, the only sign that does not lie. And the consequence for us of this dialectical assertion, which confronts its own deficiency and is enriched by recognition of it, is that we have to question ourselves in a more complex fashion about the way poetry works. What is this effect of a deeper truth, of a suddenly "open" utterance, produced by such verse? Is it something accidental in relation to poetic quality, tending only to express the indi- vidual's essential being through images and complexities of meaning, or is it the highest achievement of that much-discussed and still obscure quality? Are we to define poetry as the supreme expression of the language of an individual or a group, or, since the highest experience in any system of signs involves an awareness of its limitations, of its basic inadequacy, should we ask whether the progress from a fully and richly experienced orthodoxy to awareness of the fissure, with its dynamism, its spirit of futurity, is not an even greater richness and as deserving as any other to be called poetry? After all, even if one takes for granted that a poem is the form of a "being-in-the-world," we must admit that its author may recognize that other such forms exist, more all-inclusive, more powerful, and that he will think about these and practice them, and seek through them and far beyond the "self" of his own experience a universal self which would be, at the deepest level of perception and perhaps at the limit of history, the only legitimate plane on which being can be understood. Which means that poetry must be that forward drive of the loftiest desire, feeling its way through destiny, just as much as the organization of the poet's other desires and of their symbolic satisfaction.

We may say, to sum up, that there are two sorts of minds in the history of what is referred to, perhaps mistakenly, by the single name of poetry. Poets of one sort are satisfied with their words, and thus turn to the poem as the completed form which reflects the settled relations between words; their significance, which is infinite, exists there only like the sound passing across the strings of a musical instrument, and the unconscious has the advantage of acquiring visible form, and, in its depths, of attaining order without having to scale down its desires or confess its secrets. Poets of this sort were of course Poe or Nerval, to whom I referred earlier, and sometimes Baudelaire—as in *L'Invitation au voyage*—and even Rimbaud to some extent, since even the most determined effort to break the enclosing barrier of speech is hampered by a lingering desire, a dream from which one cannot wake. But the other sort of spirit exists and endures in many poets, if only in ambition and hope rather than in fact: those for whom rhythms and rhymes immediately and instinctively suggest the form beyond all forms, the word that could be more than all our languages, the universal—in short the spirit that reaches its ultimate transparency through the dispersal of the illusions of the personal unconscious. Such minds indeed accept poetic form, if only as a mirror by means of which they may supervise their otherwise invisible research; but they are aware of the great danger it presents, and their first task is to reject its potential orthodoxy and thus to move on from one attempt to another in what is, finally, not the construction of a work but the truth of a destiny. They are searching and not finding. And it follows inevitably—which is where the earlier question finds its answer—that there is for them no contradiction in theory nor even in practice between their rejection of closed structures in the society they live in, and their adventures in writing. They think rather, and rightly to my mind, that far from contradicting action their experience of the limits of speech is the only possible way to protect it from the inertia of language, from the ease with which any form of words can be used to other ends than what they actually say. They do not believe in the poem, that aftermath of poetry, but they accept it and even choose it, since here alone can the human sign recognize its alienation and recover wholeness, provided, of course, that some aspiration uplifts it. In other words: when ideology, and philosophy itself, are so ready to forget their own source, which is wonder, "amazement," shock, that is to say, acts of love, of true life, these poets who are memory remind them of it.

And so we come back, for the last time, to Mme Rimbaud, since it was from her son's awareness of her restrictive use of the language and ideas of our civilization, based though this was on words of love, that his thoughts about poetry so manifestly derived. But it is time, too, for certain explanations or revisions that, by their more general character, will enable us to clarify the complex and perhaps, after all, highly ambiguous relationship we can sense underlying the antagonism between these two equally intense personalities. One first point that struck me from the outset is that when a thinking being seems dissatisfied in his relations with ordinary speech, whether he wishes for a language richer in words and resonances, or is seeking rather to break the sheath of conservatism, and hence of abstraction, in which convention enfolds even the simplest words—in order to understand him properly one needs first to study what his mother was like, and what she meant to him. For the mother's role precedes and governs the nascent relation between consciousness and the outside world, that longish period during which the child neither can nor as yet wants to be distinct and separate from things, even the most remote, nor from people, even the most frightening, and thus perceives everything that exists not only as something living but as something looking at him, as a presence bound up with his own: as, in short, a part of the relation uniting any reality with any other. Now this sort of co-presence with everything perceived, more intimate than the words that will express it, more important than they are, richer in knowledge and above all in potential, is indeed—though still wholly passive and burdened with the vain illusions and beliefs of the "magical" consciousness—an intuition of what might be, in the future, a community bound by a living language such as was promised by the founders of religions or by certain great poetic adventurers. And the mother, at this period, represents a vague conviction of this spiritual horizon, except that soon this first barely expressible feeling will be overlaid by other convictions dictated by the need to feel autonomous, by aggressive impulses and conflicting desires. By the age of seven, as Rimbaud has said, there has developed that self-assertion that requires the support of a language one can control. For within the depths of the speaking presence there has arisen that need for self-sufficiency which seems to be inherent in any condition of speech. There is thus a danger here, although it has no clear outline. But the mother remains implicated in the coming transformations, where she will still have a role to play. Before, she simply needed to *be*, in that loving act—and with words, in words, as well—which counteracts the tendencies of egocentrism. Now her task is to understand what she had been doing, to go deeper into it, to transform it radically within herself as well as teaching it to the other person, by disclosing, for instance, a readiness to leave to his own judgment, when he wishes it, the choice of other affections. More than ever, as the child grows up, and above all in our forgetful societies, where the father is obliged to inculcate in his son a law that by now reflects only external necessity, the mother retains for a long time the function and power of preserving speech. We may thus expect to discover in her a major cause of the possible appearance of the poetic vocation.

Yet, even if she is all that she should be—giving, and thus encouraging the other to give: trusting, and thus releasing trustfulness—so that the child thus attaining self-awareness will be enabled to respond to another's presence, now or later, and to the most inward revelations of the simplest feelings, such as can be expressed every day by the commonest words, still nothing implies thereby that he will ever take an interest in poetry, or at any rate in the creation of poems, the ambiguous nature of which I have already referred to, involving as it does an almost obsessive awareness of the paradox of signs, and the practice of writing. Indeed, I see this practice as entailing the concentration, the focusing of the self, conscious or unconscious, upon itself; and if it seems thereby to challenge the law—other people's law—it is in order to maintain one's own secret world, of whose frailty one is aware, rather than to begin the experiment on language by the destruction of what I have called orthodoxy. Writing has its links with childhood, obviously, but it seeks to safeguard the child's illusions, the dream of a magical mastery over things and destiny, rather than the happy moments of unconstraint, of trustfulness, of sharing in the joy of another's presence.—But poetry involves a longing for full communication, a will to "reinvent" it by way of the written word, and to become a poet one needs to have met, at the outset, at once and doubtless in equal measure and in a single person, so that one senses a mystery, both the evidence that one is loved and that restriction of words I have called the cult of the image. That disturbance that is poetic sensibility will be aroused by people who show themselves torn between the two modes of being of the sign; the creative vocation—that energy that surges in from elsewhere—will be stimulated by people whose violent but uneasy assertion of acquired values renders them unable either to develop fully their power to love or to destroy it completely.

Now—and this suggestion is the final and most important correction added to my earlier portrait of her—this was more or less the case with Mme Rimbaud: her acceptance of the principles of a narrow milieu was, as I have stressed, total and violent, but its very violence implies that a struggle, "brutal" if not wholly "spiritual," had taken place at some point before her choice of an arid existence could triumph. She worshipped the Law, of course, but less with the cold, unquestioning piety of a bigot than with the live fervor of a convert, whose vehemence, severity, and immoderateness in the assertion of her faith suggest a hidden ambivalence, a repressed dis-respect. And although that afternoon in 1861, in front of those children "conversing" (as Rimbaud says) in low voices, she displayed a sullen strict-ness that masked an underlying anguish, yet a season or two earlier there must have been something tender and tolerant all the same, otherwise would Rimbaud have experienced his nostalgia for the *années enfantes* or retained in their immediacy and purity the *délicatesses mystérieuses* of his moments of trust? Mme Rimbaud had been *the other*, and even in her worst moments she kept a trace of this, elusive and glowing like the primal grace that remains unalterable even when sin seems triumphant. She had had her *tour de bonté*, her turn of kindness, of which her son was still conscious even at the nadir of the present dreariness, even if its light passed so low in the darkened sky that it would be "slower to come back than a star." Who knows? Perhaps, on one occasion in particular, shortly before Arthur reached the age of seven, she may have been surprised, taken aback, not so much because he and his brother were becoming budding adults whom she must hurriedly subject to the law, but from a private resentment and anger that betokened—and this was the unsuspected and humiliating factor—that she had loved, and still did. . . . We know scarcely anything about the exact circumstances of her separation from her husband, except that it occurred a few months before the moment described in *Les Poètes de sept ans*, and after sharp quarrels. But we can have no doubt that the "very intel-ligent" child who was watching her understood what was going on—and *Mémoire* indicates clearly that if "Madame" stood "too upright," cold and black-robed among the flowers, it was after "the man's departure." That final break was the moment when, hurt, her pride wounded, "Madame" must have decided that men represented an evil, uncontrollable force, and pledged herself to what was better and safer: the moment when, unfortu-nately, she may have done what was worse, if we now recall the strange sentence in that late letter about her children having caused her "so much suffering" and thus prevented her from being happy with Captain Rimbaud. A strange remark indeed, for how could Arthur's escapades, years later, have damaged her previous happiness? Or, if she was thinking of him as a small boy, how could a four- or five-year-old have so powerfully disturbed the peace of her life? Vitalie may have realized that this transient husband had no use for so large a family, she may have begrudged her elder children their existence, while justifying this embarrassing indictment in her own eyes by criticizing their conduct. This may have been one of the reasons for her severity toward them in subsequent years: such moral rigidity possibly concealed a desire to believe herself beyond reproach.

As a result of many factors combined, the end of Arthur Rimbaud's early childhood was not that commonest situation where falling ash stifles a fire, but for Vitalie a moment of crisis and for her son, on the other hand, the questions raised by apprehensive affection as much as by the *répugnances*, the loathing so loudly—too loudly—proclaimed. A crisis, the intensest point in the battle for the Law, vengeful and self-protective, while the disappointment that had caused it was still a raw wound. As yet nothing of that peace the Law is to bring, but meanwhile the turmoil of an acceptance no less difficult when made unreservedly, even overzealously. And in the case of the puzzled child, the undeniable realization that a change has taken place, a never-ceasing uncertainty: the perplexity, the bafflement that drive him to such provocation, to actual experiment and to hope. Is that "blue, lying gaze" really lying? Will it always lie? Isn't that all-pervading aridity, in spite of appearances, just a pose, a mask—just a meaningless artificial discourse that a few true words, unexpectedly provoked, could dissolve at one blow? Such is the mystery of that total acquiescence in which, nonetheless, a fissure can be sensed: the mystery of sin abounding, with an unshakable conviction that superabundant grace might touch it: the mystery of speech.

Thus I suggest the hypothesis that Rimbaud benefited—if that is the right word—from one of those examples of conversion, of repression, of tension, terms that suggest hostility but that convey a lesson of energy when we decide to interpret them differently. Very unlike the language of real love, but poles apart from the ignorance and apathy of a naturally servile mind, Mme Rimbaud's mode of speech was of the sort that alienates and yet suggests a great deal, laying bare the dialectical connection between the two levels of the mind. By listening to such voices one may be roused to metaphysical or religious speculation; one may also grow toward that rare but very specific sensibility that likes to probe the depths of language, whether with a conscious aim or not. By heeding them too often, wondering at their paradoxical nature but fascinated by their power, one is correspondingly in danger of being captivated by their idiosyncrasies, their deficiencies: that somber fervor, that pride, that desire to dominate which will not yield even to love. Indeed, many dangers threatened Rimbaud.

In conclusion, however, I shall not dwell upon these but on one or two others which, in such heroic relationships, spring from the simple fact that love has failed to mature there.—Any child, I assume, any adult reflecting on his childhood, longs passionately to find his parents equally impassioned. When, having lost them, and brooding over their relics, he discovers or confirms with emotion that his mother or his father once loved, really loved, it matters little what—some thing, some place, their childhood home: it is as though this would be a retrospective proof of his own existence, of his right to feel a living person. And should it happen that one has at some time experienced one's mother's aridity of soul, and then decided to become not another devotee of that religion of absence but the hero of the spirit who is to free language and change the destiny of all men, all the more will one seek to rediscover the spiritual truth about the person whose attitude is still so disturbing. What would one have gained if, while she was still closely present, one failed to make contact with her essential being and restore her to freedom? Such must only too clearly have been Rimbaud's way of thinking, from the *Étrennes des orphelins* to *Mauvais Sang* and *Enfance*. Not *Mémoire* alone but the whole fabric of his writing is alternately lit up and harshened with moments of severity and hope, daydream and exigency. And when, in *Première Soirée*, the boy describes his dream-lover as

> *assise sur ma grande chaise,*
> *Mi-nue.* . . .
>
> seated on my big chair.
> Half naked. . . .

or tells us in *Les Déserts de l'amour* that if he was so disturbed when "the woman" approached him, it was "mainly because it was at home," we must recognize here among other causes of anguish his desire to seek reparation for that "theft of the heart," that loss of trust for which his mother was responsible, in the very place where it was first committed, and with her full agreement.

But in that case, the danger is that by too anxiously seeking a reconciliation, by trying to understand her where she is most at fault, one is liable to take on that fault oneself and thus lose confidence in one's own power to amend it. Does Rimbaud become his mother simply by process of heredity, as he believed when writing his poems, or because of that fascination I spoke of earlier, exerted by the tension of voices? The fact remains that he also has his own way of assuming responsibility for certain aspects of Vitalie that he condemns—and for that very reason. It is noteworthy that when in *Les Poètes de sept ans* he refers to those eyes of his mother's as representing a lie, he leaves them undefined as "the blue gaze," whereas his own blue eyes are mentioned at the outset of the poem, at the very moment when he tells us he was concealing something. Is he not perhaps persuading himself that he shares with his mother the *oeil bleu-blanc*, the pale blue eyes of that "inferior race," the "bad blood" of those who, he reflects with painful resentment, have understood nothing of Christ's message: who are incapable of love? And when he reached Paris a few months after that great truthful statement, he behaved in such a way that Mathilde Mauté, Verlaine's young bride—a poet's wife—was convinced that, as she writes, his eyes were *bleus, assez beaux*, blue, rather fine, but with "a shifty expression." He had gone there in quest of a word, a spiritual revival, and he had already come to doubt and despise himself, since he displayed (his gaucherie contributing) such an uncharacteristic expression, which in Carjat's photograph was to be replaced by his real, poet's gaze.

Meanwhile another trap awaited him, due to the ambiguity latent in all poetry but intensified in his case because of his complex response to his mother's intentions. Remember those deplorable lines of Reboul's in which an "angel," speaking it seems on behalf of the little child's mother, wishes that he may die before reaching the age of defilement. Had this just been a short-lived suggestion, a danger over which Rimbaud had triumphed in spite of everything? Yet already, in another of those Latin verse compositions whose themes were in such strange concordance with his potential destiny, the memory of some lines from an ode of Horace had led him to dream of becoming a poet, to which we may suppose him consenting willingly, though not without a foreboding of the disastrous temptation to which such a vocation would expose him. For where the Latin poet merely says that doves will bring branches of olive and myrtle to the child chosen by the gods, Rimbaud chooses to introduce—after these messengers which were but the disguise and the epiphany of Phoebus Apollo himself, symbol of virility and adulthood—"all the Muses" who clasp the child in their "tender arms" and fondle him, as though he were still in the cradle. . . . Sadly, for one who is too starved for maternal affection, the heroic project of reforming and purifying speech is liable to take on dubious attractions. It is easy to see that, to one's unconscious satisfaction, the very words that, in poetry, condemn the closed circuit of other people's speech can become fixed, in their turn, in that private language that a poem becomes; and then can dwell on the imagined superiority of that idiom, fancying it a reflection of some divine speech among poorer languages: in short, however concerned one may have been with others' salvation and with the future, one may think of oneself as a sort of angel. And is not that what one's mother wanted one to be or to become, at the time of one's most trustful and intimate relation with her? So doesn't this daydream, which by an unconscious decision can become a settled project, provide a means of reconciliation with her? Her anger will be appeased as soon as it is aroused. And then one can be revenged on her for triumphing yet again, by becoming in the angelic transformation she has brought about, the bad angel, the fallen one; the angel that disappoints her, flagrantly coarse at the very moment when he might be thought to be casting off his material state forever. Remember the lines in the *Album zutique* about the *angelot maudit*, the accursed cherub; they express the whole ambiguity of Arthur's fate in terms that would shock Vitalie.

For a further proof of how this sense of angelhood, with its suicidal tendencies, frustrated his loftiest intentions, we may note the various alterations to which, in his lines on "The Angel and the Child," the boy subjected the unwholesome theme he had been set. If we glance at this little piece, composed at speed while the writer's mind was preoccupied with other problems and thus a fertile field for the expression of psychic automatisms, we notice the addition of a few lines that show how Rimbaud identified, concretely and existentially, with the doomed child: its setting and the dramatic situation are those of the *Étrennes des orphelins*, written in the following months. Instead of the unconscious baby envisaged in Reboul's highly abstract text, Rimbaud describes a child who is already aware that he has a mother and remembers the presents she has given him—and here we can surely recognize the earliest years, the *trésor à prodiguer*, the treasure to be squandered, referred to in *Jeunesse*. Then Rimbaud expresses precisely that anxiety *Les Poètes de sept ans* conveys with such intensity, his obsession with people's insincerity and the lying nature of appearances. "Here on earth," he reflects (in Latin: I retranslate), "no one is to be trusted (. . .). Even the scent of flowers exudes bitterness." And in conclusion he develops Reboul's *Pauvre mère, ton fils est mort* ("Poor mother, your son is dead") in eight highly equivocal lines in which we catch a noble echo as well as some disturbing aspirations. The mother is seen mourning her child, who then appears "on his wings of snow" in all her dreams, and she "meets his smile with a smile," *subridet subridenti*; after which the son "joins his own divine lips to his mother's lips," *illaque divinis connectit labra labellis*. The noble echo here is from Virgil's "Fourth Eclogue"; in that poem, too, the closing lines speak of the smile with which a little child responds to his mother's smile, deriving from the knowledge of the love borne him that intense confidence in himself—and in life as such—which will eventually gain him access to the table of the gods and even to the beds of goddesses. This smile, conveying in its authentic purity an assurance of mutual love, had in Virgil no ambiguous sexual undertones. But with Rimbaud! With all his unhappy sensuality aroused and yet ravaged in that relationship that thwarted his development and his destiny, he reveals the reasons that have governed his dreams of angelhood, paradoxically physical reasons, very much of this world in its ultimately perverted state; reasons so compelling that the need to obey them seizes him like a frenzy—witness *Vierge folle*, but also Ver-laine's *Crimen Amoris*—whenever he tries to "change life," his own to begin with. An acceptance of incestuous feeling amid the ashes, or shoals, of revolt. A few of the *Illuminations*, deep-searching, with a fleeting snatch at remote glittering treasures, instead of the *Premières Communions* or the *Mains de Jeanne-Marie* or the great truthful poems of 1872. . . . We can have no doubt that it was in the most obscure and intimate depths of his relation with his mother that there gradually developed in Rimbaud's life, just as much as his need for speech, his renunciation of freedom, and those words that are only dream, and that mute future.

Translated by Jean Stewart

8   Paul Valéry[1]

THERE WAS A FORCE in Valéry, but it went astray. A will and an energy always ready for the most exacting labors of language; but French poetry that he thought rational and that is in fact far from clear did not really suit his purposes—for it is drawn to what is dark, and accords so little in substance or in depth with the birthplace of his thought, that cloudless coast, the dangerous horizon of the obvious. Clarity, too, has its mirages. Poetry, in any case, feels disappointed, deluded by a certain terrain, whether real or imaginary: the Mediterranean of the mind. A place where sensation is so easy, so elementary, so pure that it seems to lead directly to the heart of things: to an eternal sea, to the sun, to the wind. Where the light neither veils nor is veiled. Where sight lays claim to knowledge and imposes its way of knowing on the mind, where the olive tree standing near the broken stones or by the edge of the water is, of course, the archetypal olive tree. Having come thus far, we think we are touching the intelligible, which is scarcely disturbed by matter, that we are journeying back to the house of the Idea. That is indeed the illusion that Italian, for example, with its obvious and closed words, neither suspects nor condemns—but there is another way. There is this extraordinary thing: there is, however formless and dark, a being who is born, who is carried along by time, and who will die. There is a living being in this very place before me. There is the olive tree as well, this very olive tree, but in its profound difference, its existence *hic et nunc*, its being which will fall to fire or to the axe. Valéry never understood the mystery of presence. One feels Aristotelian opposing him. For the revery of the Idea carries a great risk for poetry, that the word will no longer be a scandal. I say: flower, or sea, or olive tree, or wind. And these words that seem to have caught only the essence of the thing, its monotony, its eternity, correspond all too easily to what Valéry thought real: *the* sea, *the* olive tree, *the* wind. This may be a great blessing for language, but at what cost! There

1. "Paul Valéry" was first published in the revue *Lettres nouvelles* in September 1963. It was subsequently reprinted in the various editions of *L'Improbable et autres essais* already referred to. It is, as always, the version of the text published in the Gallimard edition of 1983 that we have translated for this volume.

96

is peace—repetition, imitation, description—but a peace without act or soul, quite the opposite, for example, of what Mallarmé wanted! He, too, equated word and Idea, the flower with that which is "absent from any bouquet," but he knew that the Ideas do not exist, or do not yet exist, and asked of the "book," with its virtue of gathering and establishing, that it bring about a time when they would exist. An admirable project, and quite poetic as well, since it aims at salvation! And in this step toward being, colliding with and thus crying out what opposes the Idea—matter, place, time—all that Mallarmé summed up in the single word *chance*. Then the scandal I have mentioned broke out in our speech: the distance between the word and *this* real thing. The confrontation of intellectual knowledge and this invention of the object which may surely be called love.

From Plato to Plotinus and to early Christianity, the philosophy of the Idea has always come to be healed by this more living water.

And it is, I think, the absolute originality of modern French poetry, the poetry begun by Baudelaire, that it recognized this secret wish in the poetic moment of speech. Poetry like love must decide that beings truly exist. It must pledge itself to this Here and Now which Hegel proudly revoked in the name of language, and make of words that, indeed, abandon being, a profound and paradoxical return to it. What concerns the poem if not the naming of what perishes? The charter of this recovered poetry is the sonnet *À une passante*. The subject to which poetry must return after so much wandering is the meditation on death.

But Valéry was unaware that death had been invented.
He wrote his least insightful pages on Pascal and Baudelaire. He was content with a world of essences in which nothing is born or dies, where things persist without accident, even if they do not truly exist, a world of delicate paintings on the opacity of night. A world one can sleep in, yes, if it is true that a certain drowsing in the light, the pleasure of which Valéry has evoked in so many poems, a drowsing that filters sensations and retains only their extract, both sensible and universal, seems to savor what is archetypal, as animals and plants do—a pleasure sought after by that sleeping thought that is Greek art. The sleeper is a shade, who opens his door to shades. And Valéry loved the matterless world of dreams, where actions never trouble the surface of what is—because it is the nature of his universe that our acts are unreal in it. "All is that will be," he wrote in adolescence, and he was charmed by the thought. The symmetry of the universe (in the Greek sense), its consistency (in Poe's sense), reduce our freedom to nothing, our acts and what they might grasp to the nature of a shade. Then Narcissus can be astonished by a vacant ardor and beauty. He gazes into pools, but he sees

no matter in them, he is not exalted by the enigma of the water's presence; he finds there only his own belaureled image and the other, poorer enigma of his existence which has no destiny.

While the one real act is to go out of oneself, to come as close as possible to the world where we are not and cannot be, the one act possible for Valéry is to hold back from all action in order to enrich our limited condition with a bit of the divine intelligence. Sleep once again, the sleep of an attitude that in order to persist, dreams of a pure act and a rational law. Monsieur Teste, insubstantial as he is, would be the virtual image of God in the pupil of the universe's eye. The dim candle flickering in the semi-darkness of his alcove would concentrate the rays of God reflected by all that is. And his very existence, that dead gesture, would reproduce the desireless freedom, the omniscient immobility of the Creator. What grandeur to attribute to the operations of "the mind"! But it is also true that this creature of reflection has nothing to say, that words do not exist for him! Our language belongs to a time when geometry and existence have parted ways, when the search for laws is no longer undertaken with words but against them, when speech has been raised to the level of mere chance, but this Valéry did not understand. When he should have restricted himself, like Monsieur Teste, to silence (meaning abstention, or algebra), he returned to this speech. At the risk of being surprised by poetry.

He contemplates this reality of the poem, ungraspable and impenetrable; he attempts to subordinate it, by means of poetics, to the truth of science or the purposes of knowledge; and occasionally, with a somewhat timid fervor, he consents to be a poet but is always kept from remaining one by a skeptic's taste for illusion. What, in his eyes, can the language of poetry do except simulate and seduce? Perhaps it can tighten the bonds between Beauty and Truth, those two aspects of the Law, but the body in which it is held—the sensible figure of the poem—is none the more necessary for all that; it is merely one possibility among many others in an evasive roundabout of things, a temptation to deceive. The work of poetry, like the grapes of Zeuxis, is an appearance without being, it invites nothingness into the house of essences; is it not simply a ruse of this "nonbeing," which suddenly seems to be a positive force, a malignancy, a will? Thus the poet is required, by the poem itself, to embrace the wrong cause. He, the subtle idler, discovers in himself, between thought and sun, the devil's nature, though of course he need not take entirely seriously the mocking serpent who haunts him, more disillusioned than wicked, who never plays out his whole game, who only "sketches," out of boredom, ironic variations on what God has willed—a dilettante, almost a dandy of the possible, who knows perfectly well that if seduction is pushed too far it will always end in blood and death, which is to say, again, in being, a place he wants nothing to do with. There is no profound fascination in Valéry. He does not suffer enough from the scant reality of his existence to turn the machinery of illusion against it, like certain great baroque artists, or to choose blasphemy, like those who cherish being and weep in their exile.

Yet what decadence of poetic ambition! In the modern poetry which claims succession from religious thought, in this profound French language, almost awakened, which Baudelaire reminded of the place it once held open for the unknown God, who might be *this* woman passing by, *this* swan, *this* ivy leaf splashed with mud, in this discovery and this new beginning, Valéry is the apostate, a new philosopher of enlightenment, a man who speaks of clarity of mind when he has consented with body and heart to be a shade. Once again I recall the man I heard speak at the Collège de France in 1944, a man of such grace, with a mind so nimble and yet so aimless, a form as pale as the shades in his dialogues, which are now shades themselves. I think he was the one true *poète maudit* of our time, sheltered from misfortune, surely, and from the ability to imagine misfortune, but condemned to ideas, to words (to the intelligible part of the word), by a lack of love for things, and deprived of that essential joy mixed with tears which suddenly rescues the poetic work from its night. The real curse in this world is to be reduced to playing games in it. The verse of Valéry, which has no being or recourse except in its own rules, this mixture of diversion and learning, this chess match in which the play with ideas and echoes is endlessly refined, is merely precarious and sad.

What remains to us of Valéry? The game itself, since it is true that literature needs this negative activity, which gives language its nuances, which patiently prepares the exquisite resources (as he would have said) that a more violent poetry will come and spend all at once. But also, closer to what matters, the shadow cast in certain of his poems by the curse I have mentioned. There is the serpent who offers God "the triumph of his sadness," and his accent is suddenly so pure, so sincere, so fervent, that this triumph of God does not seem self-evident, and one comes to think that the glory of being perhaps cannot be received and that indifference would therefore be more truthful than denial or adoration. There is above all the *Cimetière marin*, Valéry's most beautiful poem, because here he falters. Here, in the noontime of absence, on this shore where pure sensation and pure thought endlessly turn back on each other, something unformed might have surged up. The glistening of the tombs reveals a threshold. Another face of the light, a "secret change," says Valéry, a "deficiency," offer a ground to be built on. And certainly the *possible* that Pindar speaks of could be bent in this direction. But to the creative anguish that drinks from finitude, Valéry once again chooses to prefer a colorless sadness, the unreality of heat. He comes back to the brightness that blinds us, to sleep-like sensation, to this wind which is not the wind. . . . Such were the affirmation and reaffirmation of an art of closed form. In his language which lacks the "mute *e*"—that rift between concepts, that intuition of substance, that extraordinary chance for French—this intellect identifies form with diagram, with the fleshless gesture of the ballerina, with speculative hypothesis, not knowing that there is form only in stone, that is, in stone arched over brokenness and night. We must forget Valéry. We must try to see form as the figure of the praying woman on the old frescoes, but this time with her face uncovered, a new figure that man, beyond theologies as well as science, must invent for himself.*

Translated by Richard Pevear

* Have I "found fault" with Valéry? It seems to me that I have taken him seriously, which is an honor one can pay to very few writers.

And these writers exist *in us*. We must fight against them, as we must choose, in order to exist. It is a private struggle. It is perhaps a wager, in the rather serious sense this word has acquired. [Y.B.]

9   The Act and the Place of Poetry[1]

I SHOULD LIKE TO bring together, almost to identify, poetry and hope; but to do so indirectly, since there are two sorts of poetry, one of them chimerical and untrue and fatal, just as there are two sorts of hope.

I am thinking first of all about a *great refusal*. When we have to "take on a burden," as is said of someone smitten with misfortune, when we have to face up to a person's absence, to the deceitfulness of time, to the gulf that yawns in the very heart of presence or maybe of understanding, it is to speech that we turn as to a protected place. A word seems to be the soul of what it names, its ever-intact soul. And if it frees its object from time and space, those categories of our dispossession, it does so without impairing its precious essence and restores it to our desire. Thus Dante, having lost Beatrice, speaks her name. In that single word he evokes the idea of her and solicits rhythms and rhymes and all the solemn devices of language to raise up a pedestal for her, to build for her a castle of presence, immortality, returning. One kind of poetry will always seek to detach itself from the world, the better to grasp what it loves. And that is why it so readily becomes, or seems to become, a form of knowledge, since the anxious mind, separating what is from natural causality, immobilizing it in absolute form, can no longer conceive of any relation between things except by means of analogy and prefers to stress their "correspondences" and their remotely envisaged harmony rather than their obscure mutual antagonism. Knowledge is the last resort of nostalgia. It emerges in poetry after defeat and might confirm our misfortune, but its ambiguity—its fallacious promise—lies in maintaining our awareness of the situation in which we were defeated, and even of its future, from which we expected so much and which has vanished. Such is the theme of *Mémoire,* the most "daydream-like" of Rimbaud's poems:

1. "The Act and the Place of Poetry" ("L'Acte et le lieu de la poésie") was first given as a lecture at the Collège de Philosophie in Paris. It was subsequently published in the revue *Letters nouvelles,* 4 and 11 March 1959. The essay was then reprinted in the various editions of *L'Improbable et autres essais.*

Jouet de cet oeil morne, je n'y puis prendre,
o canot immobile! oh! bras trop courts! ni l'une
ni l'autre fleur. . . .

Plaything of that eye of dull water, I cannot reach
o motionless boat, o arms that are too short!
either this flower or that other. . . .

O motionless boat, arms too short! I can hear this fervent voice regaining control even as it makes its admission, and separating a concept of itself that it thus knows or feels to be its essence, its divine part, from the degradations of lived experience. In the castle of the poetry of essence, when some weakness is admitted it is in so archetypal and pure a fashion that instead of a desire accepting failure we find a soul breaking free of its earthly fetters and thus seeking salvation.

Such poetry is forgetful of death. And so it is often said that poetry is divine.

And indeed when there are gods, and when man believes in his gods, this spiritual impulse may bring some happiness. That which we have loved, and which has died, finds its place in a sacred order. Nymphs are bearers of earth's waters. All that has shocked and disturbed us in this world is resolved in a wise acceptance; or, if one chooses death, or rather the anguished anticipation of death, one will die with the god who is dead. It is easy to be a poet among the gods. But we come after the gods. We can no longer have recourse to a heaven to guarantee our poetic transmutation, and we must inevitably question the seriousness of the latter.

Which brings us to the question: What are we concerned with? What are we really attached to? Are we entitled to reject the contamination of the impermanent and to withdraw into the stronghold of speech, like the king in Poe's tale, far from the plague-stricken land? Or did we love the lost object for its own sake, and do we want at all costs to recover it? Of course, I don't think there has to be an answer. But I have no doubt that modern poetry—poetry without gods—has to know what it wants in order to judge the power of words with full knowledge. If we only want to save ourselves from nothingness, even at the cost of possession, then perhaps words are enough. Mallarmé thought so, or rather he suggested such a hypothesis. But his unbounded honesty contradicted his attempt.

Yet he had taken enormous precautions. Through intransigence of mind, and doubtless also as a deliberate method, he had consented to abandon almost everything to the nothingness he saw everywhere at work, to finitude and chance. Appearances banished, pleasures and feelings disdained, no part of reality is required to found the new domain except the form of things, which is above suspicion, which outlasts their death and even the obliteration of their memory—the *presque disparition vibratoire,* the all but disappearance of what is vibratory, that the word, by chance, seems to have the mysterious power of inventing. Mallarmé seeks to preserve only the kernel of being, but since the word seems identifiable with this he really believes he can do so. Should some demiurge have abandoned this world to be undermined by darkness, speech would undertake to restore the lost creation. In spite of halting syntax, speech will endeavor through its lucid patience, through its discretion, through the gradual elimination of what is risky and irregular, to convert those essences that were mere flotsam of a great vessel into the Idea become at last immanent, and the Book into the holy place which will retain that Idea amongst us. Poetry must save Being, which in turn will save us. Was it from blind pride that Mallarmé undertook such a task? Of course not; it was from disgust with illusory satisfactions, from love of poetry, from the feeling that someone must at last assume responsibility for restoring poetry, at least to truth.

For it was only to truth that Mallarmé attained.

Language is not the Word. However distorted, however transformed our syntax may be, it will always remain merely a metaphor for the unachievable syntax, signifying only exile. And what a sentence reveals is not the Idea, but our aversion from facile speech, our reflection so to speak, the confirmation of exile. And there is worse: the corpus of Ideas, being self-contained and self-sufficient, can only be born of itself, without contact with emotional vagaries and errors; and such purity, such coldness oblige the poet not to tolerate at the inception of his work that "inspiration" that, in the poetry of the past, did at least bring passion to sustain the concern for intelligibility. This is the meaning of Mallarmé's well-known recourse to the pretext, a significant renunciation which binds us entirely to poetic invention, sacrificing pain, the poet's "illustrious companion," for something almost non-existent which vanishes as soon as it is stated, which ceases to concern us, frivolity or perhaps scatology being the bleak conditions of that will to break the initial impure link. Mallarmé's poetry represents the defeat of existence, impulse after impulse, desire after desire. "Fortunately," he writes to Cazalis when initiating his great plan, "I am perfectly dead." We have here, indeed, the ancient baptismal concept that one must die to this world in order to be reborn in a higher, holier one. The fact remains that Mallarmé could only hope to gain a foothold on the threshold of being by silencing the original desire within him toward anxiety and understanding. What is the value of a gift conferred only on one who is already dead?

Stéphane Mallarmé demonstrated the failure of the old impulse of hope. We can no longer ignore the fact that it is impossible to escape through speech from the nothingness that consumes things, ever since *Un Coup de Dès* celebrated this irremediable fact. And those of us who have sought to evade it, such as those to whom I referred earlier—those seeking to retrieve from nothingness not their own lives but the object, those who are anguished at the thought of losing rather than of being lost—we are all tossed out of the safe harbor of speech into a land of dangers, where, moreover, the premonitions and the dissatisfactions of many great poets will recover their meaning and their authority.

For poetry, despite its great design, has always preserved within its closed dwelling the sense of an unknown existence, an alternative way of salvation, a different hope—in any case, of a strange and inadmissible pleasure.

How indeed can we forget the fascination exercised on poetry by blood and death, the wounding of Clorinda, the dying of Eurydice and Phaedra, situations of misfortune, dispossession, farewell? How can we fail to recognize, behind all its idylls, poetry's predilection for something sinister wandering among eternal woods like the ghost of the limit one would like to forget? The truth is that there is something ambiguous about all great works. And this makes them more deeply akin, among all edifices, among all mansions whose eternity is assured, to a temple, to the dwelling of a god. For the temple. through the rules of proportion and number and the essential economy of form, seeks to establish in the dangerous region the security of a law. Here we escape from the shadowy and the indefinite into the crystal clarity of the timeless. But in the secret heart of the temple, on the altar or deep in a crypt, the unforeseeable is present. Just a gleam on a stone face—but it reawakens all the storm within the symmetry, as though a well had been pierced in that luminous enclosure to reveal the unknowable depths of the place.

It is the destiny of every work of art to create a ceremony from that which is obscure. But often poetry does not admit this to itself, does not know itself, does not consent to release and name the mysterious powers it celebrates. This is the case with Racine, whom I take as an example of that central region, of those high places inhabited by incessant thunderstorms, where the symmetry of the facade tells nonetheless of the impossibility of rest.

What admirable coherence there is in Racine's capacity for denial! Never has prosody been so strictly confined, the vocabulary so lofty, meanings so pure and so controlled. Nothing can be said unless it conforms to the inflexible economy that the word sets against reality. Racinian man is by divine right remote from things. Or rather, nothing remains on his diurnal stage but a specimen of each thing, which has been assigned to him so that he may accomplish, outside of space and time, the essential actions of his immanent royalty. Here death serves only to punctuate great actions. It takes place in a single moment, without defilement, by means of poison, as one slips into the wings—and when something dark and formless, like the thought that obsesses Phèdre, is revealed, death is seen not as annihilation but as the victory of being, since the dying Phèdre cries out that she restores "all its purity" to the light of day. The Racinian hero dies, it seems, to simplify the universe, to give greater weight to being, offering sacrifice to an aulic conception of the sacred in which the smallest possible number of figures are set out in the glorious sunlight. But this highly abstract death assumes a terrible importance. It seems as though by reducing it to pure act we merely precipitate its rhythm; it seems as though the quintessence of man, freed of its lees, has become an unstable substance which vanishes as soon as it appears; it seems, in a word, as though the essences cannot cohabit without eternally destroying one another and that if Racine is led intuitively, and by a supreme yearning, to that garden in the evening sunlight where characters stand motionless, these will only be able to move again for immediate death. Thus, in *Bérénice,* the opening words of those lucid, generous, and faultless beings give free rein to disaster. Thus, in *Iphigénie* or in *Phèdre,* we find that doom-laden heredity, that incestuous blood, as though, on the one hand, even the splendid background of the great ancestral figures were marked by disquiet and guilt, as though, on a deeper level, the dimension of time inevitable revealed the existence of a material element where poetry had thought to attain the inaccessible empyrean. Within the transparency of his pure crystal Racine recognizes a shadow and cannot cease seeing it. And this may well be one reason for his notorious silence. Had he not undertaken to portray Alcestis on the stage, and then failed to triumph over death?

Meanwhile, however. he had consented, with an absorbing passion he doubtless considered sinful, to the dark night that terrified him. He speaks with voluptuous decorum of that which kills the thing it loves. He brings it almost to the daylight of speech, with what would be unparalleled lucidity, were it not that the death he contemplates can only be expressed negatively, as an inconsistency in existence, a privation dissociated from the deep eternal object which is man dying *under our sky.* From within the world of essences, death is imagined as the unseen, as absence. That, I assume, is how in that supposedly sunlit century, passing over the rustling sand, one drew near to the closed orangeries. For I consider these the emblematic key to the period, its latent conscience; their great windows under admirable semicircular arches let in the daylight of being; they have no dark areas, and housing as they do choice specimens of plant and flower they prefigure

Mallarmé's garden of the future—yet night, or the memory of night, fills them with a faint odor of sacrificial blood, as though some deeply significant act had once taken place there. The French orangery is the index of darkness, one of the "thousand open ways" that Racine admits, and even more that *vacant self* that is classical French poetry itself, almost self-aware but inactive, waiting for an intuition to complete it, and which doubtless for that very reason was to exercise an irreducible fascination on later poetry.

One must go to the orangery and press one's brow against its dark panes. I can see Baudelaire as a child in the garden of essences. I mean that Baudelaire accomplished what classical prosody had always required, or rather what it had inaugurated. For on the way toward what Kierkegaard has called *purity of heart,* one inevitably encounters the classical concern for unity, even when it does not represent the most essential intuition. The Racinian concept of speech also means simplifying consciousness, confining us to certain thoughts which are indeed the most serious ones, and looking beyond the irrational light shed on everything in this world by false romanticism Baudelaire recovers this decisive poverty. His prosody has the same spiritual monotony as Racine's. Simply, however, whereas the latter conceives of unity as an ideal sphere, infinitely separate, Baudelaire brings it—or seeks it—within the physical world, outside of consciousness, outside of the self. I take *Le Cygne* as an example. Whereas Mallarmé, with *Hérodiade,* was to make a last attempt to suspend human action, to unite it with the stars, to transform the Racinian heroine—still too shadowy—into an Idea, Baudelaire subtitutes for the classical archetype a real woman seen passing in the distance, not really known but respected for her essential fragility, her contingency, her mysterious grief. Baudelaire does not create this Andromache, he "thinks" of her, and this means that being exists outside one's consciousness and that this simple fact, with its hazardous basis, is of far greater importance than the stable dwelling place built by the mind. For all around this wounded woman, and through the sympathy she arouses, the world—rather than being abolished as it once was, or proliferating senselessly as in picturesque poetry—suddenly opens onto the plight of all lost beings, the "captives," the "vanquished," as Baudelaire calls them, all those whose very exile renders their presence still less explicable, less reducible. The swan, a bewildered castaway, an enigma to the poet as much as to itself, destined to die and yet capable, in its extreme distress, of giving life and expression to the paradoxical song, represents individual existence recognized for the first time in sovereign manner in a poetic tradition that was dying. It is the *here and now,* our limitation; which poetry must ceaselessly rediscover in a pure and violent crisis of the feelings and of the mind. For this act which we expect of poetry, and which was finally achieved by the poet of *Les Fleurs du mal,* is primarily an act of love. Baudelaire speaks

> *A quiconque a perdu ce qui ne se retrouve*
> *Jamais, jamais!*
>
> To whoever has lost what can never, never be recovered!

and declares with that sufferer that the one irreplaceable reality is this particular being or thing before us, and if he dedicates himself to words with unchangingly impetuous passion, he never forgets that while they enchant us, they rob us and that they are not our true salvation.

Thus Baudelaire, ascribing supreme value to that which is merely mortal, showing human beings against a background of death and through death, can indeed be said to have discovered death, having understood that it is not that simple negation of the Idea that Racine secretly loved but one profound aspect of the presence of individual beings, in a sense their only reality. And Baudelaire seeks to make his poetry express that absolute exterior, that great wind against the windows of speech, the *here and now* on which any death confers a sacred character. A new and a thankless task. For as Hegel has shown, seemingly with relief, speech can retain nothing that is immediate. *Now night has fallen (Maintenant, c'est la nuit)*: if by these words I claim to express my sense-experience they promptly become merely a frame from which presence has disappeared. The portraits that have seemed to us the most lifelike turn out to be mere paradigms. Our most private words become myths once we have let them go. Are we then condemned to be unable to speak of what we love best? At any rate, Baudelaire endeavored, by means of those *chevilles* for which he has been so much blamed (though they are surely the only valid response to the traditional closed prosody), by those muffled blows struck against the wall of speech, by the shattering of formal perfection and the collapse of Beauty which, in spite of himself and perhaps of ourselves, he envisaged for the poetry of the future, to suggest the way in which words dedicated to the universal are brushed by the wing of real life.

Baudelaire did more than that. I maintain that he chose to die—to summon death into his very body and to live under the threat of it—the better to grasp in his poetry the cloud looming on the boundaries of speech. Dead, already dead, already the one who has died in a here and now, Baudelaire no longer needs to describe a here and now. He is within them, and his works carry them.

And, I believe, that almost satisfied desire to attain to presence in language means that intelligence must efface itself in love, which is greater than intelligence, even if love can only take the form of pity or regret, *amer savoir,* that bitter knowledge, ineluctable and despairing.

But if poetry has to be this sort of stoicism, what is the meaning of the strange joy that often surges up in Baudelaire's work when it is closest to the doomed object? In *Un Voyage à Cythère,* in *Une Charogne* or *Une Martyre,* it is unquestionable that when dealing with the most horrible things, the most cruel degradations of humanity in existence, this poet displays an ardent joy devoid of sadism and not exclusive of the most earnest pity—with all the energy of an initiation. Indeed, there is nothing in this sudden, feverish excitement that recalls the lamentations of a Dostoevsky or a Shestov faced with intolerable truths. Baudelaire, who wrote *L'Irréparable, L'Irrémédiable,* and so many other poems in which he admits defeat, who lacked all resources of strength and was always acting and thinking on the very verge of exhaustion and anguish, seems to glimpse a gleam of light and to identify the perishable object, in spite of its profound precariousness, with something precious. This is what he so rightly called the *new sun;* and we could trace its rays through the twilight of his work—yet it is better to note that he did not seek or dare to understand it fully nor to probe the problem, rather enduring it as a kind of enigma, a secret forever lost and a source of remorse. I am sure—and I want to put this statement at the center of my remarks—that Baudelaire sensed at the very core of that which exists, through its death and because it must die, that it may prove our salvation. And for the sake of poetry we have to ask this question anew, trying to found a gnosis of passion, to invent a way of knowledge. Baudelaire himself left the privilege of that mysterious act to a legendary past or to the paradise of childhood.

> *Je n'ai pas oublié, voisine de la ville. . . .*
> I have not forgotten, nearby the town. . . .

The house described in one of the most beautiful poems ever written, is it not the crystal of some beneficent reality, steeped as it once was in "the streaming splendor of the evening sun" ("le soleil, le soir, ruisselant et superbe") that all day long has witnessed everything and now comes to settle on the "frugal cloth," the purest inclination of our hearts, the place for welcoming what is substantial. Here, or at that time, the servant is the *desservante* or officiating priestess, and in another poem of *Les Fleurs du mal* which forms a diptych with the one I have just quoted, *La Servante au grand coeur. . . ,* we see that priestess of a bygone rite bring against poetry the grave indictment of forgetfulness.

In the dawn of consciousness there is the promise of a good which is later submerged by reason, as though by sleep.

And the muted prophecy we find in Baudelaire, once uttered, was to spread its message unceasingly. It is surely to Baudelaire that Rimbaud owes, if not his uncompromising exigency, at any rate the notion that poetry has the power to satisfy it. Rimbaud is convinced that poetry can be a practical action; he has no use for the traditional sort that is bewitched by illusions, that is content to lament the poet's sufferings, the sort of poetry he calls "subjective"—he believes that a place and a formula, in poetry and, if need be, beyond it, will bring about the transmutation of dispossession into a benefit. Rimbaud was less savant than Baudelaire, less the cunning chemist, being less close to reality and less able to gauge it in its deep transparency, because he had been deprived of love at the most vulnerable moment of his childhood. But for that very reason he demanded more. It is thanks to Rimbaud that we know, we *really* know that poetry must be a means and not an end, and we owe him the immensity of what we might ask for—those demands, that thirst that have proved so alarming.

For it is not true that the poets who followed Rimbaud and Baudelaire understood their problem or maintained their attitude. It seems, on the contrary, as though they had taken fright and chose rather to listen to a message of pessimism that may be found in Mallarmé and that exists, in any case, in the great space of our modernity, under the "dead sky"—a twofold or perhaps just a single crisis, which offers the legacy of an empty world. And if it is true that no god any longer sanctifies created things, that they are pure matter, pure chance, why indeed should one not seek to escape from them? The end of the idea of divinity may bring about a revival of puritanism, of the fear of existence, since it completes that dissociation of the human being from nature which a certain form of Christianity had inaugurated. And among the most brilliant poets of our time we find, at the same time, a certain pessimism and skepticism, and the wish for a discipline by means of which to withdraw from the world as it is. The useless dwelling that Baudelaire had abandoned is inhabited once more. But this time it is not, it is less than ever, in order to save one's existence; it is rather to save oneself from existence in a purely formal act, secret and immobile, what I might describe as the wrong sort of death (*la mauvaise mort*).

Indeed, as I must now admit to myself, I mistrust those disciples of Mallarmé who in different contexts, with contradictory intentions, have also turned away from their master's conclusions. Valéry, who for his own peace of mind and in order to forget the tragic awareness of the Greeks, spends his time seeking rules for the making of a poem. Claudel, fettered by orthodoxy, with his list of things. Great minds, certainly, profuse and subtle personalities; but in fact *personality,* with its marked features, its authority, its latent mannerism, is the basic resource of a negative idealism. Absence here appears creative. Such poetry achieves a moment of glamor at the cost of true passion and real experience. On the other hand, what is valuable in our age has often been characterized by its distaste for the rights or privileges of a markedly personal intelligence. There was the impossible Surrealist dream of collective invention. And in some of the best poetry of our century—I think of glaciers, of deserts, of forgotten crafts, of moments of dry stone or mist—we find that the object has become hollow like a wave, separate from its body like a flame in the light, to imply the essential fluidity we share, both it and us, when we meet. Then there is the attention that speech pays to its most obscure strata. And finally, above all, we find younger poets scrupulously examining, with an almost moral end in view, the pretensions of that ego that had so often asserted without proof, written without believing, and misled. They will not accept without extreme prudence and reservation, and after careful verification, the necessary impulses of their own minds and voices. They have made a clean sweep of self-confident gestures, and then reinvented those few elementary gestures that unite us to things, in the ceaseless cold dawn of a life anxiously seeking the absolute. Thus poetry is today returning to a profound realism. This, needless to say, is not that self-styled "objectivity" with its precise inventories, of those "new novels" in which the authorial voice is muted. When there are no more desires, mistakes, or passions, even wind and fire lose their reality; the whole world becomes the home of absence. And it is the final result of the shattering of Providence, but also the dangerous contradiction of atheism, that we should have destroyed divine machinery only to deny all subjective life to things or happenings.

Already in *The Castle of Otranto* the strange sight of a huge helmet or an enormous iron arm in courtyard or hall implied man's bewilderment, confronted with a world abandoned to itself and with the mutely enigmatic presence of a real object. And possibility—that most precious of our assets—suddenly deprived of its religious dimension, was degraded into a mere vicissitude. The difficulty facing modern poetry is that it has to define itself at one and the same moment through Christianity and in opposition to it. For Baudelaire's discovery—to return to the truly decisive moment—of the *individual* person or thing is indeed Christian insofar as Jesus suffered under Pontius Pilate, endowing a particular place and moment with dignity and every human being with reality. But Christianity only affirms individual existence for a brief instant. The created thing is brought back to God by means of Providence and thus deprived once again of its absolute value.

Thus in order to complete Baudelaire's revolution and strengthen hesitant realism we must also carry out a criticism of the religious thought we have inherited. The duty of giving a meaning to existence and to all that exists—the private destiny of every work of art—is intensified today by the urgent and imperative need to rethink the relation between man and those "inert" things, those "remote" beings which the collapse of the divine may lead us to think of as mere material.

In other words, we have to rediscover *hope*. In the secret region of our contact with being, I believe there is no true poetry today that does not seek, and will go on seeking to its last breath, to found a new hope.

T. S. Eliot in the *Waste Land* expressed the real myth of modern culture. But he ignored, or sought to ignore, one paradoxical resource of that culture.

We now know the meaning of that desolate land, where a spell has dried up the springs, disrupted the harvests: it is reality, if I might so put it, *realized*, concluded; a reality endured by the spirit without a quest for possibilities. A realm of essences and the knowledge of essences. Man has embarked on the wrong path. Is it from despair at the lack of a higher life? But suppose the contrary were true and metaphysical sterility only the consequence of a bleak lack of curiosity? Was it not said at the castle of the Fisher King that a single question would be enough to break the spell?

The honor of conceptual thought—of all thought—lies in asking rather than in answering. The West began badly with Oedipus.

However, I have in mind a very different question, and the most fundamental one, bearing on the presence, not the nature, of things. The Percival in each of us, the consciousness that is to be, would not have to ask what things or beings are, but why they are in this place we consider our own and what mysterious answer they might give to our call. He would have to wonder at the chance on which they depend; he would have suddenly to *see* them. And of course this would mean, in the first stage of this groping knowledge, recognizing the death, the anonymity, the finitude that dwell in them and that destroy them. . . . I suggest today that we should once more follow Baudelaire in his love for what is mortal, stand once again on the threshold he thought was closed, facing the most distressing proofs of darkness. Here all thoughts about the future, all projects vanish. Nothingness consumes the object; we are caught up in the winds of that shadowless flame. And we no longer have any faith to sustain us, any formula, any myth; our most intense gaze ends in despair. Yet let us not abandon this blank and empty horizon; let us hold our ground, *le pas gagné*, so to speak. For it is true that already a change is taking place. The mournful star of existence, the elementary Janus, turning slowly—but at this instant—on itself, reveals its other face. A possibility appears on the wreck of all possibilities. And the horror of *Une Martyre*, or the "green gloom of moist summer evenings" ("les ténèbres vertes dans les soirs humides de la belle saison"), or anything else that is real, whether tragic or pacified, will emerge in the sacred heart of this instant for an eternity of presence. I resent using this approximative language when I should really be *telling*. But what words would henceforth not betray us? Here—and it's still the same here—and at this moment—also still the same—we have stepped out of space, we have slipped out of time. All that we had once lost is restored to us, still and smiling at the gates of light. All that passes and never stops passing pauses, postponing night. It is as though sight had become substance, and knowledge possession—but in fact what do we possess? Something has happened, something of infinite depth and gravity, a bird has sung in the ravine of existence, we have touched the water which would have allayed our thirst, but already the veil of time has wrapped us in its folds, and as the instant draws near we are exiled anew. Something was offered to us, we are sure of that in spite of Baudelaire, but we were unable to grasp it. Were we so ill-prepared? No doubt we were like Lancelot in the *Quest for the Holy Grail,* who, having come to a closed chapel and fallen asleep on its threshold, suddenly sees it lit up by a great fire, sees the Grail issue from its gates and hears a knight cry out, as he suddenly emerges from the darkness: "*Ha, guéri suis!* I am cured!"—while he himself remains sunk in the lethargy of his fatal sleep, remote from God.

And yet, in spite of this missed opportunity, we are no longer the same, we are no longer so poor, some hope remains. Although indeed the question of what might save us remains unanswered, although we have had to doubt insofar as, and almost at the very instant when we were given to believe, we have nonetheless received the boon of certainty; and, even as the view of the purpose of man is revised, we know on what basis we can build. Henceforward we have a reason for existence, which is that sudden act. And a duty and a moral goal—at any rate provisionally—which will be to recover it. And all our actions, lost, crippled creatures that we are, should be a call to this; or rather should recognize that this is what they have always been, in depth, else why do we love those lighted lamps in empty rooms, those statues whose faces are obliterated by sand, those lifeless cloisters? Is what we are seeking there some sort of beauty, as we are told? Of course not; it is rather something eternal which we share with these things.

And of speech, too, this is true. Speech is the same quest, without knowing it. Has it not waged a long war against nothingness? Perhaps the act of presence—that lost light of Baudelaire's poem—may be its origin too. And I myself am prepared, envisaging the future of poetry, seeing speech as invention or recovery, and pursuing the path which is the only possible one, to affirm passionately this *here* and this *now* which, indeed, are already an elsewhere and a past, which no longer exist, which have been stolen from us but which, eternally in their temporal finitude, universally in their spatial limitation, are the only conceivable good, the only place that deserves the name of place. In modern French poetry we see the Grail procession passing—the most vividly perceptible objects of this earth—a tree, a face, a stone—and they must be named. Therein lies all our hope.

But the difficulty confronting language, its well-known incapacity to express the immediate, has not been solved, as I well know. At best it has been clarified or emphasized, since I have only asked of words that they put their trust in silence. What can they retain or say, when presence is offered to us in the universe of the moment? Speech can indeed celebrate presence, sing of its being, as I am doing now; it can prepare us spiritually for encountering it, but it cannot in itself allow us to achieve it. Speech implies forgetting; it may even explain our fall. At any rate, it is denied contact with being. Must we not, yet again, condemn the pretensions of poetry?

I think rather that we must recognize its limitations and, forgetting that it may once have been an end, take it merely as the means of an approach, which, given the limitations of our perspective, is actually not far from being the essential thing. Deficiency has one virtue, which is to recognize itself as such and thus lead us to a passionate knowing. And if language is as incapable of the Idea as it is of presence, if the reflected light of the one hides from us, in the words of poetry, the finitude and death that are the steps to the other, we are still able to recognize this and to direct our anxious lucidity of mind against the facility of speech. I should like poetry to be above all a ceaseless battle, a theater in which being and essence, form and formlessness wage strenuous war. This is possible in a number of ways. Poetry in the past has taken risks where truth is concerned. And the fervent empiricism we shall need will have to admit that in any serious work all the "devices" of poetry are maltreated and almost destroyed. Thus we shall learn that words can above all be an action. Their potential, their infinite future of associations, considered merely verbal and assumed to be gratuitous, will turn out to be only a metaphor for our endless connection with the slightest thing that is real, for the subjective nature of everything that is profound—and in a moment of unreality, of free decision about the physical world, we shall be able to release what is from the sleep of its stable forms, in which nothingness triumphs. Thus, too, the facile delight of rhythms will be denied. Formal beauty is the dream on the edge of an ideal world. It found expression in regular verse with an even number of syllables, but it was here, in the realm of abstraction and forgetfulness, that Rimbaud dealt the fatal blow of the irregular line. He made possible a conflict and, beyond it, an understanding, of which the silent "e" is the secret link. Moved both by desire and by clearsightedness, he made it possible for the thoughts nurtured by poetry to be realized at last. The myths to come will tell of death or will admit that they are concealing it. The adventure of meaning will begin at last. Or rather, *the hypothesis of meaning,* our frantic need to organize our knowledge within the space of a poem, to formulate the myth of what is, to construct the concepts, will be subjected to diffraction by the formless. And this poetry which cannot grasp presence, dispossessed of all other good, will be in anguished proximity to the great accomplished act, as its *negative theology.* When, in relation to what is, all landmarks, all frameworks, all formulae have been questioned or obliterated, what can we do but wait, hoping in the substance of words?

And it is true that in authentic poetry nothing remains but those wanderers of the real, those categories of possibility, those elements without past or future, never entirely involved in the existing situation, always ahead of it and promising something else, which are the wind, fire, earth, the waters—all the indefinite offerings of the universe, concrete but universal elements. Here and now, but everywhere beyond the here and now, under the canopy and in the forecourt of our place and our moment. Omnipresent and alive; one might say that they are the very speech of being that poetry draws forth. One might also say that they *are* words, being no other than a promise. They appear on the confines of the negativity of language, like angels telling of a still unknown god. A negative "theology." The only universality I recognize in poetry.

A knowledge, negative and unstable though it be, that I may perhaps call the *truth of speech.* The very opposite of a formula. An intuition, complete in each word. And a "bitter knowledge" certainly, since it confirms death. It knows that the healing power of presence evades us. It rediscovers and relives past failures. It has brought no proofs to the reawakened hope. Yet is it true that it does nothing toward that salvation with which we are obsessively concerned? And is poetry merely one appeal among all the others, with no privilege, no future? We must ask ourselves, and this is a distinction that is surely not useless, since here lies perhaps our only recourse—whether in addition to the negative intuition which a poem is *for all of us,* poetic invention brings nothing to the life of the writer other than aimless desire, unrest, and futility.

I should like to show, by way of conclusion, that this is not the case. To think so would be to misunderstand this world of expectancy in which, having reached this point in the invention of speech, we are involved. Here, where nothing is considered, sought, or loved but the act of presence, where the only valid future is that absolute present where time evaporates, all reality is still *to be,* and its "past" as well. We conceive that the past event, that apparent proof of death, is only an action initiated or veiled, possessing its glorified body in the depths of the future; and that it is thus a test for us. For its nothingness is definitive only if we betray our hope. Out of respect, I speak thus curtly of that which exalts the spirit at the highest point of poetic experience. For it is true that the past and death, however manifest, however acutely present to our minds, no longer overwhelm the lover of what has been lost. He can contemplate the traces of them. And although these are nothing, having failed to preserve presence and being unable to restore its scattered essence to our inert memories, he will understand why he guards them so jealously as being the key to an unknown future. He may meet with words; they, too, are what remains of what has vanished. Let us take them as tokens of a good and not of a quiddity. And let us try to understand that they, like the past, are a test for us, since, given the recurrences of the future, they require us to act instead of merely dreaming.

They require us to act. And first of all to imagine what is very deep, to remove the contradiction between the lightning flash and our night. Logically (if I may use the word) to conceive of a true place. For if it is certain that here, in the everyday world, the only good worth wishing for is evanescent, so that we are in disarray and divided within ourselves, why should we not ask some other place in this world to restore us to our law? Another place, beyond other encounters, beyond the war of being alone. Having now discovered that travel, love, architecture, all the efforts of mankind are only so many ceremonies to summon presence, we have to bring them to life again on the very threshold of that deeper region. And in the changing light of its dawn, to fulfill them absolutely. Is there not somewhere a true fire, a true face? I can almost see those stones in the daylight, and for a whole day of this world, a day redeemed, after which, if the word still has a meaning, one will only have to die. This is, if you will, the blessing of the torn ivy leaf, given and possessed at last.

The true place is a fragment of duration consumed by eternity; in the true place time is annulled within us. And I might equally say, I know, that it does not exist, that it is only the mirage, against the background of time, of the hours of our death—but has the term *reality* still a meaning, and can it free us from the engagement we have contracted toward the remembered object, which is to go on seeking? I maintain that nothing is more authentic, and thus more reasonable, than to go wandering, for—need it be said?—there is no method for returning to the true place. It may be infinitely close. It is also infinitely far away. So it is with being, in our moment of time, and the irony of presence.

The true place is given by chance, but in the true place chance will lost its enigmatic character.

And for the person seeking, even if he is well aware that there is no path to guide him, the world around him will be inhabited by signs. The least object, the most ephemeral creature, because of the good they do him will arouse the hope of an absolute good. The fire that warms us tells us that it is not the true fire. Its very substance proves this; it is here, it is not here. We recognize again those wanderers through the great space of reality, those promise-bearing angels of which I spoke. In the true place, elementary realities reveal that they are not confined to place and moment; that they partake less of the nature of being than of that of language; that they can compel whatever appears beside them to speak to us, in a whisper, of an unforeseeable future. I have rediscovered the point at which, by the grace of the future, reality and language have united their powers. And I say that a longing for the true place is the vow made by poetry. Having conferred the energy to undertake the journey, poetry provides the path. Words appearing before us in the space of our waiting, words being only a matter of waiting and knowing, poetry will know how to dissociate, at the most important moments, quality that is ephemeral from meaning that is vigilant. It will search the horizon according to the wish of our hearts. It will question all that pass by. And when certain things reveal themselves to be *openings,* signs consumed by the close proximity of the good they have called forth, poetry will keep these keys in mind in its strictest economy; it will establish the word *lamp* or the word *ship* or the word *shore* in the stronghold, this time, of a memory that is striving between dispersal and recovery. These things are, in fact, the buttresses of the true place, and their names will come together in poetry to form what is intelligible, *subjectively intelligible,* or a necessary hypostasis before the unity we desire. Thus speech is the sense we make of our involvement in the obscure possibilities of earth, of our relation with what is. And certainly, in our twofold journey, speech is likely to lead us toward an increase in consciousness rather than toward a place. But the whole spirit must keep watch, waiting for the decisive, chance moment. . . . The poet is the person who "burns" with expectation. The truth of speech is a proximity—when essential realities are so clearly the threshold of the true place, and yet all the more opaque and strange in that they always conceal, through their chance dispersal, the next step, which remains a secret. There is a cloud in the light; something elusive, dark, and formless in the purity of the crystal. This is why words offer to the anxiously questing mind of the poet not only the clarity of the concept but also their material opacity, their arbitrary and fascinating letters. I say *a flower,* and the sound of the word, its mysterious figure brings back the enigma. And if opacity is joined with transparency, if a poet is able to write "Le pâle hortensia s'unit au myrte vert," there can be no doubt that he is as close as possible to those elusive gates. Of such a poet it will most frequently be said that he is "hermetic."

For his only object, his only lodestar is beyond any expressible meaning, even though his quest requires the full richness of words.

The process of poetry takes place in the field of speech, but each of its steps is verifiable in a world newly affirmed. Poetry brings about the transmutation of the finished into the possible, of the remembered into the expected, of the waste land into a journey, into hope. And I might speak of it as an *initiatory realism* if, in the end, it gave us reality. But how can one answer that question, which is the first one I asked? This poetry will prove to have been our destiny. For *in the meantime* we shall have grown older. The act of speech will have taken place in the same space of time as our other actions. It will have given us one kind of life rather than another, amidst the perils of poetry and the contradictions of exile. What indeed shall we have had if we do not reach the true place?

I think of that poet whose hope was the clearest, whose suffering was the keenest; the most secret of those who, in nineteenth-century France, formed that sort of quadrangle in which all thoughts are lost and then recovered in endless refractions. Purely, like poetry incarnate, he became totally absorbed into the hopeless love that is love for mortal beings. But his desire remained desire, and his impulse toward plenitude maintained in honesty of heart the sense of the unpossessable. This union of lucidity and hope is what I call melancholy. And in the world of Justice nothing comes closer to Grace—whether truth or beauty—than this ardent melancholy. This at least is the gift that a true poet can offer. And in his poverty, giving remains his wealth.

For a long time, poetry sought to dwell in the mansion of the Idea, but, as it is said, was driven out and fled, uttering cries of pain. Modern poetry is far from its possible home. The great four-windowed hall is permanently closed to it. The repose provided by form in poetry can no longer be accepted with honesty. But the opportunity of the poetry that is to come, its good fortune (and I can admit that good fortune now) is that it is on the point of realizing, in its enduring exile, the issue offered by presence. After so many hours of anguish. Was it so difficult, then? Surely it was enough to glimpse, on some mountainside, a window gleaming in the evening sun?

Translated by Jean Stewart and John T. Naughton

10 French Poetry and the Principle of Identity[1]

OF WHAT VALUE is the French language to the experience of poetry? We know that Baudelaire and Rimbaud, among many other witnesses, were sometimes given to fits of anger against it. Baudelaire writes, for example: "I am bored in France because everyone here resembles Voltaire." And in a letter to Ancelle, dating from the last months of his conscious life, a letter that is in truth his spiritual testament, Baudelaire again writes: "And you were enough of a CHILD to forget that *France* ABHORS poetry, *true* poetry, that it admires only bastards like Beranger or de Musset." Some years later, Rimbaud spontaneously finds similar words: "French, that is to say, detestable. . . . Yet another work of that odious spirit that inspired Rabelais, Voltaire, Jean La Fontaine explicated by Monsieur Taine! . . . French poetry will long be savored, but only in France." These insults, I admit, are aimed more directly at society than at language. But can one truly make a distinction between civilization and its mode of expression? Is not the latter, at least, one of the causes of the former and thus of the difficulties of its poetry?

But listen to how Baudelaire, and Rimbaud also, correct themselves. "French, not Parisian!" the latter exclaims, referring to the "odious spirit." And in the draft of a preface to *Les Fleurs du mal*, a book, incidentally, that is dedicated to a "pure magician of French letters," Baudelaire writes: "Like the languages of Latin and English, how mysterious and unappreciated is the prosody French poetry possesses." There is thus a city of poetry in the land of prose, a rhythm in our language whose quality cannot be squandered by so many ignorant "bourgeois." In truth, it is to a certain esoteric quality rather than to a deficiency that Baudelaire and Rimbaud allude. French poetry should exist, but it hides itself or, in any case, keeps its distance. What it most hates is what is called poetry.

Therein, however, lies a problem. If our language is capable of poetry,

1. "French Poetry and the Principle of Identity" ("La Poésie française et le principe d'identité") was first published in the *Revue d'esthétique* 3–4 (July–December 1965) and then in a signed and limited edition by the Galerie Maeght in 1967 with two watercolors by Raoul Ubac. The essay also appears in the various editions of *L'Improbable et autres essais*.

why does it make contact with it only in these obviously reciprocal misunderstandings and deprecations? Is this the fact of all culture since Romanticism, perhaps? Or is it a characteristic peculiar to the French language alone?

I believe it is the former; but in order to explain why, I have to define what seems to me one of the initial movements of the poetic intuition. This is also its first contact with language: namely, its reaction to the most simple reality, that of the word.

It is important to stress that this approach differs radically from what is ordinarily considered the only conceivable explanation of the sign. In fact, this difference is so decisive, and so consistently unrecognized, that there may perhaps appear one of those persistent nodes of dangerous certainty that for many authors makes the *reason* for poetry so difficult to understand.

From this perspective, moreover, how little progress has been made in recent critical theory! Saussure and his followers have shown that the sign is determined by a structure, thus adding a new dimension to meaning and consequently to the knowledge of literary works. But they assign to the word the unchanging task of merely signifying, and the very richness of their discoveries has become a danger for a meditation on poetry.

For all linguists, so it seems, the word *horse* represents what is, let's say, neither donkey nor unicorn. Its content is a quiddity, nothing else; thus, in its destiny to evoke, as a proper noun can evoke when one shouts it out, it does not express the actual existence of the "horse" that is here before me.

That seems obvious. What would "the horse" be if not a concept? *A* horse, yes, before me; and "the horse" as its idea, by whatever means this idea may be determined. I admit that this point of view allows one to describe correctly the way language is available for most uses. But poetry is, precisely, not a "use" of language. Perhaps, it is a madness *in* the language, which we can understand only through its eyes of madness—only through poetry's way of understanding and taking hold of words.

This, I believe, is what initiates poetry. If I say "fire" (yes, I am changing examples and that already in itself means something), poetically what this word evokes for me is not only fire in its nature as fire—what there is about fire that suggests its concept—but the *presence* of fire in the horizon of my life, and certainly not as an object, analyzable and usable (and, therefore, finite, replaceable), but as a god, active and endowed with powers.

But I fear I am becoming unclear, so I will use another example.

And I shall imagine or remember—we will perhaps see later that the two ideas are equivalent—that one summer's day I enter the ruins of a house and suddenly see a salamander on the wall. Surprised and frightened, it remains motionless. And roused from my reverie I, too, am ready to be held captive. I look at the salamander, I recognize its distinctive features, I see the narrow neck, the gray face, the heart that beats softly.

So, several paths have opened before me. I can analyze what my perception has shown me, and thus, profiting from the experience of other beings, mentally separate this small life from other realities in the world, categorize it in the way the prose word might, saying to myself "*A* salamander," and then absentmindedly continue my walk, as if I were only superficially affected by the encounter. But other, more profound reactions are possible. For example, I can keep my eyes on the salamander, pay particular attention to the details that had enabled me to recognize it, think about continuing the analysis that makes it more and more into *a* salamander, that is to say, an object of science, a reality structured by my reason and penetrated by language—but with the immediate result that in these appearances that have been abruptly separated one from the other, in this contour of an absolute, indisputable, barren leg, I no longer perceive anything but a terrifying bundle of enigmas. These things have a name, but suddenly become strangers to that name. And these concepts, these definitions, these appearances are for me no more than an empty coherence, unresponsive to any question.

What is a salamander? *Why* this salamander rather than the hearth, or the swallow, or the cracks in the wall? *Where* is the origin of what lies before me? In sum, I have just discovered the agonizing tautology of language by which words only speak themselves, having no real hold on things—which can move away from words, remaining distant from them. I shall call *bad presence* (*la mauvaise présence*) this latent muteness of the world. And I am even tempted to call it the devil, for there is a power, a strange appeal, hidden in the depths of this void. It is as if nothingness mimicked our most familiar realities and by the darkness of its night penetrated the closed form of being. I experience the idea of death. I am fascinated, as surely as if by a snake. But, fortunately, at this moment I find in myself the freedom that denies it.

For here is the third path. By a sudden act, this reality (*ce réel*), which has divided and exteriorized itself, *comes together again*, and this time in a plenitude where I am taken up and saved. It is as if I had accepted, *experienced*, this salamander. Henceforth, rather than having to be explained by other aspects of reality (*le réel*), the salamander, here present as the softly beating heart of the world, becomes the origin of what is. Let's say—although this experience is barely describabable—that it has revealed itself, becoming, or becoming again, *the* salamander—as one says *the* fairy—in a pure act of existing where its "essence" is contained. Let's say—for one must also save the word, above all from the fatal desire to define everything—that its essence has flowed into the essence of other beings, like the flux of an analogy by which I perceive everything in the continuity and sufficiency of a *place* and in the transparence of *unity*. The wall is justified, and the fireplace, and the olive tree outside, and the earth. And having again become one with all that, having been awakened to the essential savor of my being—for this space arches in me as the inner world of my existence—I have gone from accursed perception to love, which is prescience of the invisible.

How, indeed, to express true reality (*le vrai réel*) through another word? This *invisible* is not a new appearance that will be revealed beneath other imperfections. Rather, it is that all appearances, all coagulations of the visible, have dissolved as particular figures, have, like sloughed-off scales, fallen into knowledge, *have found the body of the indissociable*. The salamander has freed itself from the world of objects created by an analytic reason that runs the risk of remaining on the periphery of things. And before me, in me, it is no longer anything but pure *countenance*, although its features remain material. It is the *angel* that drove devils away, the angel that is unique; for the One is the great revelation of this limitless moment when everything surrenders itself to me to be understood and bound together.

"Mine the sun," writes St. John of the Cross, speaking far ahead in the distance on this faintly traced road, "mine the moon and the stars, mine the mother of God."

This reestablished or, at the very least, emerging unity I shall call *presence*. And now I can return to the subject of words and better define their appeal for the consciousness of poetry.

What I have briefly tried to show is that in unity, or in any event under its sign, there is no longer *a* salamander at odds with this hearth, or with one, or even, a hundred swallows, but *the* salamander, present at the heart of other presences. The idea of a creature on this path—it matters little whether it is illusory or not—implies its existence, and this defeats the concept, which must abolish that existence if its forms of expression are to flourish. In the expectation of presence, one does not "signify"; one lets a light disentangle itself from the meanings that conceal it.

But that does not mean that one turns away from language. For language, and this is the other point I wanted to emphasize, is naturally continuous with the experience I have described—in one as well as the other of its aspects. On the one hand, there is dissociation, which occurs when words become concepts. In language, especially analytical language, there is certainly this potentiality for muteness, against which feeling, desire, humor—the beginnings of poetry—rise up. But since language is a structure, it can become—even before any form of expression has begun its work of death—a *cipher* for the unity that every form carries within itself. In this instant when everything is decided, it can thus return with me to an encounter with being. Language—and this is why one spoke of *logos*, of "Word"—seems to promise the same unity beyond its conceptual moment as life offers beyond the fragmented realities of its presence. It seems to invite us to carry in its depths the word that will give being to what it names. And the word, a flashing of unity, will henceforth suggest that I no longer assimilate existence to language but, on the contrary, assimilate language to my participation in the real. Every language is thus the field for the elaboration of a kind of order; for the establishment of the sacred in the destiny of the person who speaks; for, at least, the efforts of a poetry.

For I can now define what I mean by poetry. It is by no means, as is so frequently asserted even today, the creation of an object in which meanings are given structure, whether for the purpose of capturing moments of revery or for the deceptive beauty of having fused into the mass of these meanings—into their elusive particles of "truth"—the appearances of what I am. This object exists, of course, but it is the castoff skin of the poem and not its soul or intention. To attach oneself only to it is to remain in the world of dissociation, the world of objects—of the object that I, too, am, and do not wish to remain. The more one seeks to study the subtleties and expressive ambiguities of the object, the more one risks overlooking an intention of salvation, which is the poem's only concern. Indeed, the poem aspires only to interiorize the real. It seeks the ties that *in me* unite things. It must allow me to live my life in justice, and sometimes its finest moments are notations of pure evidence, where the visible seems to be on the verge of being consumed in a face; where the part, devoid even of a metaphor, has spoken in the name of the whole; where what has been silent in the distance rustles once again and breathes within the open, the whiteness, of being. The invisible—it needs to be said again from this perspective of the word— is not the disappearance but the liberation of the visible: space and time dropping away in order for the flame to arise where the tree and the wind become destiny.

I recognize that the paths leading to this liberation will in fact be quite different. Language is not the same as word. The most important word, since it is at every moment involved in acts that analyze and dissociate, can only share this alienation; and thus it must run the risk of exhausting itself in perhaps endless preliminary work. The clearest danger the poem faces is to let itself be mastered by an exterior vision that may contain a great deal of "art." But there is another, even more profound, danger. Recalling the phenomenon of "bad" presence (*la mauvaise présence*), I believe I am justified in fearing a specious imagination that, while captured by appearances and terrified by the nothingness that dwells within them here, in proximity to us, is going to delight in giving them another life, a *raison d'être*, a plenitude "somewhere else," continuously endowing them with qualities of exteriority that are all the more alluring for being somehow touched by enigma. Thus, chance, space, multiplicity surge into existence *here* as magical powers that keep appearance from dissolving into presence. The good, for which one always dreams, is assumed only to exist beyond this curtain of matter. And this dreaming, since it is passionate for being, will therefore appear "poetic." But compelled to imagine the interior with the exterior—whether through the idea of some illusory perfection of measurable form, or the idea of the distant lady of medieval imagination, or the idea of a Faustian depletion of the possible—this dreaming, deprived of the unique threshold of the absolute that any ordinary thing, truly loved for what it is, can be, is the *evil* inherent in poetic intuition: the burning, "luciferian," highly pernicious form of its innermost and, perhaps, fatal flaw.

One should perhaps name this flaw "symbolism," because of the naive confidence one finds in the "hard lake"[2] of the visible, in the gold and pearls one encounters there, and in the beauty of appearances, this illusory marble. These played a large part in fin-de-siècle poetry; in its shimmering surface and its ever so narcissistic and sterile essence.

I will have to come back to reconsider, from the point of view of the French language, this aberration of poetic intuition. But for the moment I will content myself to show the change and significance that it introduces into our relationship with language. In the form of poetry that I consider the only true one, fundamental words—they vary of course from person to person—bear the promise of being. They preserve the idea of a voice, in which an order will be clarified that, as Mallarmé would say, "will authenti-

---

2. This is an allusion to the frozen lake in Mallarmé's sonnet "Le vierge, le vivace et le bel aujourd'hui":

> *Le vierge, le vivace et le bel aujourd'hui*
> *Va-t-il nous déchirer avec un coup d'aile ivre*
> *Ce lac dur oublié que hante sous le givre*
> *Le transparent glacier des vols qui n'ont pas fui!*

> The virginal, lively, and beautiful today
> Will it with drunken wing tear us and
> This hard, forgotten lake that is haunted beneath the frost
> By the clear ice of the flights that have not escaped.

cate" our life. But in the same instant the inward character of this experience of order, of the sacred, dissipates any feeling by which this voice, imminent in the substance of words, can organize itself into forms of expression. The most intense sentences speak of our proximity to transparence and of something like its savor—the taste of fruit dissolving in the mouth—but nothing more. They evoke order, yet without revealing its structure. And this is because true experience, which only searches for the absolute through the threshold of finitude, is in any event only our necessarily relative consciousness, experienced to its innermost depths as such. On the contrary, he who, like Mallarmé, has dreamed of an "elsewhere," where certain aspects of this world can at his pleasure be resignified in keeping with another order, in itself more "true," more "real," will opt for rare words or even rarer sensations and will seek the form of expression best able to make this secret order reveal itself to the mind. His prescience of the *logos* is that it might be absorbed into a speech that is at once utterable and definitive, and is stronger than the chance that governs this bleak earth. We know about these plans for the *Livres*.[3] They are only one of the ways to seek presence by means of appearance, which is, however, the salt that eats away at it.

But from the perspective to which I would now like to return, this may not be important. To summarize, then, I will say that what poetic consciousness has hoped for in words—in some words at least—is that unity, divinity shine in them, that there be true presence. And this should be enough to catch a glimpse of certain of the relations existing between poetry and languages, in particular, the French language.

It will seem perhaps obvious to remark that not all the words of a language lend themselves in the same degree to poetic intention.

Wind, stone, fire, Rimbaud's "mazagran coffee,"[4] Baudelaire's "train

3. Mallarmé sought unsuccessfully for most of his career (especially after 1866) to make possible the creation of *Le Livre*, which he envisioned as the orphic explanation of the earth. The writing of the Book, transpiring without the active intervention of the author, who surrenders himself to the power and initiative of words, would occur only when the real world, the individuality and personality of the authorial self, and the role of chance were reduced, until they ultimately disappeared. Mallarmé's Book would be objective, impersonal, pure, and unreadable; it would deal with no particular object but with the totality of all existing things; and it would be organized according to a structure in which various elements moved and changed places in a quivering mobility. "Everything, in the world," he wrote "exists to end up in a book."

4. In the poem "Après le déluge" from *Illuminations* Rimbaud writes that "Les 'mazagrans' fumèrent dans les estaminets" ("The mazagran coffee steamed in the coffeehouses"). "Le mazagran" is a coffee served in a glass and mixed with water or brandy. Its use and name date from the siege of Mazagran in 1840 during the French campaign to colonize Algeria.

carriages" and "gas," or any other name for the most banal realities can become radiant with light—as long as, through these realities, we have experienced in some small way our attachment to the world. But from this very fact it follows that the call will be heard all the more intensely when words will speak more clearly of "essences"—and by that I simply mean those things or creatures that seem to exist per se for the sake of our naive consciousness in ordinary life. Thus the word *brick* speaks less clearly to the spirit of poetry than *stone*, because the calling to mind of the manufacturing process prevails, in the reality of this word, over its own being as "brick"—and all the more so because it is the opposite of *stone* in verbal structure. It is perhaps only a nuance. But *silicate* has less appeal than *silex*. And the verbs *to grimace*, *to sneer* will lend themselves less well to the poetic process than *to cry* or *to laugh*, because those words take hold of the human act too clearly from the outside; they only describe it; their only signified is an *appearance*, which is difficult to maintain through the interiorization that is poetry's task to accomplish.

Of course, numerous words that seem to express this appearance can be taken up again and redeemed through poetic interest: one will have learned that such words can name something that "is" and that lies beyond external appearance. From the verb "to grimace," Laforgue could have created one of the fundamental, *irreducible* components of his existence in an ambiguous world, between irony and desire. But finally, if I want to rescue the word *to sip*, for example, I will have to struggle long against the winds of exteriority, whereas *to drink*, since it expresses an essential act, will surely maintain its capacity for the absolute, even during life's most disillusioned moments. In spite of the caricatures presenting Rimbaud prostrate before the glass of absinthe—caricatures that he provoked and sought—Rimbaud *will drink*, he will not *sip*, because as a poet he dwells within the gravity of destiny. Poetry desires words that one can make part of one's destiny.

But if that is the case, then one of the points linking the intention of poetry to the fact of language becomes clearer. In this encounter one will be able to tell whether language abounds in words that express appearances or in words that name essences. From the comparative relationship of exteriority (which language on the whole imposes) to interiority (which, despite an habitual decline in use, language accepts), one could derive a sort of *poetic coefficient* that has steadily and significantly influenced the development of poetry.

And if there is some doubt about the import of this point of view, allow me—in order to show the gap it reveals between two kinds of poetry—to stop a moment and consider the English language.

What strikes me the most about English is its great aptitude for noting appearances, whether they be of human gestures or of things. A host of expressions allows one to grasp precisely and quickly the way in which the event—everything becomes event—proposes itself to immediate consciousness. And as a great number of words also express "realities" that apparently differ from other realities only by the slightest nuances—for us, this would be different appearances of the same essence—one quickly has the feeling that English seeks to describe what consciousness perceives, while avoiding any preconception about the final being of these referents. It may be true that languages are structures, but this is hardly felt in English! The words are there, so numerous, so unclassifiable, so difficult to define, and so elusive in their usage. Often as related by their form as they already are by their meaning, and without an obvious derivation or an etymology that could be called meaningful, they press against each other in opaque continuity, like the crystallizations of a dazzlingly beautiful substance—in fact, like the flashes of intelligibility extracted from a real that one has deliberately approached by empirical means. The power to photograph, so to speak, is boundless, but the capacity for hyperbole is less apparent; and yet, a few great essences—the sea, the bird, the springtime, which are at the universal heart of our relation to the world—are there to reveal the radiance of an epiphany, which they alone keep pure.

So, it is very probably from this tension that English poetry has drawn its remarkable energy. The consciousness of the One is alive here; this is what Blake's poetry proves with a violence and a clarity of purpose that have no equal in our own language. And it is Coleridge who has given us the most poetic definition of the Beautiful, asserting that Beauty is that by which the many becomes the One, even as it is perceived as the many.[5] From Marvell to Wordsworth to Hopkins, this prescience is constant. Yeats can oppose it only with rage, overwhelmed as he is by its irrefutable reality. But if poetic intention is the same in English as everywhere else, then, in order to develop, it will have to follow paths that, as one now perceives, will be unique to it alone—even if, in doing so, it were to provoke Voltaire's incomprehension. The contradictory metaphors, the images that were sketched and then abandoned, the interrupted verses, the obscurities, all this chaos by the "erratic" author of *King Lear*, what does it mean? Simply that Shakespeare wishes at one and the same time to interiorize the real (as *The Tempest* will come so close to accomplishing) and to preserve the richness of a language that has so many words to express the appearance of things. As a result, the assertions of the exterior consciousness are simultaneously silhouetted on

5. "The Beautiful is that in which the many still seen as many becomes one" (quoted in English by the author).

this stage and shown to be inadequate, like the figures of God in negative theologies. It was necessary for image to annul image so that the invisible could be felt.

Thus, in fact, Shakespeare's "barbarity," constitutes his greatest seriousness. And, evidently, it is the same paradox, the same 180-degree turn of the compass, that permits John Donne as well, though he is very different from Shakespeare, to lift up the stone of appearance in order to revive the absolute. One sees the absolute—a scandal for Racine almost as much as for Rimbaud—clinging to the anecdote, this "exterior" vision of human reality. But this is to show—such is the secret irony of Presence—that it is in our reaction to the inessential that our essence is revealed. It is also through existence, through being, that we must *by indirections find directions out*,[6] that is, by roundabout ways discover the way; and from this there are two consequences that ensue. On the one hand, English poetry enters the world of the relative, of meanings, of ordinary life, in a way almost unthinkable in the "most sublime" French poetry.* Its gaze at the object, at least at first, fixes on the outside appearances that our literary tradition refuses to see; for the inattentive reader it is sometimes hardly different from the gaze of the moralist, the humorist. But, on the other hand, placing itself at this common point and pursuing its own ends, poetry in English will all the more forcefully leave the mark of its difference and truth. Who has ever doubted that an English poetry exists?

But I will end these imprudent speculations here. I have offered them only to put into clearer relief the very different characteristics of French poetry.

From the outset, what seems to me obvious in our language is that its words connote for the most part not empirically determined appearances but entities seeming to exist in themselves as the props on which to hang attributes that different kinds of knowledge will have to determine and distinguish, unless—and, in fact, this is what we seem asked to believe—these attributes are already revealed in the idea of the thing. For example, we readily say "A spade is a spade" ("un chat est un chat"), and this proverb makes us think that there is a well-defined quiddity (*en-soi*), an autonomy, a permanence about the spade in a reality which thereby, and without much difficulty, becomes intelligible.

It follows that what is true in English of only a relatively limited number

---

6. These lines from *Hamlet* (II.i.66) are quoted in English by the author.

* Laforgue and Corbière, so admired in England and America, do create this kind of poetry, but only by resigning themselves to being "minor" poets. [Y.B.]

of words becomes in our language a kind of rule that tends to identify reality and reason and suggests beyond a doubt that in its structure language itself accurately reflects the Intelligible. This fundamental reality of our way of looking at words I shall call the *principle of identity*. I believe that it is profoundly accepted by the naive consciousness, for which the fact that a spade is a spade (and remains so and cannot be anything else) always seems so easily verifiable that one could not deny it, except through dishonest intentions. There is a moral corollary to the principle of identity, and it is the imperative that Boileau states—"I call a spade a spade" ("J'appelle un chat un chat")—but not without revealing almost in the same breath the dialectic of our language. From the primary evidence, two consequences follow and may appear to be in opposition. On the one hand, the intuition that there is an order to the world makes us want to preserve it and to be united with it: in French society we quickly and constantly rediscover the fundamental *word of identity*, barely transposed into oath, cry, or slogan. It is "*The king is dead, long live the king!*" of which, from the point of view of identity, a not very dissimilar variant is "*The Republic is one and indivisible.*" Like everything else that exists, institutions are perceived by the French as substances. But this sense of their being will by no means exclude a critical spirit and even a revolutionary project, since by its overall evidence the Intelligible can call into question those of its parts that have deteriorated.

Let us turn to our polemicists, and we will see that for them it is certainly not a question of empirically improving a state of society but rather of rediscovering the *true order* and of denouncing the lies that have succeeded in taking its place. Yes, this can only have been deception; intellectual error is not a convincing excuse, and we reject it. "Dissolute monks, leprous bigots, snail-like hypocrites, dissemblers, false zealots, debauched priests, self-indulgent friars, and other such sects of men, who disguise themselves like maskers to deceive the world!" Rabelais exclaims in *Pantagruel*. The order of being or of nature is obvious: to him who wants it, it is there for the taking. It will be necessary, therefore, to denounce continuously the liar, the "good apostle," the person interested in spreading confusion. And from the loyalty to essences represented by the "I call a spade a spade" will come as much an implacable psychological lucidity as the political necessity of *calling Rollet* [sic] *a scoundrel. . . .* [7]It is always the same equation, triumphantly solved. "*There is nothing like these Jesuits . . . ,*" Pascal writes, here pursuing

7. Rolet was a seventeenth-century lawyer and prosecutor who lived at the time of Nicolas Boileau, the poet and critic of French classicism. Rolet's dishonesty and lack of probity, for which he was severely punished in 1681, were so blatant that his name was used eponymously during his lifetime to designate any notorious thief or scoundrel, as in the expression, "He's a Rolet." He is remembered thanks to Boileau's celebrated, now proverbial, line: "J'appelle un chat un chat, et Rolet un fripon" ("I call a spade a spade, and Rolet a scoundrel").

the devil in one of his avatars, a devil who must have been up to his old tricks again, since what could only be clearly evident has for a moment been hidden from view.

But what meaning does the principle of identity have for poetry?

To answer this question I believe that I have to examine it again in a more historical way: for, if since Boileau or Voltaire it is associated—and if I must, from the outset, in order to simplify, also associate it—with a rational, potentially materialist vision, it is clear as well that from the very beginnings of French it has had to fluctuate in its apprehension of essences and has had to change its metaphysics.

In these beginnings, for example, who could doubt that order was experienced as a religious reality—that is to say, as an interior and even mysterious relation between forms of experience? If French is so forcefully dominated by the thought of identity, it is because as a late language it developed out of linguistic and social givens—the Latin language, Rome, Christianity—that were already clearly impregnated by the idea of a world order, with distinct essences well-established in the great chain of being and thereby all the more sacred. The priest who taught the Credo also taught essences. The belief that bread is the body of Christ may be conveyed only insofar as bread is already bread, which is to say, a clearly identified and stable reality and not some obscure and changing apparition indefinitely prone to taking on new forms. The fact remains, however, that this bread, if given its clear and distinct image, is experienced in God and under the sign of the One.

"*Clear is the night. . . .* "[8] This order is magnificently radiant in the *Chanson de Roland* where everything is simple, shadowless and perfectly mysterious. We are not surprised to discover this very "objective" decasyllabic line, whose four-initial feet firmly involve consciousness in the permanence of a knowledge, while the second part of the line, through its natural ternary rhythm, accepts human time in an act of sympathy but only in order to return it to the eternal. We are not even surprised that the poem is anonymous. When poetry becomes personal, it is because the individual, so far as he is concerned, has had to free himself from a collective forgetfulness of being, which is not initiated here. And we can observe finally that, by means of words opening themselves to presence, poetry as such, in contrast to other words, has as few distinctive signs as possible. The poetic line is undoubtedly necessary so that consciousness can find its

---

8. "Clere est la noit e la lune luisant" ("Clear is the night and the moon is shining") is the first line of *laisse* 184 of the Oxford text of *La Chanson de Roland*.

level of greatest importance. But beyond this, the simplest reality appears in its familiar expression and countenance. And the greatest poems of the French Middle Ages will perhaps be the plainest songs, where it is clear that the sacred can be experienced with astonishing familiarity and playfulness. Order, here, is given by the nightingale, figure of origin; by the garden, figure of place; by lovers, figures of the eternally renewed human effort toward Presence; by the "deceitful and jealous husband" (*le faulx-jaloux*), figure of the opposite of communion and sharing and expression of the possessive instinct by which the beloved is debased and transformed into an object. And all this is "natural," but not because one has dreamed of "nature" as later one will create it; rather, it is a question here of an experience of the whole which encompasses the sufferings and recognizes the limits of the human being, as illuminated by Christianity and as enlightened also by words.

Never better than in these poems could one glimpse how a language, by constructing itself, can construct a world and, by becoming transparent, reconcile us to the universe. From the Strasbourg oaths to *green boughs* (*la ramée*), to the *nightingale* (*l'oursegnol*), to *may songs* (*reverdies*),[9] what has grown within the substance of words is light. And I would like to assert that for my part I have always found French words, as they have grown in the past, to be half transparent, so much does the structure of the consonants (inherited from Latin with its air of erudition) seem to bear the faded imprint of an absolute root, while the vowels, which become apparent through this structure, are either like the shadows of tangible existence or, as in the case of the mute "e", like the light that comes from the One. Thus, it is in the deep spaces of the word, and not in some conventional form of expression, that the tension between finitude and presence can be resolved in a mysterious affinity. The word seems to suggest of itself the always virtual crystallization of being. Poetry can be made, as Mallarmé will say, from words. And it is this potion of furtive reflections that Rimbaud also contemplates when—at the end of his most exhausting decantations—in the new "songs" of a rediscovered communion he writes that eternity is the sea gone "with the sun."[10]

---

9. In the lyric poetry of the Middle Ages the *reverdie* was a song in which the poet celebrated the return of spring, the singing of the nightingale, and the greening of nature.

10. In the first and last stanzas of the poem "L'Eternité" of 1872, Rimbaud writes:

> *Elle est retrouvée.*
> *Quoi?—L'Eternité.*
> *C'est la mer allée*
> *Avec le soleil.*

> It is rediscovered.
> What?—Eternity.
> It is the sea gone
> With the sun.

I will say, therefore, that in these first moments of poetry in the French language, identity is at its highest point of substantial saturation, and that poetry is, in its almost invisible difference, above all a work of simplicity and seriousness. But in the original state of our language an ambiguity had already embedded itself, the consequences of which will be very grave. It is from Latin and its civilization that French received the vocabulary and syntax of an order. But, for all that, it did not receive along with this propensity for essences the legacy of a great myth that might explicitly designate earthly things as spiritual realities, since religion continued during all this time to express itself in the only existing language, Latin, and in terms of transcendence. So there ensued, first, the loss of a creative energy, since all theological or mystical minds had to abandon French; then, the absence of a belief that might lastingly ensure the sacred meaning of green leaves and the nightingale; and finally, even the condemnation, vigorously pursued, of the vestiges of paganism. All that could not but render extremely precarious, and in any event unprovable, this direct experience of the absolute in the French word.

And therein lies the ambiguity, and sometimes the drama, of our language. This principle of identity, which was so intensely experienced in medieval poetry as the axis of participation, as the certainty of being, has merit only because of an intuition that nothing in our tradition or knowledge justifies or evokes. Thus, it can at any moment lose its substantial virtue, which, in truth, it did very early on for a great many people. France could become the country of simple and rigid certainty, of "good sense." The French gaze could find satisfaction in a certain, almost shadowless picture, in which objects are clearly visible in their logical relationships and are few in number (relatively speaking), because they were carefully drawn within lines rigidly enclosing them.

But—conversely and in a totally sudden way—this picture, or one of its variants, which I will soon describe, becomes for certain minds enigmatic and nearly terrifying.

This is a fact to which Rimbaud par excellence bears witness, and, recalling the emergence and evolution of the initial gaze at the salamander, I should like now to speak about the considerable importance of some of the notations of "Alchimie du verbe" for the understanding of poetry, of French poetry, that is. In the "Lettre du voyant" Rimbaud had already with the greatest violence condemned the entire poetic tradition, and it is quite evident that he blamed it for this simple, inharmonic clarity about which I spoke a moment ago. In "Alchimie du verbe" he says, in this vein, that "he found laughable the celebrated figures of modern painting and poetry"—

but he adds, as if to counterbalance his assertion: "I liked stupid paintings, the upper parts of doors, stage scenery, canvas backdrops for acrobats, signs, popular prints in color, old-fashioned literature, church Latin, erotic books deficient in spelling, novels of our ancestors, fairytales, little books of childhood, old operas, foolish refrains, naive rhythms." And further on, he writes: "Poetic obsolescence played a considerable part in my alchemy of the Word." And finally: "The title of a light comedy caused terrors to rise up before me." We can well imagine what these readings might have been. In the country of Favart, of Mme de Ségur—can I add, of Raymond Roussel?—all of us have encountered these stories and these descriptions, in which, because the power of intelligence presented is weak, the picture of the world is reduced to a few realities, in principle simple and obvious, but so schematic, so devoid of contrast, that a fascination is in effect revealed, and, I will even say, a strange hope comes into play. Now, here is how I understand this feeling of "being on fire," this presentiment of metamorphosis. These essences, so poorly developed and so reduced in number, are seemingly stripped of the usual system of reciprocal relations—of what one could call the "depth" of conceptual description. It follows that the things these essences show reappear there before us in this "quiddity" (*en-soi*) that the concept appropriates, wears, conceals; and they reappear in the same way that, presently, in one's glimpse of the salamander one will vaguely sense the surging forth of a presence, either auspicious or inauspicious, along with "the terror" that the proximity of the sacred awakens in consciousness. In short, the mediocre text or the weak image has played the same role as the object that is *seen* suddenly, either before its meaning hides it from view or as soon as this meaning, once disintegrated, abandons it. And for an adolescent, lost here or there in the desert of the concept, all of external identity at its most empty is abruptly transformed. As for me, I felt during my childhood "the terror" of those gardens that are aptly called "French": a clarity possessed of frightening internal forces. And now I understand quite well that it was above all an event of language that transpired there. Yes, it is in a single stroke, invisibly, sometimes at the moment a simple word or a name is uttered, that absolute identity surpasses conceptual identity—that the spirit that leads toward poetry begins anew.

Moreover, it would be worthwhile for the historian to study it again from this point of view, replacing the usual descriptions of the chains of influence or of the supposed meaning of themes with an examination of the tensions that oppose or render dialectical the intuition of presence and the necessities of the concept. Thus, the same Rimbaud who, in his "delirium," which is simply the rejection of conceptual identity, wanted to see a

mosque in the place of a factory, a drawing room at the bottom of a lake—
that is to say, the other through the same—ends up in the poem "Brux-
elles"—where in a single stroke he comes close to achieving immediacy—
by declaring apropos of reality that "It is too beautiful!" which one must
take to mean that "It is too present!" Poetic modernity in every period has
its origin in this return that frees the object from hackneyed rhetoric. It is
true that poetry moves in advance of action,[11] since it is the power by which
the concept that governs action is depleted and renewed.

But it is, above all, in itself that poetry born of "terror," French poetry, is
an act, and this is how I understand it. First of all, because of the very fact
that in its absolute gaze poetry initiates the appearance of presence; it does
not have to demonstrate it, to express it through myths—it does not even
have time for this—it is compelled only to live it. And immediately, there-
fore, it is the effort by which, in the midst of "things-as-nullities," poetry
will attempt to dwell in the light of being and thus assimilate it to the
realities of a destiny. I believe that the poetry of a language of essences, like
French, has therefore, as its most urgent task the constituting or the re-
discovery of the profound, infraconceptual order at the heart of which the
poet can live his being as presence, having verified analogies, having undone
impenetrable appearances, having reopened the path that leads inward.
This is a matter of discontinuous, silent experiences, but from them will
emanate the energy that enables a few important, revitalized words to exist
together and to open themselves to endless rays of light. And the true
subject of the poem is a life that recovers its form—a finitude that becomes
limitless. As far as meaning is concerned, one is well aware of its ambigu-
ities, considering the importance of this enterprise. Sometimes, it is true,
the author of a poem has *spoken* a sensation, has formulated an idea. And one
could discern there a will either to describe what exists or to express what
one is. But, in fact, of what is it a question here? Of evoking in a savor the
deeper savor of the unity one desires. Of summoning in the palpable fruit
the supreme fruit. Of loving; or, again, of refusing—as in an act of purifica-
tion—to serve the interests of nothingness. Poetry is an oath that both
differentiates and confirms itself in the textures of spoken things. It is that
which *brings together*, like the mason who selects his stones—and who can
certainly comment on them, or even speak about them, apparently at ran-
dom, but against the background of the silence where he already sees the
emergence of the future threshold.

And as the mason demarcates the place of life, at first abstract, so the
poet, reenacting the ancient beginnings of the word—of the word as *found-*

---

11. In "La Lettre du voyant" Rimbaud writes, "Poetry will no longer give rhythm to
action; it *will be in advance.*"

ing act—changes Presence in building his poem, so as to rediscover reason, that site in the Universe of the most humble realities. It is frequently said that English poetry "begins with a flea and ends in God." I would say that French poetry moves in the opposite direction and begins "in God," whenever possible, only to end up by loving the most inconsequential thing.

But I would not want to close without anticipating some objections.

I imagine, first, that the reader, if he has followed me up until now, must be surprised by a definition of poetry where not much place seems to be given to the subject with which I began: the aversions and impatiences of Rimbaud and Baudelaire that so many other poets can identify with, because of the suffering, and sometimes the doubt or the despair. What does this reconciliation with the real or this "poetically inhabited" earth have to do with Vigny's scorn, Verlaine's renunciations, Antonin Artaud's cries of horror? When Baudelaire, stricken with aphasia, is brought back to Paris and sees Asselineau, who had come to meet him at the train station, he lets out a long, shrill laugh; Asselineau is frozen with terror. Does one find in that, and in the *cré nom* of the final months,[12] the plenitudinous silence to which the greatest perhaps of our poets would certainly have been entitled, according to my definition? And despite everything, if the French language, in its ever so formidable essentialism, holds the key to the idea of what is sacred and ordered, how is it that our country gives the world its most celebrated *poètes maudits*?

I fear, in fact, not having sufficiently emphasized—and not only in what has preceded (which can be easily corrected) but at other times as well— that in this movement toward unity there is, alas, nothing idyllic, nothing determined, nothing that could even imagine being freed from a false life, nothing that could put its faith in dreams. To interiorize the real does not mean bypassing what prevents us from living; rather, we must reduce or

---

12. On July 2, 1866, after two-and-a-half years of self-imposed exile in Belgium, Baudelaire returned to Paris. Since the previous spring a series of strokes had completely robbed him of the power of speech, except for two words, *sacré nom* (an oath not unlike "goddamn it" in English), frequently abbreviated and pronounced as *cré nom*. Until his death in August 1867, these were to be the only words Baudelaire spoke. "With these two words," writes Enid Starkie in her biography of the poet, "he who had loved and practised the art of conversation was obliged to express the whole gamut of his feelings and thoughts—joy, sorrow, anger and impatience—and he used sometimes to fly into a rage at his inability to make his meaning clear, and to answer those who spoke to him" (*Baudelaire* [Norfolk, Conn.: New Directions, 1958], p. 512). Thus, it is with a shrill and tragic laugh that the mute Baudelaire, having no other audible means of expression, greets his closest friend, Asselineau, at the Paris train station.

transmute it. And often fire does not catch in such intractable matter, especially considering that the alienation of the other is intimately involved with ours, and it will therefore be necessary—an undoubtedly impossible task—to clarify both at one fell swoop. Poetry, or the remission it brings, is not a form of repose. What value would poetry have, for example, without union or justice? And does it not raise questions about the enigma of evil, which its own intuition cannot answer? This can be seen in Rimbaud: "I want freedom in salvation," he writes. We must take this to mean: the right to uphold my values, which are equality and justice, in the very experience of Presence. And this contradiction is not readily forgotten—as Hugo's work reveals—in a language where the universal can show that it is as much the universality of right as that of being. French has no words for evil: nothing except abstract expressions that already rationalize it. Yet, the existence of evil will for that reason alone be all the more harshly felt. It can prevent the French from finding happiness.

In truth, the word that seems to me to lend itself best to defining our poetry, in its sudden depth, in its hindered momentum, is *contre-jour*. For the light I am talking about will be discovered in the darkest poetry, in images of "vibrant violins," of "child days." Yet, the world of dissociation and evil remains present to cast a shadow; and so it is in this *clair-obscur* that wanderings and fits of anger occur—an order simultaneously building and demolishing itself in the often proclaimed persistence of hope. "Can one light up a black and muddy sky?" Baudelaire asks, while Rimbaud writes: "And at dawn, with a burning patience we will enter the shining cities." The metaphor of the *spiritual dawn* is common among French poets. It aptly corresponds to this gleam, this *luster* of language. And if it rarely has the chance to transform itself into the truth of noontide, except perhaps through dream—or maybe through deceptive illusion—it is sometimes possible for it to be recognized in that most ardent *contre-jour*, the red light of evening.

The other remark I will make will relate to what I had earlier called the *flaw* inherent in poetry. Perhaps in reading the preceding pages, one will think that I was not sufficiently concerned about it or that I consider it absent from French poetry. That is not the case, and I will even say that, to my way of thinking, this "flaw" is more common in our language than in many others. This is because, if in the words we use there is this virtuality of presence, this great hope, it will therefore follow that we will speak under this sign, as if intoxicated, without having critically examined, as we should, our experience of things. To name the tree too easily is to risk remaining captive of a weak image of the tree, or in any case of an abstract one, which in the space of the absolute could only grow from one of the inadvertently remembered appearances of the object. And thus, Presence is no longer envisioned except as a fabulous unfolding of this appearance, as a profusion of marble. No longer anything but a décor, from which the *I* also is absent, it is soon nothing more than a convention and the refashioning of a rhetoric. This is what Romeo unknowingly reveals when he thinks he is in love with the "beautiful" Rosalind, the symbol of appearance, of what one has imagined and not experienced, and of the object that disappears, therefore, beneath the myth. Fortunately, he has Mercutio close by—Mercutio, that incarnation of the English language—to remind him of the obligations of "triviality."

French poetry has no Mercutio. In our language it falls to the poet alone to regain self-control in this beauty of words where so often he has placed the ghost of things. And our poetry also has, as a dimension of its history and diversity, moments of deviation and return. Some—the moments of recovery—are found in Baudelaire's "Le Cygne," in Rimbaud's "L'Eternité." The others, sustained by pride, are found in Racine's tragedy, in Mallarmé's "pure idea." Between the *exterior* identity of good sense and the *interior* identity of presence, there was for a long time—from, let's say, the poets of the Pléiade to Paul Valéry—this proud and very alluring appearance of the flaw: the claim of the Idea to be its own proof and the illusory materiality of the dream's figure.

Translated by Richard Stamelman

11 Translating Poetry[1]

YOU CAN TRANSLATE by simply declaring one poem the translation of another. For example, Wladimir Weidlé once jokingly said to me that Baudelaire's poem, "Je n'ai pas oublié, voisine de la ville . . . ," renders the *sound* of Pushkin: it has his clarity, it is the "best" translation of him. But is it possible to reduce a poem to its clarity?

The answer to the question, "Can one translate a poem?" is of course no. The translator meets too many contradictions that he cannot eliminate; he must make too many sacrifices.

For example (drawing on my own experience), Yeats's "Sailing to Byzantium": straightaway, the title presents a problem. "L'Embarquement pour Byzance"? Inconceivable. Watteau would get in the way. What's more, "sailing" has the energy of a verb. Baudelaire's "A Honfleur! Le plus tôt possible avant de tomber plus bas" comes to mind, but"A Byzance" would be ridiculous: the myth rules out such brevities. . . . Finally, "to sail" makes one think not only of departure but also of the sea to be crossed—difficult, troubled like passion—and the distant port: commerce, labor, works, the conquest of nature, spirit. None of the things *appareiller* might convey, and *faire voile* isn't strong enough over these distances. I resigned myself to "Byzance—l'autre rive." A certain tension is perhaps salvaged but not the energy, the (at least unconscious) wrenching away that the verb expresses. As so often when we pass from the language of Shakespeare to French, still subject as it is to the harsh restrictions Malherbe imposed on it, lived experience is transformed into the timeless and the irrational into the intelligible. Another solution might be to gloss the title with Baudelaire's phrase. Then it would be necessary to experiment with open-ended translation (*traductions developpées*): one would allow into play all the associations of ideas called up by the work, laid out on the page like Mallarmé's "Coup

1. "Translating Poetry" ("La Traduction de la poésie") was first given as a lecture in Paris to the *Association des traducteurs littéraires de France* in 1976. The essay was then published in *Entretiens sur la poésie*. The English translation by John Alexander and Clive Wilmer was originally published in *PN Review* 48 (1985), the "Special Cambridge Poetry Festival Issue." Slight revisions have been made for the present volume.

de dés." But Yeats is *speaking* of the moment—unique, urgent—and one must be faithful to that too.

In the same poem, another sacrifice that can't be avoided: "fish, flesh, and fowl." Yeats crams the variousness of life into three words—its energy, its seeming finality—and does so above all by means of alliteration. Already quite a problem!—but worse is to come. The expression is ready-made, which is why we can dream—and taking it up into the poem suggests this—that everyday language preserves a little of the primordial language, fundamental and transparent, whose return or advent so many poets have longed for. "Sailing to Byzantium" is therefore concerned with the folk wisdom of the race and the here and now, at the very moment when it is a matter of tearing away from these things toward pure spirit. This is a paradox, which in Yeats is profound and ever present, but one that is necessarily lost in French where a comparable concision is not possible: the "felicities" of languages do not coincide. I translated it "tout ce qui nage, vole, s'élance," which retains that vitality in the sense but not in the substance of the words. What is more, the verb form in this instance is weaker than the nouns— "fish, flesh, and fowl"—which seem to repeat the first divine bestowal of names. Where a text has its felicities (accidental or not), its cruxes, its density—its unconscious—the translation must stick to the surface, even if its own cruxes crop up elsewhere. You can't translate a poem.

But that's all to the good, since a poem is less than poetry, and to the extent that one is denied something of the former the effect can be stimulating to the latter. A poem, a certain number of words in a certain order on the page, is a *form*, where all relation to what is other and finite—to what is true—has been suspended. And the author may take pleasure in this: it's satisfying; one likes to bring things into being, things that endure, but one readily regrets having set oneself at odds with the place and time of true reciprocity. The poem is a means, a spiritual statement, which is not, however, an end. Publication puts it to the test: it is a time for reflection which one allows oneself, but this is not to settle for it, to make it hard and fast. And, of course, the best reader is similarly the one who cares for the poem: not as one cares for a being but in response to the irreducible content it addresses, to the *meaning* it bears. Let's neither make an idol of the written page, nor, still less, regard it with that iconoclastic distaste that is inverted idolatry. At its most intense, reading is empathy, shared existence. And, in a sense, how disturbing that is! All that textual richness—ambiguities, wordplay, layers of meaning, etc.—denied the privilege of obliging us to solve their crossword puzzles. In their place, darkness and dull care. I will be reproached for impoverishing the text.

What we gain, however, by way of compensation, is the very thing we cannot grasp or hold: that is to say, the poetry of other languages.

We should in fact come to see what motivates the poem; to relive the act which both gave rise to it and remains enmeshed in it; and released from that fixed form, which is merely its trace, the first intention and intuition (let us say a yearning, an obsession, something universal) can be tried out anew in the other language. The exercise will now be the more genuine because the same difficulty manifests itself: that is to say, as in the original, the language (*langue*) of translation paralyzes the actual, tentative utterance (*parole*). For the difficulty of poetry is that language (*langue*) is a *system*, while the specific utterance (*parole*) is *presence*. But to understand this is to find oneself back with the author one is translating; it is to see more clearly the duress that bears on him, the maneuvers of thought he deploys against it; and the fidelities that bind him. For words will try to entice us into behaving as they do. Once a good translation has been set in motion, they will rapidly begin to justify the bad poem it turns into, and they will impoverish the experience for the sake of constructing a text. The translator needs to be on his guard and to test the ontological necessity of his new images even more than their term-for-term (and therefore external) resemblance to those of the original poem. This is uphill work, but the translator is rewarded by his author, if it's Yeats, if it's Donne, if it's Shakespeare. And instead of being, as before, up against the body of a text, he finds himself at the source, a beginning rich with possibility, and on this second journey he has the right to be himself. A creative act, in short! Playing tricks with the lacunae of his language, tinkering (*bricoler*), to use the fashionable word, he now finds himself reexperiencing the restrictions first encountered by his author, insofar as he attends to what the author learned from them: which is to say that you must live before you write. You must realize that the poem is nothing and that translation is possible—which is not to say that it's easy; it is merely poetry re-begun.

Isn't this all out of proportion though, laying claim to a power of invention comparable to Yeats's in order to get back in this way to the source of his poem? But to put yourself forward is not to imply that you feel assured of success. The writing of poetry is invariably ambitious, and, even for the real poet, this ambition must proceed in uncertainty. There is no poetry but that which is impossible. And to fail, let us say, over certain specific details at least leaves one room to attend to unity, or transparency—and destiny.

Indeed, practically, if the translation is not a crib, nor mere technique, but an enquiry and an experiment, it can only inscribe itself—write itself—in the course of a life; it will draw upon that life in all its aspects, all its actions. This does not mean that the translator need be in other respects a "poet." But it definitely implies that if he is himself a writer he will be unable to keep his translating separate from his own work.

Some examples of this interdependence—personal ones, since they are nothing to pride oneself on (nor to be alarmed at: discrete fragments, with no value except as tokens).

Horatio, talking to Hamlet about his companions of the watch after the ghost has appeared. They were "distilled," he says, "almost to jelly with the act of fear. . . . " The meaning is clear. But "the act of fear" introduces an intensity that is tragic, in which context "jelly" (literally gelatine—so English—in French, *bouillie*) seemed to me problematic. Why? The obscenities at the beginning of *Romeo* are translatable. But an obscenity is a pointed linguistic device, clear-cut and self-contained, while here "jelly" is everyday speech used without special care and not charged with meaning. Now I think my tendency here is very French: given such contexts, which are after all tragic and exemplary, I want a heightened consciousness and, accordingly, an economy of meaning, and so too a vocabulary if not restrained at least tried and tested. Of course, vulgarity must have its place, but simply *as* vulgarity—think of Rabelais and Rimbaud—and here I am at one again with Racine or Nerval and what is called elevated, or literary, language, but which is no more than language at its tautest, most highly serious. The English (look at Mercutio) expect less from language. They want direct observation and uncomplicated psychology (in short, "jelly" where a soldier would say it) rather than heroic reconstruction.

And I admit they're right. But while I am thus undecided, should I meet the challenge without more ado and speak of *la bouillie*, or even of *l'eau de boudin*? It would cost me almost nothing to be literal. But if it's true that, even in accepting this, I remain however slightly the disciple of Racine, it's also true that what looks like accuracy will lead to quaintness. This is the vice of Romantic translation—badly hewn from an earlier rhetoric—which always seems to me to evade the problem without resolving it. Even Duçis[2] would be better than that! Better still, listen to Shakespeare until I can anticipate him in all my own writing and not merely mirror him. And meanwhile, with full knowledge of the case (I will add a note), translate "jelly" with my own word, derived from another set of associations: *cendre* ("ash"). . . . Locally, the translation fails. But the act of translating has begun and will be concluded later elsewhere—that is, still *here*.

And now back to Yeats again, to "The Sorrow of Love," where he says of

2. Jean-François Duçis (1733–1816) was a dramatist who adapted five Shakespeare tragedies for the French stage. According to the *Oxford Companion to French Literature*, the adaptations were "feeble": "To suit French taste he introduced confidants in the classical manner, and provided *Othello* with an alternative ending in which Othello discovers his mistake in time and does not murder Desdemona."

the girl with "red mournful lips" that she is "doomed like Odysseus and the labouring ships." "Labouring": the word conjures up long, difficult sea crossings and the rolling of the ship, but also emotional distress and grief—not to mention "to be in labour," that is, the process of giving birth. Not to mention, either, that the archaic sense of *labourer*—that is virtually *ensemencer* ("to sow")—is still current. All these senses have weight here, so what is to be done? But this time I wasn't even able to ask myself the question; irresistibly I translated "labouring" with *qui boitent / au loin*, thereby immediately rejecting some of the senses in my translation. And I would be equally able to justify or criticize these words: Odysseus did not flee, the children of Priam did—in quest of another Troy—and the death of Priam occurs in the next line. But that's not the point here. For these words did not come to me by the short circuiting that people think of as running from text to translation by way of the translator. They came by a more roundabout route that took in my own past. I've often thought about the limping of a ship. . . . Once even, coming back from Greece in 1961, with my heart full of the memory of the Sphinx of Naxos, whose smile expresses ataraxy, that music, I imagined that the boat—labouring in just this way, by night, off the coast of Italy—was itself fleeing and searching. With Verlaine at the back of my mind, I sketched out a kind of poem, in which the ever-rolling sea also played its part, "comme du fer, dans une caisse close" ("like iron in a closed chest"): a poem I've never since completed—and which, twelve years later, on an impulse, I tore up to give life to my translation. The relationship between what was there feeling its way and my concern with the poetry of Yeats became the most important, the true development. It was the English-speaking poet who explained me to myself, and my own personal experience that imposed the translation upon me. It is in the sympathy of destiny for destiny, in short, and not of an English phrase for a French one, that translations unfold, with lasting consequences one cannot foresee (the boat and its limping appeared in my last book).

Following the logic of these remarks, I ought now to ask myself how my translations have fed back into my own poetry; and how the poetry of other languages has contributed to the development of ours.

For want of time, I will do no more than raise another preliminary question. Under what circumstances is this type of translation, the translation of poetry, not completely mad? "Translate poets who are close to you," I once suggested. But what poet can be close enough?

The irony of Donne, the luminous melancholy of Eliot—or Baudelairean spleen, or Rimbaud's *mauvaiseté* (and always, too, his hope)—are they not impenetrable worlds? And as for Yeats—the aspiration toward the Idea, toward Byzantium, on the one hand, but on the other "blood and mire," both mud and ecstasy, even the fury of passion, and Adonis as well as Christ—can that be shared?

But in poetry, necessity is the mother of invention. What one has not tried is sometimes repressed, and translation, when a great poet speaks to us, can bypass censorship—this is part of the feedback which, as I was saying, the translated work may generate. An energy is released. So let us follow where it leads. But let us follow only this. If a work does not compel us, it is untranslatable.

Translated by John Alexander and Clive Wilmer

12 The Origins and Development of My Concept of Poetry: An Interview with John E. Jackson (1976)[1]

Yves Bonnefoy, I am particularly interested in understanding how you went from Surrealist writing, which you practiced for awhile, to a very different use of the image in the poems of Douve[2]

The image is what had touched me most especially and right from the beginning, in Surrealist works—both in poetry and in painting. All the more so, probably, because I had not yet really seen anything of what greater poets or painters had been able to do or were still doing with appearance, how they discovered—as I learned later—an entirely different kind of intensity in appearance, the intensity of evidence, of the simple. In fact, my interest in Surrealism developed while I was still a *lycée* student in my provincial city, where what does not attract attention, where what is perpetuated without any real becoming, and without unsettling any established habit, was the law—and where the bookstores were empty. One day, my philosophy teacher, a very young man who had frequented a few avant-garde groups in Paris, just before the war scattered everybody, lent me a copy of Georges Hugnet's *Petite Anthologie du Surréalisme*, and there I discovered, in one fell swoop, the poems of Breton, of Péret, of Eluard, the superb verbal masses of Tzara in his Dadaist period, and Chirico's *Mystère et mélancolie d'une rue*—a real thunderbolt—and Giacometti's *Boule Suspendue*, the collages of Max Ernst and the paintings of Tanguy, the first Mirós: in short, a whole world. I was immediately fascinated and felt as though summoned—precisely by the strange situations in these works, the unimagined objects, the altered aspect of things; in a word, by what is called the image, in Surrealism, even if it is in fact a denial of coherent representation. "If only there were sun tonight," I read, and it seemed to me that a road whose presence I had not even imagined opened in front of me, in this night I recognized as my own, and as deep as ever, but now suddenly murmuring,

1. The interview with John E. Jackson first appeared in the review *L'Arc* 66 (October 1976). It was reprinted in *Entretiens sur la poésie*, at which time it was followed by an important sequel titled "Lettre à John E. Jackson."

2. *Du Mouvement et de l'immobilité de Douve* (*On the Motion and Immobility of Douve*), Bonnefoy's first major book of poetry, published in 1953.

initiatory—the first step toward the first true light. . . . And yet, I should like to emphasize that for quite some time my adherence to these intuitions and momentary visions, exalted as it was at the time, was not in the least exclusive; I was reading other poets, for example, Valéry, and, what is more, I loved the sky's and the sea's identity with themselves in "Le Cimetière marin," the heat without anything in the background, the sparkling light in which dreams are dispelled. Was it simple incoherence, or were these needs, and each one true, which I would have to synthesize? In any case, it was only later that I became a militant, with all the seemingly ferocious exclusions that word implies.

Was there a new and specific occasion that led to this more radical commitment?

No, unless it was the state of mind that prevailed after the Liberation, that mixture of vague hope and ideological naiveté, with all the side-taking, all the regrouping it caused, and all the bad poems as well, over-loaded with fine sentiments that had become clichés, that had become, in fact, wretched, unbearable images. There was much in all that to refuse, especially for one who instinctively associated the idea of poetry with an intensification of consciousness and of speech, whatever its values and principles in other respects; and there was also the temptation to take sides oneself, to bring—for the second time, since there had been those writings of the Resistance, but this time on the true plane—the writing of poetry into contact with collective preoccupations, and it was the Surrealist tendency in me that profited from this ambition when I came to Paris, since Surrealism had spoken so often of revolutions in the domain of the spirit; and so I founded what was, it goes without saying, a very slim review[3] which also encouraged peremptory judgments from me. In addition, I met some former members of the group right away, people like Victor Brauner, for instance, who was one of the greatest, and then in 1946 I met Breton, just after his return from the United States—and here were examples of uncompromisingness and of vigilance the high quality of which scarcely incited me to question what these men affirmed, the one so simply, the other so haughtily still, despite his obvious sadness, and enveloped in the aura of legend created by the distance of those five years of interruption and exile. But my fidelity to the movement was not without contradictions, even in this second phase. In fact, as much as I saw myself, and felt myself to be violently Surrealist in my publications and in my writing, I still remained at a certain distance from the group which had re-formed around Breton. I did not associate with his young friends; I did not invite them to publish in my review (nor Breton for that matter, but in his case it was out of admiration; I

3. *La Révolution la nuit.*

thought him too great a figure for the review, at least in the beginning); and on the other hand I had friendships, for example, with Christian Dotremont, among the far more independent, more ironic members of the Belgian group, which was always very distinct from the one in Paris, and which Breton was coming to appreciate less and less. I also saw a great deal of Gilbert Lely, himself a friend of the Surrealists but not devoted to them, and he encouraged me to make judgments. As for my personal relations with Breton, well, for some reason they ended abruptly. I admired him, as I have said. Hadn't he written *Les vases communicants*, *L'Amour fou*? These I preferred to *Nadja*, which had disappointed me, and to the poems of *Revolver*, which I had tried to force myself to like—but there was also *Pleine marge*, his masterpiece. All the same, something about him sent a chill through me, with all his distant courtesy, "attentive" to me as he said, but somewhat taken aback and clearly on his guard: probably I had a sullen air which he must have taken as a sign of antipathy. On the whole, I must have passed for a rather marginal member of the group, and when the day came, just before the exhibition of 1947, when I refused to sign the manifesto of that moment, which, as it turned out, was called "Rupture inaugurale," everything just ended, without any of the dramatics of disappointed hope. As we left the café, Breton simply made no effort to shake my hand; there was neither exclusion nor insult.

For what reasons did you refuse to sign "Rupture inaugurale"?

For a reason that will surprise you and that no longer has the slightest merit in my eyes. Despite a great many pages that André Breton had written, and on the strength rather of a few solemn declarations that had come down to us from the group's past, I imagined that Surrealism was exactly the opposite of any occultism; in other words, that it only intended to reveal the riches of the world that strikes our senses, and of the life that might be led there, without any belief in hidden powers. It is true that the Surrealists had called upon the Dalai-Lama during the twenties, but they had subsequently declared themselves Hegelians and even Marxists, which mattered to me because I came to poetry from a region of thought dominated by my earlier study of mathematics and the history of science, interests I still pursued to some degree—and of formal logic whose difficult relation to the dialectical method we were taught to revere had already caused me enough real concern. This being the case, to see Breton and his new friends become enthusiastic about magic, and make Leonie Aubois d'Ashby into a sort of demon, preparing to raise an altar to her at the next exhibition, was disconcerting, and all the more so in that I was not myself without an elective fondness for certain concrete forms—we can come back to this—of ancient thought and religious speculation. I loved the Alexandrian sects that Georges Bataille's study, among others, had revealed to me—the one about Gnostic intaglios, in *Documents*, the most beautiful review of the period between the two wars—and I was ready to accept the Osiris, the "black god" spoken of in *Arcane 17*, out of affection for the Pharaonic period. Caught between a kind of spontaneous materialism, which has remained natural to me, and an innate concern with transcendence, a deep interest in the categories and even the myths that give expression to it, I had to find an acceptable compromise; and incapable as I still was of understanding what could form this compromise, I had at least decided that it must exclude belief systems and repatriate all the experience of the old correspondences, all the fantasies of occult powers, into an ontology, simply, and the pure act of poetry.

Isn't this relation of Surrealism to science—and it does seem a contradiction—what you were already trying to clarify in the page from 1945, entitled "La Nouvelle Objectivité," which appeared in the first issue of La Révolution la nuit?

Yes, and the notion, which seemed most important to me from this point of view, was certainly that of the object, since it had become as problematical in the new physics, after Heisenberg's discoveries, as it was central to Breton, who had invented the Surrealist object and had involved his entire group with it. I was struck by the fact that modern knowledge, founded on atomic physics or on biology, passes across the level of the objects of our existence without really seeing them—the objects our eye perceives, the objects we can love and which can help us to live—while ancient science knew how to keep hold of everything, charging everything with meaning in the network of correspondences. And what I valued, on the contrary, in Surrealist poetics, which loves unexpected discoveries, coincidences, encounters, is that this poetics was supremely attentive—think of Breton wandering through Paris in his great prose works—to those thousand things, at once furtive and insistent, that earlier poetry had never sought to question, even during the Symbolist period, had not even suspected. To my way of thinking, here was a compensatory practice which was historically necessary and already highly effective, and which had to be thought through, deepened, but, as I have said, without once again falling into fantasies of magic which could only reseal the forces at work in the infraconsciousness. This being said, "La Nouvelle Objectivité," as far as I can remember, was only a very confused intuition, written furthermore in just a few lines, that lacked some important additional categories which only came to me a little later. For instance, if I were still interested in pursuing the question, the idea of presence would enable me, I think, to more precisely define the relation of Surrealism to scientific thought, or let us say to thought that concerns itself with the object as such; in other words, to thought that does not unduly existentialize our material environment, our earthly place. Today I would say that there isn't a real and a surreal, the one structured and overemphasized by science, the other overflowing science with its irrational characteristics, which can only be perceived by the "primitive eye"—this could lead me to despise the table on which I write, the amorphous stone in the ravines, in favor of the lyrebird—but rather the sense of *presence* that imposes itself at times in the face of the transitory signifieds of conceptual thought. And this is how I might establish my differences and my detachment from Surrealism, recognizing of course that I loved the Surrealist object and the image in which it appears, for a certain intuition that projected it, an intuition of its presence, thanks to which the object is there in front of us, resistant to all analysis, one might even say conscious—but that the Surrealist approach to reality through presence is also as if deformed, and so deprived of its virtue.

I see that we have reached the heart of your attitude toward Surrealism, in which one can sense both an attachment and a refusal. . . .

I will now in any case be better able to tell you what Surrealism brought me, and if you will let me, I will give you an example which could be taken from Chirico—since you seemed to want to know why I was so fond of his work—but which I will take instead from Max Ernst, because I have a very precise memory of the encounter I want to describe. In Hugnet's *Anthology*, there is a collage by Ernst, taken from *La Semaine de bonté*, a collage that shows a young girl bound and gagged beneath a yellow light bulb in the compartment of a train at night. Around her are the other passengers, who have the heads of lions. And one can feel her terror, which clearly goes beyond the danger to her life, if there is a danger to her life, and which rather bears on the most fundamental relationship one can have with the real, the one that reveals to us the alien character of the world, transcending all our representations and thus throwing us back into nothingness. This said, if Max Ernst's image arouses us to such an immediate sense of metaphysical horror, it is because the artist, who was a great poet in this respect, has taken as elements of his collage the kind of woodcuts found in the *Magasin pittoresque* in which very practiced, fast-working engravers— they had to finish their work by dawn like the modern journalist—were able to evoke current events or far away places just as the newspaper photographs would soon do in their place. In the line or the play of light and dark there is already the camera's vision which simply registers things without knowing anything of their significance or of the symbols which coordinate them for us, and which even the most pessimistic painting of earlier times had noted instinctively in its representation of the world, thus bringing us a sense of peace. All that Max Ernst did with his collages was to make explicit and dramatic a perception he found, diffuse but deeply rooted, in the prints he loved, an intuition still only in latent form there, but which it was going to become easier and easier to develop—with horror or with anguish—in the period of dying theology, and that one might call the experience of nothingness—very precisely that and nothing else—since when things, when beings no longer speak to us, no longer collaborate with us, it is our faith in ourselves that, in the collapse of meaning vanishes too, unless we think of ourselves simply as exiles groping in a universe of shadows. And for my part, there had certainly been enough empty houses in my childhood—enough petrified alcoves haunting the immobility of houses in the country that had long been closed up, and enough old magazines as well, the ones from the end of the last century, whose scenes, convulsed in the gaslight, I would study in the attic—for this way of looking at things to seem natural to me the moment it was put forward by the Surrealist poets, and for me to be moved by these icons of blackness, for them to show me to myself, suddenly, and with a real disquiet. It should be noted that such thoughts about being, especially signified so directly, didn't exist in the art and poetry that were the most widely accepted, the only ones I was aware of in 1942 or 1943. Surrealism, on the other hand, was nothing but that, paintings and poems both, and this is what led me to try to designate my experience with some of these ideas and to refer to these kinds of apparition as "object" or surreal quality, as Surrealism itself did, with all the vague hope that, despite everything, one puts into such words. But with richer categories—and this example is meant to lead me to them—I could have more readily understood that the gagged look of the nocturnal train, that increase in intensity perceived in the object that a moment before we were still seeing absentmindedly—but a negative intensity if I might so put it (the Surrealists loved the word *black* which gave such apt expression to this negative luminosity)—this was not the revelation of richness dwelling behind sensory experience and unperceived by our ordinary reason but rather what I would call *la mauvaise présence*, a spectral presence under whose influence what is seems to fall into absence at the very moment it appears before our eyes and to shut itself off from our reading of it—so that we must seek, beyond the night it casts about us, some shore where meaning—and this is the new idea, the essential one—might reemerge in simple things, assuring each one a place, a reason for being, in the unity that is more than being, that is in itself the light.

Where did you find these categories you speak of, that are different in the final analysis from what Surrealism has to offer but that allowed you to decipher it?

It is difficult, I must say in passing, to go back as we are doing to earlier periods, even and perhaps especially if it is a question of what mattered the most in the formation of our way of thinking. I don't keep a journal; I note nothing of what was; I forget a great deal. And so I run the risk of revising, on the basis of my present values, what I once lived in a confused and contradictory fashion and with perhaps other tendencies I misunderstand now or even repress. Dream sometimes likes to disguise itself as memory, don't you agree? Furthermore, the influences that acted on me were too complex for me to be able to disentangle them so quickly. At the time, I read extensively—Baudelaire, Kierkegaard, Hegel, Plotinus—and each of these played a role. And there isn't just intellectual life, there is also daily life that little by little turns the theoretician of twenty or so, given to abstraction and with his head in the clouds, into the more conscious and responsible person who begins to understand a little better what life is, and destiny, and what priorities must be established in order to be worthy of them. The Surrealists were children; they played games, which is, I realize, of irreplaceable importance, but for me existence after 1947 was very difficult for quite some time—work, suburb, isolation—and what is more, the education I had received encouraged me to accept these humble tasks, these anonymous finalities that are so far removed from the egocentrism that can often open the mirages of the infinite to poetic creation. Yes, it was in the course of the passing years and the trials they brought that I learned what time is, and chance—what I call finitude—in their absolute irreducibility which is being itself. Still, I think that I will not be far from the truth if I mention the decisive importance of my discovery during this period of formation (and it was, I suppose, a somewhat unexpected enthusiasm for a young Surrealist, but chance led me to this discovery very early in my development) of the Russian theologian—if the word can be applied to him—Lev Shestov. As early as 1944, I had found a secondhand copy of his *Potestas Clavium* in the bookstalls along the Seine, in Boris de Schloezer's admirable translation, and something began at once to work in me. Shestov teaches that what we love is by rights what has being, in the strongest and most "objective" sense of that word. It follows that Job is right to demand that his children and his goods, which God had taken from him, be returned to him by that same free power that is beyond all causes; just as we would be right if we demanded, if we dared to think and to will that Socrates whom we loved, and who died unjustly, not be dead, that he begin his work once more, free from judgment and from the deadly hemlock. And this because the kind of representation that philosophers call essence, and that science would call causality or necessity, is only, as Shestov insists again and again, a form of retrospective consolation—as devoid of truth as it is disastrous— which our eternal stoicism invents in the situation of seeming misfortune. Shestov's whole philosophy—or I should say the essence of his thought, for there is no system to it, and for good reason—is oriented, as is easy to see, by the idea of resurrection, or rather by the idea that the past can be gradually effaced, that the irreversibility of history can be abolished, that it can be rewritten by our authentic desires. And though it might seem crazy, this is only in fact because it insists on conceiving of the absolute—with which it is justifiably obsessed—in the context of the admittedly naive notion of temporal eternity. Shestov himself is afraid of time; he remains outside the moment, the value of which he does not really feel. If one only retained his valorizations—presence over essence, what is loved over what is, or seems to be—one could end up with a negation of absence, the simple resurrection of what is lost, which in my opinion are better founded on the understanding that the absolute that we desire resides in the fullness of a second, during which intensity has the value of eternity. In short, it is only a question of disposing ourselves with respect to what is real in such a way that our complete adherence to it allows the universal to consume in us all differences, all the vain desires that are born of fear, and all our regrets as well, in moments of such depth and power that what comes after them little matters. And though this is doubtless difficult, it is here that the light dwells, the goal. Shestov, by asserting his right to eternity with such force and insistence, opened me to what was missing in Surrealism, so that reality, which is more than the surreal, could flourish; and this, in the final analysis, I would call hope.

Have we reached the origins of your preoccupation with the sacred, with what you sometimes don't hesitate to call the religious, although you have indicated that the idea of God, that unduly fixed signified, is immediately apt to provoke the absence of God?

Yes, I think so, but with a few nuances. In the first place, this "religious" concern—why refuse the word?—didn't really begin there, at least as far as lived experience was concerned, or the kind of vague premonition one can have. From early childhood, a certain idea I had of place, for example—"here" blighted and colorless, but elsewhere (or rather "over there") rich in substance—had all the characteristics, it now seems to me, of an intuition of transcendence, even if in this case transcendence inhabited aspects of our world. And it seems significant to me that the first text I ever published, an answer to a survey from *Savoir-vivre*, one of those extremely short-lived reviews of Belgian Surrealism, was an evocation of this "background" which I described much later[4] and which is at the very least a demonic phantasm. Furthermore, nothing could be farther from my vision of Surrealism than to interpret it as a form of secularism against which I needed to oppose my more extensive knowledge of transcendence in order to be true to myself. If it had occurred to me, in 1947, to use the word "religious"—which was so suspect, so often insulted—I would have used it, in fact, against Breton and his followers, in my criticism of "Rupture

---

4. See Bonnefoy's autobiographical work *L'Arrière-pays* (Geneva: Éditions d'Art Albert Skira, 1972).

inaugurale," for example, inasmuch as I did not like their occultist inclina-
tions. Those archives of "spectral" presence that I received in abundance
from Surrealism, and which did open my eyes, as I have said—there was
certainly a religious dimension to all that, and even in the only living form
that modern poetry has known, with the exception of Georges Bataille (I
had read *Le Coupable*, then *L'Expérience interiéure*, as early as 1944, and I
had felt that he was speaking of what is essential). But both the occultism of
André Breton—what Jean Starobinski has characterized so well, so con-
vincingly, by recalling the influence on Breton of Myers's "subliminal
self"—and the ethics of paroxysm in Bataille's work were—how can I put
it?—a kind of misguided sense of the religious, and it is for this reason that
separation from Breton was certainly a beginning, an origin.

What do you mean by a "misguided" religiousness?

Alas, something that was in me as well, and still is to some degree,
and that also explains my first adherence to Surrealism—or in any case is the
overdetermining factor: so that when I mobilized myself a bit later against
the demons and the "black gods" of the 1947 exhibit, it was less against
some alien thought than against an inner heresy to which I had at times
surrendered a great deal, and that I was trying to combat in its most au-
dacious forms, the ones that are easiest to criticize. The "misguided" sense
of the religious is what I have sometimes called "gnosticism," especially in
L'Arrière-pays, by which term I seek to indicate an intuition of transcen-
dence, yes, but one that has attached itself too exclusively to a certain object
or aspect of our universe, chosen at first to account indirectly for transcen-
dence, by analogy for example, but quickly seen as carrying at least the traces
of some superior reality in its being; which means that all the other things in
the world lose their value and that the earth becomes a prison since down
here it is the lower forms of reality that predominate. Thus divinity is seen as
an absence that manifests itself only at certain times and in a veiled way; we
live, then, in exile and our moments of lucidity only come in flashes of
momentary, incomplete freedom. Now it is certainly true, for example, that
the experience of being can sometimes seem a kind of ardor that one lives as
a sort of adolescence carried, in its very difference, to a level of unknown
intensity, and thus it is perhaps legitimate, based on this kind of thinking, to
make the adolescent a figure of the good, and even to dream of angels or of
spirits released from time and age, for such notions allow us to speak
symbolically of mental attitudes difficult to express in other ways. But what
I mean by "gnosticism" begins when someone like Breton writes, mytho-
logically, that Rimbaud was, for a period or two, a true god of puberty and
that he should always have remained so, refusing the limitations of finite
existence, and of destiny, even if it meant suicide I suppose, as soon as the
weight of the world became too great. The gnostic attitude, in other words,

substitutes an image, which is thought of as the only reality, for all things, and above all for other people. Thus there is gnosis, to my mind, or at least the risk of gnosis, the moment there is writing, since the writer is preoccupied with the facts, the objects, and the beings that he loves and that he therefore invests with his desire, abolishing them in their own being and deifying them according to the laws of his own heaven when they are in fact creatures of this world. If he is not careful, the author will think that his text has sorted out from the world what is true and pure in it and that these few words of his are a reflection or an expression of the absent god (Mallarmé would say a copy in which an Intelligible is revealed). I believe that one can affirm—and this would assist the task of criticism—that all literature, especially all poetry, is in part gnosis, since it is in part writing. But for the Surrealists, ah, how much more so than for other poets, except perhaps for their immediate predecessors, the later Symbolists! Breton is completely immersed in this illusory sovereignty that denies Nadja the right to her own truth, though, he thinks that he recognizes her as a free presence; her truth is too simple, too ordinary; she has to be a fairy or else she will be cast out among the millions of other contemptible beings. I said that *Nadja* had disappointed me. It is precisely for this reason. It is because the book sacrifices too obviously to a generalized kind of writing, to a way of listening to the world which only retains what is desired from the perspective of a self that is, moreover, content to be, itself, no more in the final analysis than the sum of its own images.

You were saying that this "gnostic" tendency was also present in you?

In that I write; perhaps also as the tendency that first led me to write. But what separated me from the Surrealists in the end is that I believe, through another kind of experience at work in me, that the "gnostic" dream is an intuition gone astray, as fallacious as it is intense, and that there can be true presence only if sympathy, which is knowledge in action, has been able to pass like a thread not only through those few aspects that lend themselves to our fantasies but through every dimension of the object, and of the world, taking them on thoroughly and reintegrating them in the context of that unity I for my part feel is guaranteed to us by the earth, in its evidence before us—the earth which is life. In my eyes this unity—and it was in this way that I read Plotinus—is the foundation of being, the reason why anything at all is able to participate in a place that has being, instead of falling once more, through fragmentation and inner opacity, into its nothingness and our own. It is this unity that asks us to give ourselves with trust to finitude, because there is no totality except in the mutual recognition of each of the parts that make up the whole, and this recognition has limitation as its essence, but a limitation that earns us the right, through the very assumption of our nothingness, to accede to the universal. And here is the act I would call religious, here is the potential sense of the sacred, and here is what encourages the break with Surrealism, since the major error of Surrealism was its lack of faith in the simple forms of life, preferring as it does the opening of the imaginary to the tightening of the obvious, the peacock's fan to the stones of the threshold. Finitude, which can help us accept a place and therefore live in that place and thus see it in its depth, in its resonances, is not the land of exile feared by the gnostic vertigo, clinging to its rock of infinity; nor is it the misfortune Shestov speaks of, which one could reverse if one had enough faith and courage, and which is accepted, but with suffering, by the stoicism of the philosophers. No, it is once again, and from within, the infinite that we thought was lost, the plenitude that saves—the moment replacing the eternal. And this is why, shortly after my Surrealist exercises, I could place as the epigraph to my first book, *Douve*, or rather on the threshold of the thinking that led to it—and not without irony, because of its original context—that sentence from Hegel on death, and finitude, which he tells us that human thought must always remember.[5]

You evoke your work from the period after you had left Surrealism, as I did myself, at the beginning of our discussion. But how was the transition accomplished in practice? Not so much in abstract thought now, as in the writing itself where the danger lies?

I believe that this transition occurred because of a contradiction that exists in Surrealist writing, a contradiction that Breton preferred not to acknowledge, or rather that he perverted—I won't have time to fully explain what I mean here—a contradiction that for my part I discerned little by little, sensing rather quickly, I think, that it might have a positive quality in the search for meaning. Let's go back to the image we evoked at the beginning. The Surrealist image is the most effective instrument of the gnosis I mentioned because it subverts the principles that allow us to decipher the world, because it is indifferent to time, to space, to causality, to the laws of nature and being; and so it blurs the form of where we are, deprives us of the music of the place we are in, while its origin in the author's unconscious, the significance, which can be considerable, that it has for the author's psychic life—though he may not be aware of it—give it the appearance of something that concerns us but that is beyond our grasp, of something mysterious and to be deciphered. Thus it is easy to take it as a sign that is sent to us, an appeal, another proof that there is some other level of being. Remember that poem of André Breton's which I cited at the beginning, with the sun in the night, and that other poem as well, "Tournesol"—they both have the same idea of another light which Breton

5. "But the life of the spirit is not what flees from death or seeks to keep apart from it; it is rather the life that confronts and maintains itself in death."

imagined was prophetic of his life to come. In this surreality that seems to come to life as he passes, he feels that forces are waiting for him, watching for him; something knows more about him than he knows himself. In short, what I denounced a moment ago as *la mauvaise présence*, as the syncope of meaning that reduces the object to its slough, leaving it bare in front of us— Breton interprets this as the vigilance of great and secret forces from whose perspective our ordinary idea of reality is only a veil. But precisely to the extent that the Surrealist text is burdened, as I said, with unconscious determinations, it becomes, as soon as it is finished, the concrete expression of the author's deeper personality, and this—his obsessions, his needs, his eccentricities, sometimes perhaps his neurotic traits—is part of the reality we live in; in other words, the laws, the values, the restrictions of our world, refused but nonetheless active, and even present and pressing as never before in poetry, since the older introspection did not allow the unconscious to speak its language so freely. In automatic writing there is certainly no danger of hiding what one is beneath some conventional figure. The reality denied image after image by Surrealism "comes back" as the sum of these imaginings, these sketches of dreams, and in the end one can even see working in each of André Breton's books—to return again to the great example—that finitude that may perhaps be refused but never avoided. . . . This is the ambiguity of Surrealism, and from this ambiguity we may deduce several consequences for the necessary next step. First of all, why not establish oneself in ambiguity, taking it as a given of experience, instead of refusing any knowledge of it, as the Surrealists did, with the possible exception of Eluard? In other words, if man is the perpetual dreamer, the "definitive dreamer," as Breton would say, why not remain within the dream writing opens to us, but in order to watch it live and to "criticize" it, as I said before—which will mean to work on oneself, and therefore on the dream as well, which might become simpler if it is elucidated in this way, and make the writing more transparent. And so one shouldn't refuse the image, which is an un-leashing of our secret language—this dash is meant to diminish any impression of paroxysm that, in my view, is simply one more strategy of censorship—but rather analyze it as if with a prism and thus liberate the forces that shape themselves there in too limited a fashion. And so, too, one shouldn't refuse oneself the desire that carries the image, but rather disentangle it from the too specific objects in which it becomes estranged and lead it inward toward the universal. By the end of my Surrealist period, I was beginning to sense the possibility of a poetry that would not try to formulate our existential problems—that is the business of conceptual thinking—nor seek to present me in some distinct form of individuality (which is often seen as the standard of truthfulness), as was the case with Verlaine and Laforgue (I won't say Baudelaire since he was so much more)—this would be, in spite of how it seems, a presence seized from without, a kind of rhetoric—but rather would from the outset try to bring consciousness in action into the field of the forces that are at work, the forces that determine as well as those that desire, the forces of the unconscious as well as those of being, and would seek to harmonize these forces while fading into them, the self becoming more extensive, detaching itself from name, from psychic past, through a consideration of the effects of finitude on the infinite that is language. This is the direction I tried to follow, which means that there really was no distinct break between my attempts in this new period and my earlier writing but instead a recentering, thanks to which the images, in their sustained irrationality, offered themselves to the act of poetry, about which I still had everything to learn—and I have groped about a great deal since.

Translated by John T. Naughton

13 "Image and Presence": Inaugural Address at the Collège de France[1]

MONSIEUR L'ADMINISTRATEUR, My dear colleagues, As I appear before you now, let my first words be to tell you how much I appreciate your confidence, and how grateful I am for it, for myself personally but also and especially for the great cause which you have called on me to represent. I extend this gratitude, entirely, to each of you, since I have already had occasion to notice that, in spite of the extreme diversity of your research, each of you takes an interest in poetry.

And since through your various researches you all manifest an exigency and a rigor—those which characterize science in its concern for method, in its passion for truth—allow me to tell you as well, and this is my second wish, that I take on the task that you have defined with the keenest sense of a new responsibility which is both distinct from and related to my preoccupation with poetry. There is a point, in fact, about which I no longer have the slightest doubt and which I feel it necessary to stress at the outset. Although I place above all the kind of thought characteristic of the great poems, which strives to base itself on nothing if not on the purity of desire and the fever of hope, I know that our questioning of it is fruitful, that our teaching about it has meaning, only when they ripen in the midst of the facts which the historian has come to recognize, and when they are formulated with words in which are heard, in echoes more or less distant, all that has been acquired by what we call the sciences of man. The impatience of intuition, but close beside it the preciseness of careful study—these are the "loyal adversaries" which must be reconciled if the statements of an epoch are not to fall as quickly as dying embers go out; and I am the more convinced that they are in fact reconcilable, in the case of poetry, and that it is therefore worth the trouble to attempt this exalting synthesis, as I know of several examples of these achievements in this very assembly

1. Yves Bonnefoy made his inaugural address to the Collège de France in December 1981. A slightly revised version of the address was published as *La Présence et l'image: Leçon inaugurale de la Chaîre d'Etudes comparées de la fonction poétique au Collège de France, 1981* (Paris: Mercure de France, 1983). The English translation by John T. Naughton was first published in *New Literary History* 15, no. 3 (Spring 1984): 433–451.

where, to my joy, are active some of the great scholars who encouraged me to think in this way. One of you[2] was my guide through the world of Renaissance studies, and I owe to him irreplaceable moments of growth as well as of discovery. And as for Georges Blin, who proposed the project of this Chair, is it necessary to recall, since all of you know his great books, the first of which virtually reinvented Baudelaire, what a model of clear-sightedness but also of scrupulousness he offers to all who are attentive to poetry?

But is it enough to aspire to this double postulation to guarantee that one will be capable of it? And is it not imprudent to hand over to someone who writes poetry—and even if he knows the value of scientific reflection—the problem of analyzing the very act he is in the process of performing? Many critics claim, as you know, that the author knows less about what he is doing than his writing does; that writing possesses a finality and follows paths which the writer as he writes cannot but misunderstand: and so, if he happens to formulate some statement about poetry, this evaluation should only be considered at best as another dimension of his own creative work, as a further manifestation of the forces which are brought to bear upon it—in short, as one of the byroads of a creativity whose totality is best grasped by those standing on the far shore, looking from a distance. This is a fact: the observations of the author are somewhat casually collected in the laboratory where over the last few years particles of written material have been ana-lyzed, particles whose minuteness rivals the fragments of matter explored by the physicist or the biologist; and perhaps, indeed, it is simply good method that the writer of this new era ask himself, on occasions such as this one, if it would not be more rigorous to devote himself to creative passivity rather than to judgments which might prove illusory.

My dear colleagues, I am not forgetting that it was here in this room, not fifty years ago, that an idea was initiated, and with what authority—which signs of personal sacrifice made only more intense—the idea that poetry in its greatest specificity does not allow for self-knowledge, and that one can therefore only deal with it through a discarding of beliefs, where what the author takes seriously, if not sometimes tragically—let us say his feelings, his values—is reduced, under the watchful eye of an algebraic and almost ironical witness, to the level of a simple variable in the equation of the mind. This was not the way the first poets who frequented the future Collège de France thought; and when the "King's Lecturers"[3] gave new life to the

2. André Chastel.

3. The "King's Lecturers" or "Lecteurs royaux" was the name given formerly to the professors of the Collège de France because, in the beginning, all read lectures written out in advance. Originally called the Collège du Roi, the Collège de France was founded by François I as an academic body independent of the Sorbonne, whose power the king wished to uproot. In

great poems of the ancient world before these enraptured listeners, Ronsard and Du Bellay had no doubt that to be, if only for a moment, the *Vates,* the poet blessed with enthusiasm, was to attain to truth. But when Paul Valéry was called to the first Chair in Poetics at this college, he had already decided that the content of the poem—which had been regarded, doubtless with too much facility, as a veridical cry of suffering or as a premonition of the secrets of being—is in fact only another element in a play of forms and has value only insofar as it is discarded, forgotten on behalf of a more serious study of the laws of writing. A development had begun, summed up by the fact that sometimes Roland Barthes was among the young people who came to hear Valéry—Barthes who did so much thereafter to deconstruct the illusions of self-possession and of self-knowledge which beguile writers when they work; and who, consequently, carried further than anyone else the formalist exploration of writing, but not without turning away for many years—and this was no accident—from the direct study of poets. It is true that a contrary evolution began little by little to make itself felt in this lucid consciousness—you were yourselves witness to it as colleagues and friends of Barthes. After having wanted only to describe the functioning of language, of which literature would merely have been a partially unconscious intensification, he came to the conclusion—through an experience of grief which involved his whole being, which was an intuition as much as an act of reason—that all language is as such an order, that every order is an oppression, that every act of speech, be it even of scientific truths, is consequently an act of power, and that therefore to recover our freedom, to place ourselves "beyond power," we must cheat with words, make light of them while playing with them, and that this identifies the free act—and therefore true lucidity, this time apprehended as an act—with the practices of the writer who knows how to evade every formula. It was a writer who took the floor here in 1977, a writer filled with the sense that literature is a consciousness; and his last book, *La Chambre claire,* would soon show—and this touches me under the present circumstances—that he was drawing close to poetry.

The question of the author's right to claim to know some sort of truth about his own work remains, nevertheless, a valid one; for some it is even an issue already settled in the negative; and it is this basic controversy, this dispute that is sometimes violent and always secretly anguished, which I feel I must examine first of all, raising questions in this first lecture about the categories involved, which should perhaps be modified or made more com-

the beginning, there were two *lecteurs* appointed by the king, one for Greek and one for Hebrew. In 1534, a Chair of Latin Eloquence was created, and the name of the body was changed to Collège des Trois Langues. Ronsard and DuBellay, the most famous poets of the so-called Pléiade, were friends and followers of the *lecteurs*.

plete if we want a more intimate understanding of poems. In the calculations today which attempt to situate exactly the significance of poetry, it may be that one component has not been taken into account. In the doubts certain poets themselves feel about their capacity to know, it may be that we should see nothing more than a sudden moment of vertigo, brought about by the perception of the abyss which is writing, but which a more courageous decisiveness could dispel. And is not doubt itself, in this situation as in so many others, the area in which what is obvious—although veiled for a moment—can take shape again in still more striking fashion? From which it follows that doubt, in this deep sense, was also a necessary moment in the history of poetry, where it functions as a test, where it offers us a chance. I am going to try to put these ideas together and to find my way through them.

Ladies and gentlemen, My friends, One of the great contributions of our era has been the importance placed on what is called the activity of the signifier, and, correlatively, the denunciation of certain illusory aspects of our consciousness of ourselves. Where the critic or the philosopher once thought to find in the work of literature or in common speech the unequivocal and direct expression of a subject to whom fidelity to the truth would have been enough to feel present to other presences, and by degrees through these fundamental experiences the master of the world's meaning or even a divine emanation, we have learned to better perceive a maze without beginning or end of transitory representations, of fictions without any authority, where what seems to remain most worthy of being called real is this mass of words, ceaselessly changing their meaning and often their form, a mass which rolls down through the ages like a huge river across languages and cultures. Where once spoke what were called geniuses— because they were thought to have gone straight toward a higher truth— galaxies called the text have begun to glitter, more complex and resonant spaces than what not long ago was found formulated in them, but where one searches in vain among the constellations and the shadows for the being who nonetheless, in the boundless abyss of the white page, had brought together or thrown out these signs. A "hollow nothingness," said Mallarmé, and which is the more an enigma as it is sometimes a music indeed.

And consciousness has seemed, in this perspective, to have a new task to assume. Rather than evaluating in the discourse of the person speaking a statement of truth, based upon facts about the world which will be reputed to be knowable, one should analyze the way in which verbal states—signifiers briefly enclosing unreal signifieds—produce themselves one from another, using more than expressing the universe. It is here that one encounters at their origin, and with a weight of proof it would be idle to deny, the impressive programs of recent research: first, that archaeology of cultural events which seeks to unearth from our age-old neglect the interlacing strata of the concepts of a time such as they really were, that is to say, other—and yet more active, more determinant of practical behaviors than the carefully meditated notions of philosophy and science; and, second, a completely renewed method of analyzing literary creation. For there is just as much concern as ever with literature, in the new thinking, since it is in the writer's work that the life of words, constrained if not even denied in ordinary practice, achieves, with the help of dream, a freedom which seems to be the avant-garde of the world. Often without the author's awareness, but clear to the critic's scrutiny, the constant flow of change which takes place in the relationship between meanings and words pushes forward its meanderings throughout the text; one might say that it opens there onto the unknown, to such a degree that the witness to this burgeoning of anagrams, to this unfolding of polysemies—which are so many shatterings, so many centers of fleeting iridescence in that mirror where once one followed the eyes of the artist—comes to ask of avant-garde authors to finish smashing this reflecting water where Chateaubriand or Baudelaire, and Rembrandt as well as Van Gogh, sought with an anguish now considered outdated either the refinement of their attitudes or the devastations of their torment. Criticism just renewed the pact it makes every generation with the obscure need to create. But the old idea of the creative act, which had drawn so close to that of a sovereign subjectivity, is only the more severely denied thereby.

And yet, if it is easy enough to verify, in the quiet of a study, that, in the ruins of the cogito, nothing remains but thousands of levels of the fleeting clouds of this language of which, for our passing moment, we are only a slight ruffling of the structures, a mere crinkle which we cannot pretend to entirely understand, it is nonetheless true that when we speak we say "I," and we say it in the urgency of our days and in the midst of a condition and of a place which remain, whatever may be their false pretenses or their groundlessness, both a reality and an absolute. We say "I," and thanks first of all to this word, we give direction to our existence, and sometimes to that of others; we decide upon values; it even happens, strangely, that beings die for the latter through what seems to be a free choice, while others, and we know what a misfortune it is, others who are many in our time, suffer at having lost a clear and coherent relationship with something in them they might call their own being and prefer from then on, in so many instances, to simply let themselves die. This capacity to acknowledge and to accept oneself, through the agency of a few values which may be shared with others, would have been a simple fiction—we can accept this last word—

but this is also what would have given to those lives a reason for lasting and to the world around them a meaning, with a little warmth. And I notice moreover that this era, which has disqualified all inner experience, is also the period which, for the first time in history, turns with nostalgia toward the arts and the poetry of those times when the relationship of individuals and an asserted meaning of life or the universe was the unique concern of collective thought. Unless preference is given, beneath the withered leaves of "cities without evenings,"[4] to the proliferation of erratic acts whose violence seems gratuitous but in fact reveals in the desperate incendiary the ever-human desire to be a responsible subject and thus to gain access to freedom. If the deconstruction of the old ontological ambitions seems, on a certain level, an imperative of consciousness, their weakening, in any case in concrete situations, is accompanied by a risk of decomposition and death for society as a whole. And this seems to me, in the final analysis, much more the aggravation of a problem than a gain made in the direction of the truth. At best, we have become conscious of the divided character of our being-in-the-world, but we now run the risk of falling prey to its catastrophic consequences through forgetfulness of the action which once opposed this division. And while we must continue to study how the signifier ceaselessly fluctuates within the signs, it seems to me that we must also search for the way in which this élan that we are can affirm itself, in spite of being adrift in words, as an origin. What must one do, in other words, so that there still may be some sense in saying "I"?

What must one do? Well, in any case, ask questions again about poetry, which we left a moment ago in that position of tutelage where the philosophy of language, the moment it is a question of veracity, would like to keep it today.

Ask questions about poetry, which in my destiny furthermore is only the most natural reaction, since it is in the experience of poetry over the course of the years that the contradictions and the misgivings I have just tried to indicate have become clear to me, as well as the persistence of a certain hope, and of the very idea of hope. In fact, poets themselves were the first to have sensed what criticism has stressed recently concerning the role of the signifier in writing and concerning the part played by the unconscious in their decisions, and, on the threshold of our modernity, which began as a breakdown of the Romantics' absolute idea of the self, they had already made this role their principal preoccupation. Rimbaud was not unaware of the autonomy of the signifier when he was writing his sonnet "Voyelles," nor was Mallarmé when he put together his "Sonnet en yx." And this excess in

---

4. See Mallarmé's "Le Tombeau de Charles Baudelaire": "Quel feuillage séché dans les cités sans soir."

words over meaning is precisely what attracted me in my own case, when I came to poetry, in the snares of surrealist writing. What a call, as if from an unknown heaven, in these clusters of lawless tropes! What energy, it seemed, in this unpredictable bubbling up from the depths of language! But once the initial fascination was over, I took no joy in these words which I was told were free. I had before my eyes another kind of evidence, nourished by other poets, the evidence of running water, of a fire burning peacefully in our daily existence, and of time and chance of which these realities are made, and it seemed to me fairly soon that the transgressions of automatic writing were less the desired surreality, existing beyond the too superficial realisms of controlled thought whose signifieds remain fixed, than a reluctance to raise the question of the self, whose richest potentiality is perhaps in the life that one takes on day after day, without illusions, in the midst of what is simple. What are all the subtleties of language, after all, even turned upside down in a thousand different ways, next to the perception one can have, directly, mysteriously, of the movement of the leaves against the sky, or of the noise fruit makes when it falls into the grass? And always throughout this whole time I kept in mind, as an encouragement and even as a proof, the moment when the young reader opens passionately a great book and finds words, of course, but also things and people, and the horizon, and the sky: in short, a whole world given all at once to his thirst. Ah, this reader does not read, be it even in Mallarmé, as the theoretician of poetry or as the semiologist asks him to read! If he understands everything in the polysemies through comprehensive intuition, through the sympathy that one unconscious can have for another, it is in the great burst of flame which delivers the mind—as formerly the negative theologies rid themselves of symbols, and as, when one raises one's eyes at Tournus, one sees unity spring forth from what is elsewhere only space. Words are there for him, of course; he can feel the vibrations of the signifiers which lead him toward other words in the labyrinths of the signifier, but he knows that there is a signified amongst them, a signified which depends on no one of them in particular and on all of them at once, which is intensity as such. The reader of poetry does not analyze—he pledges to the author, his brother, that he too will remain in intensity. And soon he closes up his book, anxious to go and live out the promise. He has rediscovered a hope. And this is what gives us the right to think that one should not give up hope in poetry.

And yet it is not that I am trying to deny the capacity for self-deception, for spreading unreality which exists in the work of the greatest poets; and, come to this point, I even feel the need to denounce this vanity myself, convinced as I am that true power is found only where weakness also lies, and that power can only grow and have merit if it has first of all recognized this weakness through careful study.

This study of the illusory in works of poetry seems to me all the more necessary, furthermore, in that recent criticism has rather neglected it, given as it is to an emphasis on plurality in writing. Fascinated by what takes place on the level of the signifier, recent criticism fixes on what violates, in the writer's text, some previous or more ordinary state of common speech; it therefore seeks out the work of art in its deviation, or in its becoming, which thus makes of creation a movement, a dynamics, easily connected with the flow of intertextuality or the play of *différence*—and it forgets to examine the inscription of himself that the author tries to establish in the midst of the verbal turbulence. Now even if this elaboration of a definite meaning is only a fabric of illusions, it nonetheless has its own laws, the nature of which it may be important to understand. What are these laws? Above all, that writing is enclosure. A desire is in us, as old as earliest infancy, that seeks out in every circumstance what might replace the good which has been missing almost since the beginning; and as it is granted to us, through the ambiguous blessing of words, to keep in mind only a single aspect of things, the author, freer in this than the ordinary man or woman, since he works under the shelter of his white page, is going to select only those aspects which his desire can accept and use, and build with them and only with them the stage where his dream can act itself out. Much will therefore be lost from beings and objects evoked in this manner, and in particular their own inner relationship with themselves, their very act of being, this right they have to be here, in spite of the dreamer and in conflict with his idea of the world, albeit in agreement with the very necessity he denies. Let us call this region beyond our representations—this ever-censored part—*finitude,* since if we knew how to listen to it, it would assign to us our limits. A world has been destroyed— abolished, Mallarmé would say—the one in which we would be mortal; and, in return, what has taken shape in the poem is a world as well, of course, often a coherent world and, in appearance at least, complete. From this point of view the literary work is a tongue, a sort of personal language, which institutes, which maintains, which professes an autonomous reality felt as substantial, considered as sufficient; and this gravitation which retains this or that thing, this or that value, but shuts out this or that other is an iron law—let there be no doubt about it—under the semblance of a golden age. For one is sometimes led to think, in the face of certain superabundances, that the writer is free to whimsically change his imaginary world, as the scientist might methodically change his hypothesis; but beneath the sea foam which does in fact move about along the shores cut out from this ocean, how still the deep waters lie! There is something immutable about the unconscious; desire only ripens slowly or never at all. Hemmed in by the words he does not understand, by experiences whose very existence he does not suspect, the writer, and this is the element of chance which so distressed Mallarmé, can only repeat in writing that strictly limited particularity which characterizes any given existence.

Who was talking then about breaking the mirror? Perhaps one can only set down one's pen, or throw the inkwell at the looking glass. But those who truly desire this are rare, let us say now, because—and here is the second law of literary creation—this world which cuts itself off from the world seems to the person who creates it not only more satisfying than the first but also more real. And for us, as readers, it often seems so as well. Born from the impatience of a youthful mind which was repelled by artificial ways of living, by values which certainly are stifling, writing allows the author to draw out from his memory of beings those features which he thought that society had dismissed. And thus, from these refashioned beings, comes to him the voice—until then never heard by him—of an ardor, a feeling which he can believe is truer; and the earth around these imaginary encounters begins to seem a place for life—where the mountain or the sea multiply those glitterings and those flowers which, in our ordinary world, seem yet devoid of any reason for being. As for finitude, which I said was denied in and by writing, how often it is that one sees, on the contrary, in this glow of words that death is imagined—one might even say loved—as the endpoint of a plenitude! In truth, there is nothing frightening, nothing negative that one does not feel capable of accepting in the magic of the sentence, since everything takes on a new radiance there, even though it be tragic; and especially those experiences of place, of time, of the presence of others which I consider effaced by the act of writing—but which are also missing, it is true, in everyday existence, which is already devastated by so much even more impoverished writing—they seem to gather to a fullness in the sentence, they seem to reveal themselves in their unrecognized value. This impression of a reality at last fully incarnate, which comes to us, paradoxically, through words which have turned away from incarnation, I shall call *image*. Images, world-images—in the sense it seems to me that Baudelaire meant when he wrote, at the most tormented moment of his poetic intuition: "The cult of images, my great, my unique, my primitive passion." Images, the radiance which is missing in the grayness of our days, but which is allowed for by language when the unquenchable thirst of dream closes it back upon itself, when it kneads it like a mother's breast.

But what a price for this radiance, and how quickly must the debt be paid! What has been kept in the literary work is what suits desire, it is what leaves it time to drink; it is therefore an infinite, dreamt of within the very limits of things, of situations, or of beings—and it is what will be missing when we wake into real life, which has other laws. Where the writer reigns supreme, he does not live; he therefore cannot reflect upon his true condition; and where, on the other hand, he is obliged to live, he finds himself ill-equipped for this unfamiliar task. How many unhealthy dualisms, between an undervalued "here" and an "over there" reputed as richness itself, how many unfeasible gnoses, how many senseless injunctions have been poured out in this way by the melancholy genius of the Image from the very first days of our Western world, which reinvented madness if not love![5] And what an instrument these dreams are for always nihilistic ideologies, for the hunger for power, which will make of them their flags. The Image is certainly a lie, however sincere the maker of the image. Was this the intensity with which I credited the young reader? In any case, it is in the light of this ambiguity that one best understands that it really was time for textual criticism to come along to analyze and even to undermine the ever-truncated perspectives which pile up in the literary use of speech.

Except that there truly is more than the elaboration of these false pretenses in certain writings which I would now like to call to your attention as more specifically *poetic*. And I shall concentrate, in particular, on some seemingly secondary aspects of the fiction in literary works. Every poem, it should first of all be noted, harbors in its depths a story, a fiction, however uncomplicated it might sometimes be: for the personal language which structures its universe can only crystallize in the form of objects or beings which maintain significant relationships with one another and in which is manifest the very law which presided over the act of creation. Now this fiction should, since it is the quintessence of a dream, express the bliss of that dream, and indeed it does so in its sometimes surprising way: for what one might too quickly take for an expression of anguish or a declaration of suffering is often only an exterior, cruelly manipulated by desire, which knows how to use it for its own pleasure—even *Werther* is an Arcadia. But there are other wrenchings in poetic fiction than these superficial misfortunes. It happens that one notices, this time in the very heart of desire, certain hesitations, twinges of remorse—one feels that fear is at work there, that some vertigo is crippling, that an aspiration which aims higher, much higher, than the paltry scene erected is upsetting things; and as a reflection of this uneasiness in the story of which I am speaking, there is therefore some situation, some hidden dimension which cuts back through it and repudiates it.

A great deal of attention has been given recently to the "mise en abyme" in which, at some focal point of the fiction, the structure of the entire work is reflected. One should also examine the counterfiction, the *subplot* by means of which, in many cases, the work of abolition proposed by the main

5. See Rimbaud, "Délires I—Vierge folle/ L'Epoux infernal," from *Une Saison en enfer:* "L'amour est à réinventer, on le sait."

action is secretly denounced. What is Hamlet doing up there, stage front, lost in his dreams, lost in the book of himself, if not denying, as Mallarmé says, denying with only a glance, the right of others to exist?—Mallarmé who adds: "He kills indiscriminately, or at least people die." People die wherever he passes because he is the dream which only keeps symbolizations and shadows upon its stage. But at the other end of the action, here is Hamlet on the edge of a grave, his project and even his sanity stricken, crying out, with a sorrow whose expression is incoherent, that he loved Ophelia, that he has betrayed her—in a way which remains unclear to him—and that he himself, in his consciousness of himself, can now only see a series of endless contradictions. Holes thus appear in the intelligibility which subtends the worlds of speech, blackness in the clear skies of the image, even a complete tearing to shreds, no longer just of the hero in whom the poet is often reflected but of the very stage which had been erected by his language, as in *Phèdre*—while words, sounds, rhythms, all the elements of prosody which one had seen working toward the unity of the poem reveal that they can just as easily attach themselves, in the emergence of forms, to what undermines their equilibrium and create a dissonance where one had believed that one was hearing a harmony.

Now who is expressing himself in this way, who can envisage this failure in the midst of the world dreamt of by the literary work, if not someone who, though moved by this dream, yet refuses to consent to its potential for lying? In writing, which seems totally given over to the joys of its painted rooms, isn't there a captive who is shaking the door? All the more so in that this same author one saw devoting himself, in a first sketch of his book, to the logic of writing is also the person who, one day, has called his book finished, has detached himself from it and criticized it with regard to himself, and begins another where sometimes he attains even greater self-awareness. There are not only books, there are literary destinies in which each work marks a stage—which would seem to indicate that there exists an entirely different kind of desire, the desire, let us say, to free oneself from desire, the desire to grow with respect to oneself. And indeed one notices that as the evidence of the autonomy of language increases in our modernity, this maturation of the writer, who calls his writing into question, also becomes more frequent, more vehement—and more listened to as well, more passionately appreciated, as though it were for us, on the threshold of a redoubtable future, the only act with merit. Think of Baudelaire, who goes from his poems on the Ideal, and on Spleen, to his *Tableaux parisiens,* his eyes as if opened; of Rimbaud who burns up so many stages, though each is fabulous, before disavowing the seer or the angel he had dreamt of being; and think of Yeats, or Artaud, of Jouve, and others of our time whose scruples, whose long silences sometimes are our rallying point, our strength. In the very heart of writing, there is a questioning of writing. In the midst of this absence, something like a voice which persists.

What is the meaning of this persistence? At the very least that poets carry within themselves another idea of what has importance, or of what is, than the idea which emerges today from the investigations of the semiologist. In the very place where for the latter the writer's struggle with words reveals nothing but transitory structurations, shadows where the person speaking has nothing but a shadow to inscribe, there precisely the poets find something very different, since we see that they can sacrifice what they had taken for a more intense form of reality—and this in order to bear witness to an existence beyond, to a being, to a plenitude they don't even know how to name. And one might add to this first paradox that this painful discovery, which cuts into the fabric of sentences, which ravages whole sequences of images—such is the prince of the *Illuminations,* who sets fire to his palace— is not in the least a simple remorsefulness born from the sense of wrongdoing, but a waiting which is feverous, one would say the rising of a yet unknown sort of joy. Poetry is not the account of a world, however magnificent may be the forms which it alone is able to unfold; one would say rather that it knows that these representations of a world are only a veil which hides the true reality. But it is not this remanence of the old ontological ambitions which will render this testimony more acceptable to the new devotees of language. They will simply tell us that so obstinate an assertion is in itself only one more consequence of the suggestion of presence I pointed out a moment ago in what I call the Image. Not the glimpse at last of reality, but further flight into still more delusion.

And yet, my friends, let us imagine that this human community in which we observe today that ontology has been but a dream, the "main pillar" only a simple congregation of vapors, sometimes even poisonous ones, and the individual nothing but this mask which the Latin people already knew covered only an absence—let us imagine that this community be reduced, through some disaster, to a handful of survivors painfully absorbed at every second by the emergence of dangers. In those moments of deprivation and urgency, the survivors would decide upon a course of action, would assign tasks—but would not the first of these decisions, made without even thinking about it, in the once again uncontested evidence of personal existence, be that *there is being:* these people having no doubt, beneath the collapsing rock, that one's relation to oneself, even if nothing founds it, is origin and suffices to itself? And the horizon around them, though devastated, though unfit for a long while to nurture our dreams, would *be,* also, would be as one had forgotten a thing could be, from which it follows that in the presence of such things one would therefore be able to recognize that *what is* is what responds to our most basic needs, what lends itself to our project, what allows for exchange, and must first of all have done this to find a place in language: for instance, the main features of a place, the tools of labor, later perhaps the materials of a first moment of rejoicing—one will say then the bread and the wine. Being is the firstborn of emergency. Its ground is the future which calls us to its task, and its substance is the few important categories which we use to formulate this task, that is to say, signifieds which are certainly transitory, but at every moment absolute. Words which name a sacred order, words which welcome us on an earth! Being only exists through our will that there be being; but this will gathers enough reality from outside, even in this winter of ours which will be endless, to build with it this hearth—I no longer say this stage—where those who know they are nothing may come to warm themselves.

And thus it is that we can now better understand the innermost contradiction but also the stubbornness of poetry, which only refuses imaginary worlds because it knows well what our condition is and that our place is this very earth. If being is nothing other than the will that there be being, poetry is nothing itself, in the estrangement of language, but this will understanding its own nature—or at the very least, in dark times, keeping the memory of itself. Let me observe in passing, furthermore, that in so doing it only renews the very act which presided over our beginnings. When words revealed death to men, when conceptual notions put distance between them and things, hollowing out everywhere around them and between them the evidence of their nothingness—which aroused anguish and incited our species to that insane violence which distinguishes it from every other—something in fact like faith was needed for us to carry on with words; and everything indicates that it is also in words themselves—but this time understood as names, cried or called out in the midst of absence—that this faith has sought its way. The most primitive notches are a sign that speaking has always meant asserting oneself—meaning carving itself into meaninglessness; and the gravestone itself, so consubstantial with the aim of speech, is also proof of it, since it preserves a name, since it affirms a presence where one could decide that only nothingness prevailed. Indeed, every monument is the metaphor for this will to be through words and yet against them, to be as a call shouted, answered, and in spite of dream, to be through speech and in spite of the enclosures of our tongues—since the monument is erected in a desert which thus becomes a country, since all art is our way of organizing what is close by, since all beauty reflects this light—and as for poetry, it was the very act in which, throughout the ages, these certainties recovered themselves in the midst of their distortions, unity in the heart of multiplicity—at least until the confusions of yesterday, when what today we call the "text" sprang up from beneath our outworn beliefs, and at the very moment when, from every corner of society, self-confidence was wavering. Let me repeat: the moment when the labor of the signifier was laid bare was not an accident of history. At various great periods of civilization and of letters, the poets were enough aware of it for criticism to be able to describe it and for anxiety to settle in. But in fact it was then confined to the night of magic rites, it was considered the magician's book which the devil has us sign. The exteriority of words only really appeared, in Dadaism, after the first war which was worldwide; and indeed one could easily believe that in the very ardor which today affirms its irreversible advent, there are a few remnants of hope, and a call for help. You remember: when Paul was going to cross the sea which separated him from Europe, he heard a voice, in the night, which cried out an appeal from the other shore. The gods are dead; very few minds imagine even that the temple for "the unknown god" is going to receive on its steps, for the second time, some astonishing new gospel—and yet isn't there some chance that the *necessary* idea of being will revive? Is not a boatsman, still soundlessly, approaching our nocturnal shore?

Ladies and gentlemen, I think that I can return, in any case, to the two questions I asked myself at the outset.

The one regarded the contradiction which we observe today between, on the one hand, the awareness one must have of the illusions of the earlier cogito, and this fact, on the other hand, this fact which is just as obvious— and is a question of such urgency!—that in order to simply desire to survive we continue to need a meaning to give to life. To reflect even a little on this immense challenge of our historic moment, it seemed to me necessary to ask questions of poetry; or rather, having begun in adult life in this way, I was unable to prevent myself from continuing to do so, in spite of the suggestions to the contrary: but now I seem once again to have found confirmed the reason for this confidence which once was instinctive to me. Yes, there is in poets an attitude toward this impasse, an answer to this uneasiness, and it is central in them and it is clear. Whatever may be the driftings of the sign, the obviousness of nothingness, to say "I" remains for them the best of reality and a precise task, the task of reorienting words, once beyond the confines of dream, on our relationship to others, which is the origin of being. And as for the way in which one might achieve this goal, it is not so unclear, even beneath the level of the greatest contributions of which poetry is capable. For every being dreams his world, let us say at first; every being is imperiled by the words which shut themselves up in him— the writer is not the only one who abolishes, who becomes enchanted by a world-image; he simply runs the greatest risk because of his blank page.

Therefore, if he is even slightly aware of his estrangement, and this is within his possibilities, he will feel himself close to others whose situation is the same. In fact, this awareness of enclosure within the sign is the only way which allows one speaking subject to rejoin another and to share—in the void perhaps, but fully and richly—a dimension of existence. It follows that to struggle in our intimate being against the allurements of universal writing, to criticize them, to undo them one by one, to refuse in short to say "me" at the very moment when the "I" is asserting itself, is, however negative this might seem, already to go forward toward the common ground. And along this path, which is the path of salvation, poems, the great poems at least, are examples, and more: not the silence characteristic of a "text," but a voice which spurs us on.

Saying this, I have also begun, it seems to me, to answer my other question, the one I had to raise, this evening, first of all: Can one, when one aspires to poetry, when one strives after it, speak about it authentically? A great many critics of our time would answer no, as I have said, because they identify the poem with the activity of words and not with the search for meaning; but if you have found any merit in my idea of poetry as war against the Image—against the claims of words, against the weight of what is written—you will also have granted me that the poet knows exactly what he is doing, or to put it better, can only be a poet precisely through knowing it. His task, which is to reestablish *openness,* as Rilke would have said, is necessarily a meditation on what encloses his speech. And this project aims, of course, not at words in a manuscript, but at ideas, at experiences in the practice of life, which commits him to a process of becoming that can be, in the case of the greatest poets, a process of spiritual maturation. At the height of its misgivings, poetry is nothing other than an act of knowing.

And in the years to come it could accomplish this act, it seems to me, all the more effectively because for this constant goal it is going to have new means at its disposal. The paradox of the creative act of the future—and this can be its great opportunity—is that the same linguistic and semiological observations that are used today to depreciate the concentration in writing on the writer could—I have already come close to saying this—just as profitably lend themselves, and surely with much greater import, to the opposition that the writer could make, if he is a poet, to the authority of representations, of symbols which contribute to the mirages of writing. How many means have been given to us recently for deconstructing the fiction, for spotting the stereotypes, the *sociolectes,* for following in the web of sentences believed to be uncomplicated the tangle of the figures! And what intuitive shortcuts the new correspondences revealed by the psycho-analyst provide for our investigation of the imaginary! So many keys which were missing in Romanticism, in symbolism, in surrealism, to open by a few more doors the mind's relationship to itself. A lucidity, a short time ago still prohibited, except in moments of extreme tension, could become common currency. After centuries of shame which curbed or distorted desiring imagination, after centuries of ostentation which proclaimed to the four winds the most frivolous eccentricities, we are at last able to recognize the infinitely complex nature of discourse, but also that the self displayed in discourse, while thinking of itself as "seer or angel,"[6] merits—ordinary as it always is—neither Romantic deification nor, if denounced, nostalgia. Never will the "I" have been better armed for the constant struggle against the intimate, the inexorable vertigo. In my view, poetry and the new criticism are not made to contradict each other for long. They could soon constitute but a single way of living.

And only a word now, to conclude, about the potential that is there. Up until now this evening I have seemed, I suppose, to define poetry, in its relation to the imaginary, as its refusal, its transgression. Without hesitation I defined truthfulness of speech as the war against the Image—the substitution of an image for the world—in favor of presence. But this was only a first approximation, justified I hope by the demonstration I assigned myself, and I would like now to evoke what was behind it in my mind—inasmuch as the few remarks which I have just made go straight toward it. What is this second level of the idea of poetry? Well, it is that to struggle in this way, for a better intuition of finitude, against the closing up of the self, against the denial of the other, can only be to love, since it is presence which opens, unity which already takes hold of consciousness, and thus it means loving as well this first network of naiveties, of illusions in which the will toward presence had become ensnared. At its highest point, of which one can at least have an intimation, poetry must certainly succeed in understanding that these images which, if made absolutes, would have been its lie are nothing more, once one overcomes them, than the forms, the simply natural forms, of desire, desire which is so fundamental, so insatiable that it constitutes in all of us our very humanity; and having refused the Image, poetry accepts it in a kind of circle which constitutes its mystery and from which flows, from which rises as if from a depths, its positive quality, its power to speak of everything—in a word, that joy which I said a moment ago poetry could be seen to feel even in its most dreadful hours of anguish. What dream opposes to life, what the analysts of the text study only to dissolve into the indifference of signs, what a more superficial poetry would

6. The project undertaken, then deprecated by Rimbaud. See "Adieu" from *Une Saison en enfer:* "Moi! moi qui me suis dit mage ou ange, dispensé de toute morale, je suis rendu au sol, avec un devoir à chercher, et la réalité rugueuse à étreindre! Paysan!" ("I! I who called myself seer and angel, exempt from all morality, I am thrown back to the earth, with a duty to find, and rough reality to embrace! Peasant!")

have torn up with rage, even if perishing with its victim, poetry can refute but listen to, can condemn while absolving it of its fault; it reintegrates it, clarified, into the unity of life. In short, it has denounced the Image, but in order to love, with all its heart, images. Enemy of idolatry, poetry is just as much so of iconoclasm. Now what a resource this could be for responding to the needs of an unhappy society: illusion would reveal its richness, plenitude would be born from deficiency itself! But this dialectic of dream and existence, this third term of compassion, at the highest point of longing passion is, of course, the most difficult. On the level of these exalted representations, of these transfigurations, of these fevers which make up our literatures and which the wisdom of the East would call our delusions, one would need the capacity which the East seems to have—although simply beneath the leafy branches, whereas our place is history—to accept and to refuse at the same time, to make relative what appears absolute, and then to give new dignity, new fullness to this nonbeing. And indeed the Western world, which had a premonition of this deliverance with the agape of the early Christians, then for brief moments in the baroque period and on the peripheries of Romanticism, has, on the whole, made of it the very site of its failure, in unending wars between images. Poetry in Europe seems to have been the impossible: what eludes a man's lifelong search as immediacy does our words. But if it is true, as our time believes, that subjectivity is from now on fracturable, and that poetry and a science of signs may be able to unite in a new relationship between the "I" which is and the "me" which dreams, what unexpected richness for hope all at once! At the moment when so much night is gathering, could we be on the verge of the true light?

Translated by John T. Naughton